M000272119

Postphenomenology

SUNY series in the Philosophy of the Social Sciences
Lenore Langsdorf, editor

Postphenomenology

A Critical Companion to Ihde

EDITED BY

Evan Selinger

State University of New York Press

Published by
State University of New York Press, Albany

© 2006 State University of New York

Cover art by Jennifer Varn

For information, address State University of New York Press,
194 Washington Avenue, Suite 305, Albany, NY 12210-2384

Production by Diane Ganeles
Marketing by Michael Campochiaro

Library of Congress Cataloging-in-Publication Data

Postphenomenology : a critical companion to Ihde / edited by Evan Selinger.
      p. cm. — (SUNY series in the philosophy of the social sciences)
   "Comprehensive bibliography of Don Ihde"—p.
   Includes bibliographical references and index.
   ISBN-13: 978-0-7914-6787-9 (hardcover : alk. paper)
   ISBN-10: 0-7914-6787-2 (hardcover : alk. paper)
   ISBN-13: 978-0-7914-6788-6 (pbk. : alk. paper)
   ISBN-10: 0-7914-6788-0 (pbk. : alk. paper)
   1. Ihde, Don, 1934– 2. Philosophy, Modern—20th century. 3. Postmodernism.
4. Phenomenology. I. Selinger, Evan, 1974– II. Series.

B945.I354E97 2006
190' .9'04—dc22

2005023941

10 9 8 7 6 5 4 3 2 1

Contents

Preface

Evan Selinger

Postphenomenology: A Critical Companion to Ihde is unique. Although Don Ihde is widely acknowledged as one of the most important American phenomenologists, this is the first volume devoted exclusively to the interpretation and advancement of his contributions to history, philosophy, sociology, sound studies, science, and technology studies. It contains nineteen essays—most of them written by senior scholars of international distinction from across the disciplines—that situate, assess, and apply Ihde's philosophy with respect to the primary themes that his *oeuvre* emphasizes. The topics addressed include:

- Reflections on the relation between phenomenologically oriented scholarship and style.

- Phenomenologically inspired considerations of how sound is experienced.

- Thoughts on how ethicists and political theorists who are sympathetic to phenomenology might provide normative assessment of science and technology.

- Suggestions for how contemporary Heidegger scholarship should be conducted.

- Phenomenologically motivated inquiry into the nature and scope of embodiment.

- Perspectives on useful ways to integrate phenomenological insights into the study of scientific practice.

In order to facilitate new dialogue on these matters, the contributors have attended to the former topics in three synergetic ways: (1) some chapters are

textually oriented and engage directly with Ihde's written work; (2) some
chapters extend Ihde's insights into new domains of empirical inquiry; and
(3) some chapters honor Ihde's achievements by analyzing phenomena that
he has not focused upon; these domains of inquiry are discussed in connection with complimentary contributions that can be found in Ihde's corpus of
work. Ihde's concluding response clarifies how these three kinds of analyses
relate to his esteem for interdisciplinary diplomacy and his growing concern
about how "generic" continental philosophy is practiced.

    While the volume covers diverse topics, it is intended to be understood
as a work that addresses phenomenology's legacy and discusses its future
possibilities. Although Ihde identifies with the phenomenological tradition,
his approach to philosophy differs from both transcendental phenomenology
and existential phenomenology. Indeed, on the basis of years of studying
Edmund Husserl, Martin Heidegger, Maurice Merleau-Ponty, and Paul Ricoeur
rigorously, Ihde has come to characterize phenomenology ambivalently. He
refers to it as his personal "albatross" and depicts his research as owing a
critical debt to, but ultimately diverging from, the paths pursued by
phenomenology's godfathers. In this context, the American pragmatist tradition (notably, John Dewey's work) has played a significant role in shaping
Ihde's thought. Against this background, the reader is invited to consider how
phenomenology might be "expanded" into a "post" foundational form of
inquiry. Today Ihde refers to his most recent investigations—the hybrid cou-
pling of phenomenology and pragmatism—as "postphenomenology"; in the
future historians may discuss this classification in connection with a whole
generation of scholars.

Acknowledgments

This volume could not have been completed without an extended support network. Indeed, I was lucky to have diligent and patient contributors as well as an encouraging and supportive press. Everyone affiliated with SUNY Press, notably Lenore Langsdorf, the Series Editor, and Jane Bunker, the Editor-in-Chief, repeatedly went above and beyond the call of duty. Locally, Noreen Selinger, Jennifer Varn, Timothy Engström, Harry Groover, Brian Schroeder, and Peggy Noll provided invaluable philosophical and editorial support. Most of all, I wish to thank Don Ihde. His constant friendship, unwavering optimism, and unique manner of approaching philosophical issues have always proven inspirational. As a hermeneutic gesture, the volume is dedicated to him by being presented to the world.

Abbreviations

HP   *Hermeneutic Phenomenology: The Philosophy of Paul Ricoeur (1971)*

SS   *Sense and Significance (1973)*

LV   *Listening and Voice: A Phenomenology of Sound (1976)*

EP   *Experimental Phenomenology (1977, 1986)*

TP   *Technics and Praxis: A Philosophy of Technology (1979)*

ET   *Existential Technics (1983)*

CP   *Consequence of Phenomenology (1986)*

TL   *Technology and the Lifeworld (1990)*

IR   *Instrumental Realism: The Interface between Philosophy of Technology and Philosophy of Science (1990)*

PT   *Philosophy of Technology: An Introduction (1993)*

PP   *Postphenomenology: Essays in the Postmodern Context (1993)*

EH   *Expanding Hermeneutics: Visualism in Science (1998)*

BT   *Bodies in Technology (2002)*

CT   *Chasing Technoscience: Matrix of Materiality (2003)*

Introduction

Evan Selinger

Ihde's Training

Due to the traditional prejudice that philosophy is primarily a rational enterprise that aims at discovering objective and universal truth, many philosophers avoid personalizing their inquiry. Don Ihde's philosophy, however, is replete with biographical references. Taking this reflexive dimension of his style as an interpretative clue concerning his core philosophical commitments, it seems useful to begin biographically. Ihde was born in Hope, Kansas, on January 14, 1934. The son of a farmer father and a housewife mother, Ihde grew up in a rural German-American community where his education began in a one-room schoolhouse to which he commuted by horseback. While his formative years passed in accordance with the expected rustic routines, including driving tractors and threshing wheat, Ihde departed from his peers by learning to enjoy opera and engage critically with literature.

At the University of Kansas (BA, 1956), Ihde majored in Speech and Drama, served on the debate team, and took parts in the experimental theater. Although his philosophy classes focused upon the figures (A.J. Ayer and Gottlob Frege) and themes (positivist philosophy of science and philosophy of language) that were dominant in the late 1950s, his genuine philosophical interests were existential: the works of Albert Camus, Jean-Paul Sartre, Søren Kierkegaard, and Paul Tillich figured prominently.

Determined to become a philosophical theologian, Ihde received a fellowship to attend Andover Newton Theological School (M.Div., 1959), a place where Continental philosophy was taught as part of the curriculum, including the works of Martin Buber and Karl Jaspers. Ihde studied theology under Tillich, pursued his interest in higher criticism in Biblical Studies under the supervision of Norman Gottwald, and wrote his M.Div. Thesis on the philosophy of Nicolas Berdyaev.[1] By his second year in theological school,

1

Ihde was appointed to the United Ministries as a Chaplain at the Massachusetts Institute of Technology. He held this post until he completed his doctorate in philosophy at Boston University (Ph.D., 1964).

As his graduate studies progressed, Ihde's theological interests became surpassed by philosophical ones. His focus shifted to phenomenology—Edmund Husserl, Martin Heidegger, and Maurice Merleau-Ponty—even though this group of European philosophers comprised something of an underground trend in academic philosophy. Under the direction of John Lavely and Erazim Kohak, he wrote the first English-language dissertation on Paul Ricoeur.[2] Later on, during a Fulbright Research Fellowship to Paris (in the eventful period of 1967–1968), Ihde crafted the first systematic study in English of what was then Ricoeur's corpus of work. Ricoeur wrote the preface to the book, and in it he exclaims: "I am grateful to Don Ihde for having given me the courage to continue by indicating the vectors which call for further development."[3] Shortly after, Ihde edited and wrote the introduction to the English translation of *The Conflict of Interpretations*, one of Ricoeur's most renowned works.

Ihde's first tenure-track position was at Southern Illinois University (SIU), and he remained there until 1969. During this period Ihde became interested in the phenomenology of work; this, in turn, began to draw his interests to tools and other technologies. Upon leaving SIU, Ihde made the transition to his second and, ultimately, final academic post, a position at the State University of New York at Stony Brook. From the start, the Stony Brook department (which had just been scheduled to create a new doctoral program) provided him with challenging scholarly and pedagogical opportunities. During his first year there, Ihde broadened the curriculum by introducing courses in both existentialism and phenomenology. By his second year, he helped formalize the plans to make a pluralistic Ph.D. program that contained a strong Euro-American component.

Ihde continually exerted a strong presence in shaping the direction of the Stony Brook program. Not only was he the initial doctoral program director (a position that he would return to during intermittent periods of his career), but for eight years he served as department chair and for five years he acted as the dean of humanities and arts. Over the years, the Stony Brook program modified its original design only slightly and came to be regarded as one of the best North American programs in Continental Philosophy. Recently, however, Ihde succeeded in enlarging the scope of inquiry conducted at Stony Brook by founding the Technoscience Research Group. Visiting international scholars from a variety of disciplines have come to take Ihde's technoscience seminar—a forum devoted to reading only living authors, and, when possible, bringing these principals to campus for a "roast."

Although typically regarded as a Continental philosopher, Ihde's diverse philosophical corpus is unified by a rather analytic tendency. He has always been drawn to the philosophical task of problem solving, and consistently has expressed minimal interest in figure-oriented, textual analysis.[4] Thus, despite his authoritative command of Ricoeur scholarship, it appears that Ihde was always determined to avoid becoming pigeon-holed as a Ricoeur scholar.[5] Similarly, despite having written numerous essays on Heidegger throughout his career, Ihde has never integrated them into a unified collection; nor has he tried to assume a prominent role in the Heidegger Circle.

Ihde's Publications

Although Ihde's fascination with the experience of sound is already evident in many of the essays collected in *Sense and Significance*, his *Listening and Voice: A Phenomenology of Sound* can be characterized as the first monograph-length result of his decision to pursue a philosophical path that is not devoted to textual commentary. In this book, Ihde attends to concrete experiences, such as being immersed and penetrated by the sound of a distinctive voice during a face-to-face conversation, in order to analyze the phenomenon of auditory linguistic presence as an embodied experience. While Ihde is remarkably prescient concerning later criticisms of "ocularcentrism," the research trajectory that he inaugurates has not received the attention it deserves in philosophical circles. Even today the topic of auditory experience remains unduly neglected.

By the time he writes *Experimental Phenomenology*, Ihde is able to apply his style of "doing phenomenology" to an active pedagogical approach for introducing students to the study of phenomenology. While Ihde does not shirk from the responsibility of providing a succinct précis of the canonical phenomenologists, he departs radically from the typical exegetical format of introductory texts by correlating concrete visual examples to step-by-step perceptual variation exercises. By participating in these exercises, the reader learns to appreciate how the intentional act of perception is an embodied praxis, even when it is hermeneutically structured. Furthermore, by analyzing the "constitution" of multistable perceptions of ambiguous drawings, such as Necker Cubes, Ihde establishes that phenomenological analysis is an experimental form of conduct; in some instances it has more to offer epistemically than scientific analysis. (At the time that *Experimental Phenomenology* was written, scientists putatively could only explain a delimited number of possible perceptual variations through the mechanism of neurological switch.)

Above all, Ihde will probably be remembered as one of the first U.S. philosophers to make technology itself the subject of philosophical reflection. Carl Mitcham, for example, refers to Ihde as "the single most important person to develop an uniquely North American version of phenomenology and to bring phenomenology as a whole to bear on that singularly important North American phenomenon known as technology." He further insists that, "It is difficult to overestimate the importance and insights that Ihde has brought into the philosophy of technology." In 1979, the year that Mario Bunge argued that, "[Philosophy of Technology] is an underdeveloped branch of scholarship…suggested by the fact that so far no major philosopher has made it his central concern or written an important monograph on it," Ihde published his first book on the philosophy of technology, *Technics and Praxis: A Philosophy of Technology.*[6]

In this book, written during a sabbatical in Oxford, England, Ihde analyzes the ability of technology to transform perception, particularly when it is embodied in scientific instruments and imaging technologies. In arguing for the intentional and embodied character of *techné*, while emphasizing that any use of technology is non-neutral (as it always transforms experience), Ihde articulates a phenomenological framework—one that he consults not only for descriptive purposes, but also to discern and assess epistemological and ontological errors that arise from the failure to appreciate fully the concrete experience of instrumental relations. In this context his analysis of the limitations of such concepts as "objectification" and "reification" is significant. Equally impressive is his assessment of why previous praxis philosophers had failed to understand the ontological dimensions of and interactional relations to technology; his rejection of the existentialist's drive to romanticize handcraft technologies; and his indictment of technological determinism. Furthermore, the recent revival of interest in Hans Jonas (notably in the biotechnology debates) suggests that renewed interest in Ihde's critique of Jonas's ethics might develop.

As Ihde began to focus more upon human-technology relations, it became clearer to him that our involvement with technologies impacts our existential situation dramatically, particularly the way in which we understand our world and our humanity. *Existential Technics* is thus the culmination of his reflexive (or "noematic") studies on human self-interpretation. Hubert Dreyfus may be the phenomenologist most often associated with pioneering the phenomenological critique of computers, but Ihde's chapters "Technology and Human Self-Conception" and "Why Do Humans Think that They Are Machines" stand out as exemplary investigations in to the significance of human self-understanding in a technologically saturated milieu. Indeed, Ihde's thesis "that all self-interpretation takes its shape in a certain way with respect to some basic form of existential praxis which is projected upon the world and reflected back in ways which become dominant ways of understanding ourselves and our world" remains highly relevant today (*ET* 22). Whereas Ihde appreciates the value of questioning what makes it possible for humans to ask existentially if they resemble (or fundamentally are) machines, some contemporary cyborg theorists and adherents of the computational conception of mind risk reifying technology by obscuring crucial ontological differences between humans and machines.

Perhaps Ihde's most widely read work in the philosophy of technology, however, is *Technology and the Lifeworld: From Garden to Earth*, a book that incorporates cross-cultural dimensions into an examination of the lifeworld role of *technics*. In it Ihde makes the compelling case that even though the non-neutrality of human-technology relations manifests in different ways in the context of different traditions, different geographies, and different time periods, it nevertheless remains invariably the case that "*human activity from immemorial time and across the diversity of cultures has always been technologically embodied*" (*TL* 20). This emphasis upon embodiment is philosophically significant because it permits Ihde to capture the primary structural features of technological intentionality: "embodiment relations," "hermeneutic relations," and "alterity relations."[7]

While these three relations exist on a continuum, and there is no decisive point at which one relation ends and another begins, specificity can be provided. Embodiment relations arise when we enter into optimally transparent practices with artifacts in order to amplify our bodies' perceptual abilities. For example, after a very short period of user adaptation, eyeglasses enable vision to be amplified. People who wear glasses are scarcely aware of having them on; apart from occasions in which peripheral vision feels compromised, their use falls into the background of conscious awareness and the perceptual world is perceived as directly experienced. Phenomenological precursors to this view can be found in Heidegger's discussion of the "ready-to-hand" (e.g., the hammer functioning as an extension of the arm's capabilities), as well as in Merleau-Ponty's discussion of the blind man's cane functioning as an extension of his perceptual awareness. Hermeneutic relations arise when we enter into practices with artifacts in order to ascertain knowledge about the world that would not otherwise be available (or, would at least be more difficult to ascertain). Hermeneutic relations do not amplify or replicate the body's sensory abilities; instead, they engage our linguistic and interpretative aptitudes. In this context, technologies that facilitate hermeneutic relations are best understood as being "text-like"; their effective utilization requires interpretation through the activity of reading. For example, in order to ascertain precisely how hot or cold something is, a thermometer can be inserted in-between the self and the world; the significance of the numbers on the thermometer's display depends not only upon the material composition of the tool and the aspects of the world that it comes into contact with, but also upon background scientific convictions that permit one to perceive the numbers as significant data. Clearly, these two types of relations, embodiment relations and hermeneutic relations, require different levels of skill. Whereas most children can learn to use glasses almost immediately upon being given them, learning to read (the paradigmatic hermeneutic relation) typically requires considerable formal training and effort.

Finally, we enter into alterity relations when we enter into practices with artifacts that display the feature of "otherness" (i.e., an evocative quality that transcends mere objecthood but resonates with less animateness than actual living beings such as people or animals). Unlike embodiment relations and hermeneutic relations, alterity relations focus attention upon the technology itself. In a video game, for example, the field of display that captivates need not refer to the transcendent world. Of course, to play most video games, one must enter into embodiment relations and hermeneutic relations. Without the ability to use a joystick or interpret graphics as significant, the game cannot be effectively played.

Ihde's focus upon the cultural dimensions of technoscience is one of the key differences between *Technics and Praxis* and *Technology and the Lifeworld* and it was motivated by his 1982 trip to Colombia, South America. During a faculty seminar, Ihde was denounced as a cultural imperialist for failing to notice that the North American question of distinguishing science from technology obscures the fact that the two are thoroughly intertwined: both function ideologically and materially as instruments that can be readily appropriated toward the end of extinguishing indigenous culture. This confrontational experience was transformative, and, accordingly, many of Ihde's subsequent reflections have emphasized the cultural dimensions of technoscience. In *Philosophy of Technology: An Introduction* Ihde not only presents an overview of the philosophy of technology (both its classical and contemporary variations), but he also provides an extended meditation on the postmodern value of "pluriculture." Pluriculture is the relativist condition in which one performs an "identity" by appropriating resources from different cultural possibilities in a bricolage fashion. As Ihde notes in "Image Technologies and Traditional Culture," while traditional cultures are now confronting modernity after being exposed to modern secular images, so too are provincial American (as well as Eurocentric) audiences calling aspects of their own identities into question after being exposed to traditional religious iconography. A technology such as television thus presents contemporary viewers with the opportunity to engage with international affairs reflectively. For example, Americans can note that the multiperspectival, international coverage of the recent "War on Terrorism" suggests that the conflict between East and West cannot be adequately explained by the partial metanarratives that both sides present (and disguise as complete explanations).

In both *Instrumental Realism: The Interface Between Philosophy of Technology and Philosophy of Science* and *Expanding Hermeneutics: Visualism in Science*, Ihde expands upon a position that he had hinted at in his earlier work. Specifically, Ihde provides formal arguments about the historical and ontological priority of technology over science. He contends that the philosophy of science, as traditionally conceived, is an incomplete enterprise because it fails to examine critically the role of technology in scientific contexts. By focusing upon the phenomenological theme of embodied perception—both micro- and macroperception—Ihde establishes the importance of interpreting science in terms of the concrete technologies that frame the manner in which scientists perceptually engage their research. In emphasizing how the use of instruments makes scientific observations possible, Ihde demonstrates that our understanding of the production of modern scientific knowledge is obscured when it is characterized as a process of representing a reality that putatively exists and can be known without reference to human intervention and the limits of human representation. In rendering aspects of reality visually perceptible that would otherwise remain invisible, scientific instruments (such as computer tomographs and ultrasound scanners) limit how reality can be understood; interpretative possibilities are materially and conceptually constrained.

Ihde thus develops a material hermeneutics that enables instrumental presence to be interpreted as a nonlinguistic analog to textual presence. In doing so, he provides a framework for understanding how the reality that scientists study and intervene in is constituted by a matrix: the world, the technological instruments that scientists use, and the interpretative biases that render this conjunction between perceiver and perceived meaningful are all constitutive. This stance differentiates Ihde from the neo-Diltheyan critics who maintain that while hermeneutics and the natural sciences might have some superficial similarities, they remain, at bottom, fundamentally separate and distinct enterprises. For example, Karl-Otto Apel argues that it is possible to conduct a hermeneutic history of science or a hermeneutic sociology of science, but a hermeneutics of science proper (or of its objects) is impossible. For Apel, but not for Ihde, the distinction between the *Geisteswissenschaften* and the *Naturwissenschaften* is absolute.

As a metaphilosophical framework, Ihde's hermeneutic analysis of material culture also reveals why the image of science generated by the logical positivists continues to circulate in Continental circles. Continental philosophers tend to characterize the historically sensitive, reflexive nature of the hermeneutic enterprise as one that is essentially antithetical to the scientific goal of formally generating universal, covering laws. This tendency resonates as much with Wilhelm Dilthey, Husserl, and Hans-Georg Gadamer as it does contemporary discourse; proponents of the hermeneutic enterprise continue to depict the world of science as fundamentally divorced from, and derivative of, the lifeworld. By endorsing the primacy of the lifeworld in a manner that renders science an abstractly rational, hypothesis generating domain, hermeneutic theorists continue to obscure the phenomenological dimensions of scientific *praxis* (i.e., the embodied activities, typically instrumentally mediated, that enable scientists to capitalize on and expand the Gestalt tendencies of perception). For example, recent programs of the Society for Phenomenology and Existential Philosophy reveal that the topic of science arises in Continental circles typically in the context of papers and panels that criticize how the sciences define human activity and human nature in a reductive manner. In this way, "science" becomes translated into "technoscience" in the Heideggerian sense of *Gestell*: the goal of scientific inquiry is presumed to be oriented by the putative essence of technology, and the only philosophical story worth telling concerns how it transforms all of reality into "standing reserve."

In his most recent work, *Bodies in Technology*, Ihde develops further the distinction between the phenomenological body, which he calls "body one" (i.e., the body that corresponds to our motile, perceptual, and emotive being in the world) and the social and cultural body, which he calls "body two." What is unique about this book is that it contains his first critical assessment of some of the leading science and technology studies (STS) practitioners. This trajectory, in which philosophical concerns are applied to STS theorists and their treatment of the topic of "symmetry," is developed further in his coedited collection, *Chasing Technoscience: Matrix for Materiality*. That Ihde is willing to use "postphenomenological" resources to engage with a new group of interdisciplinary interlocutors at this stage of his career demonstrates the lasting value of treating the visual as complex, synesthetic, and always referring back to the active and embodied manner in which the world is perceived.

Ihde's Philosophy: A Gestalt

Ihde's success can be attributed to many factors, perhaps the most prominent being his sense of interdisciplinary diplomacy. This trait is most evident in his philosophy of technoscience where he has demonstrated that different types of inquiry will be unable to fulfill their own disciplinary ambitions without collaborating better with other styles of investigation. On the one hand, Ihde warns us that it is problematic to allow scientific and technological development to occur without the aid of critical philosophical examination. His longstanding plea for philosophers to enter the research and development phase of innovation challenges those who believe that philosophy should play "second fiddle" to the more "technical" disciplines.[8] On the other hand, Ihde has always insisted that in order for scholars in the humanities to actively participate in a meaningful conversation on science and technology, they need to refrain from succumbing to an overly dystopian perspective. The godfathers of Continental interpretations of technology, for example, attempted to legitimate themselves as proxies for high culture by focusing solely upon the worst aspects of science and technology. By substituting sweeping ontological analysis and nostalgic rhetoric for careful attention to empirical research, they attempted to inaugurate a historical reversal in which the irrelevant humanist transformed into the authoritative critic. In doing so, they exacerbated the "two-culture" view of dividing intellectual labor and perpetuated a divisive academic environment in which scientists and engineers could feel justified in ignoring philosophers and other critical theorists. By contrast, while Ihde insists that technoscience critics should indeed play a necessary and valuable social role, he also maintains that such critics need to be "lovers" of the fields that they appraise. From Ihde's perspective, a genuine technoscience critic would not feel justified in appealing to a labyrinth of textual citations in order to bypass a more direct engagement with diverse empirical complexities that affect cultural practices in varied and complex ways.

In emphasizing Ihde's diplomacy, it is important that we do not lose sight of his proclivity toward iconoclasm. Much of Ihde's recent energies have been devoted to developing an account of "epistemology engines." An epistemology engine operates when some particular technology, in its workings and use, is seen suggestively as a metaphor for the human subject and often for the production of knowledge itself. Although to date Ihde has focused predominantly on the relation between the *camera obscura* and the invention of modern epistemology (in both its rationalist and empiricist variants), it appears likely that he will continue to develop this trajectory of returning the history of ideas to the lifeworld from which they initially emerge. We can, perhaps, look forward to a volume provocatively titled *Against the History of Philosophy.*

In closing this historical introduction, it seems apt to return to the origin of Ihde's scholarship by considering a comment that David Carr once made about Ricoeur: "In spite of his shifts away from traditional phenomenological concerns and his critical reservations about Husserl's original method, Ricoeur never totally gives up his allegiance to phenomenology."[9] Although Ihde has used many labels to characterize his style of philosophical inquiry, although he has rejected the foundational enterprise of traditional phenomenology, and although he has discarded much of the traditional tribal language found in the historical phenomenological discourse, he has always remained loyal to the spirit of phenomenology. The present volume is thus titled *Postphenomenology* and is as much about future transformations as it is about historical legacies.

Notes

1. During this time, Tillich taught at Harvard Divinity School.

2. Ihde's dissertation is entitled, "The Phenomenological Methodology and Philosophical Anthropology of Paul Ricoeur." It is worth noting that during the time in which Ihde was writing his dissertation, Ricoeur was not well-known. Only a few publications had been translated into English.

3. Don Ihde, *Hermeneutic Phenomenology: The Philosophy of Paul Ricoeur* (Evanston: Northwestern University Press, 1971), xvii.

4. Ihde's first post-Ph.D. article is entitled, "Some Parallels between Phenomenology and Analysis."

5. Ihde has written numerous essays on Ricoeur after his early Ricoeur period, such as "Interpreting Hermeneutics," "Variation and Boundary: A Problem in Riceour's Phenomenology," "Text and the New Hermeneutics," "Paul Riceour's Place in the Hermeneutic Tradition," and "Literary and Science Fictions: Philosophers and Technomyths."

6. Mario Bunge, "Five Buds of Techno-Philosophy," *Technology in Society* 1 (1979): 68.

7. Although this taxonomy was developed in earlier writings, *Technology and the Lifeworld* remains, perhaps, the most frequently cited text by scholars who discuss this dimension of Ihde's corpus.

8. See Don Ihde, "Technology and Prognostic Predicaments," *AI and Society* 13 (1999): 44–51.

9. David Carr, "Husserl and Phenomenology," in *The Columbia History of Western Philosophy*, ed. Richard Popkin (New York: Columbia University Press, 1998), 680.

Part I

Phenomenological Style:
Ihde's Unique Voice

1

Simple Grounds:
At Home in Experience

Vivian Sobchack

> Sometimes he envied the boy, who could with equal enthusiasm
> enjoy the lizards sunning themselves on the rock wall by the
> house, the loud MTV channel, and his toy computer.
>
> —Don Ihde (*TL* 218)

Don Ihde's work is particularly significant—and unusual—for what might be
called its grounding simplicity, its capacity to make his readers comfortable
enough to follow him anywhere—outdoors, indoors, home and abroad, and
always, or at least, into micro- and macroperceptual adventures that expand
both their embodied presence to the world and its "possible reciprocities of
experience" (*BT* 32). His mode—indeed, his style—is to settle us, first, in
domestic and felicitous places and experiences, attuning us to our everyday
perceptions in and around our homes and offices as we engage what we think
of as the "natural" world and as we use and incorporate a common array of
low and "high" human artifacts and technologies. That accomplished, he then
entices us, ever so casually and always without threat, into the phenomenological complexities and multistabilities of what seems familiar to us and then
further—into the less "homey" places and practices of cultures and histories
that we do not experience in the "natural attitude" as remotely our own. In
a straightforward manner that is less deceptive than seductive in its promise
that we can and will understand what follows, his philosophical (and literary)
persona is relaxed, steady, and unpedantic. Even as his descriptions accumu-
late in phenomenological complexity and rigor, his tone, attitude, and autobiographical grounding remain purposefully "unacademic." Like the boy (his
son) in the epigraph above, with "equal enthusiasm," Ihde fully enjoys himself wherever he goes: listening to himself listen on a dark country road or

13

in a concert hall, exploring variations of ocean navigation, cooking a meal, describing an array of perceptual technologies and "epistemology engines,"[1] or thinking about his own embodiment as male in our culture. We get the sense that he has lived not only a full life but also has lived life fully. In sum, throughout his books and essays, Ihde offers us the friendly guidance, companionship, and presence of (dare I use the term with admiration?) an "armchair philosopher." Indeed as one commentator has put it, "the overall points almost sneak up on you, they are so gently and gradually offered."[2]

In this regard, Ihde provides us an extraordinary and exemplary phenomenological pedagogy—a pedagogy that can be "inhabited" and lived as well as abstractly learned and thought. His unadorned prose, his autobiographical vignettes, his use of narrative and thought experiments to open up perceptual possibilities, and his call for readers to test the precision of his descriptions against their own concrete empirical experience, all find expression in, as Ihde describes it, "a nonfoundational and nontranscendental phenomenology which makes variational theory its most important methodological strategy" (*PP* 7). Indeed, it is this emphasis on variational method that leads his readers to an active appreciation of the open possibilities of embodied perception as it is enabled, shaped, and regulated by human and natural history, cultural traditions, and (as Ihde titles one of his books) "existential technics" (*ET*). However, while variational method forms the core of his phenomenological investigations, what enlivens it (what makes it seem methodologically achievable to his readers) is an underlying—and rare—sense of existential presence. The autobiographical vignette only the most obvious of its signs, this sense of presence informs and animates Ihde's work—grounding us in personal (and personally possible) experience but, as well, demonstrating that the "personal" is neither synonymous with nor reducible to the "individual," and that, instead, it provides the very intersubjective basis for further investigation of more general forms and structural variants of lived experience.

In its clear call to an awareness of our lived experience and existential presence, Ihde's pedagogy seems to me of the utmost importance in the contemporary context of the commonly abstractive practices of the humanities disciplines in today's research university—the latter now an environment (as Hans Ulrich Gumbrecht eloquently decries it) "filled with the technological and epistemological noise of our general mobilization," "an environment that will not let us pause for more than moments of presence."[3] Indeed, in today's university, most graduate students, encouraged by most of their professors, are in such a hurry to "professionalize" and to "understand" that they sometimes forget to attend to their "experience" and to "see." This is as surprisingly true of the students of film and media studies that I teach as it is of those in other less "vision-focused" disciplines also informed by "critical theory" of various kinds and articulated in the embrace of such figures as

Foucault and Deleuze and such contemporary terms (now rather bloated "floating signifiers") as "multiculturalism" and "globalization," "constructivism" and "situated knowledges." These are students who cultivate and display hermeneutic sophistication but who are secretly insecure and worried that everyone else (their professors, their theoretical role models, and their classmates) knows and understands more than they do. These are also students who, intellectually aware of "perspectival relativism" and suspicious of their own "subjectivity," so mistrust their own objectively perspectival perceptual experience that they immediately dismiss it as trivial, wrong, or—even worse for its inherent denial of intersubjectivity—singular. Thus, ignoring the apodicticity and presence of their own embodied experience in the world, their thought about the world has no existential ground of its own from which to empirically proceed.

Ihde's pedagogical method and his particular style of first engaging his readers in investigation of familiar (and too quickly discounted) experience serves as a "life-saving" antidote to this general loss of existential grounding—a loss, I might add, that over the last few years a growing number of professors and even more graduate student have begun to feel deeply and attempted to redress. Hence, on the one hand, the relatively recent flurry of scholarly work on "the body" across the humanities—although, dare I say, this is the body most often held at arm's length and safely at a distance. Indeed, as Thomas Csordas writes, most of this work tries to redeem the body but does so in analyses "without much sense of bodiliness," and thus dissipates "the force of using the body as a methodological starting point," "objectifies bodies as things devoid of intentionality and intersubjectivity," and "misses the opportunity to assert an added dimension of materiality to our notions of culture and history."[4] And hence, on the other hand, the even more recent scholarly turn to autobiography and personal anecdote—although these most often serve no significant methodological purpose. Usually inserted with an "apology" or serving as an "interruption" of abstract argument rather than its ground, at worst, the effect is less illuminating than narcissistic (that is, less about what it means to be an embodied and perceiving "person" than about what it means to be "me"). In a few recent (and extreme) cases, this turn to the autobiographical has been explicitly rebellious against the academy and its dominant pedagogy of professionalization, but unfortunately its extremity has also thrown the baby of scholarly investigation out with the bathwater of (as Ihde has decried it in his own work) the "anonymous voice of technical writing that . . . employs rigorous avoidance of all anthropomorphisms, . . . is usually cast in terms of formal or abstract. . . . formulations, and . . . reduces all entities to [equivalent] variables within its system" (*BT* 79).[5]

Nonetheless, while this contemporary turn toward the body and toward autobiography and personal vignette is symptomatic of an academic dis-ease with prevailing scholarly methods in the humanities, it has had no method of its own. It is precisely here that Ihde's "fleshing out" of variational method is of particular significance—for it grounds both the body (and its various incorporations) and the autobiographical in an accessible and rigorous phenomenological practice that connects the particularities of experience with more general existential structures. Ihde writes in *Bodies in Technology*: "How can one combine the richness of autobiographical concreteness with wider implications of the general patterns, even universality (within the one remaining human species, *Homo sapiens*)? My own partial answer is that all structures and patterns—and there are these—display multistable sets of limited possibilities. This is clearly a phenomenological notion derived from variational theory, but set in a nonfoundationalist context" (*BT* 33). Thus, for Ihde, representations of personal or "subjective" experience provide the beginning of inquiry rather than its end. Indeed, as he moves from such familiar experience into variations upon it, he demonstrates that grounding more general description and interpretation of embodied perception and cultural experience in autobiographical and anecdotal experience is not a "subjective" substitute for rigorous and objective analysis. Quite the opposite: it purposefully provides the phenomenological premises (a quite concrete and embodied starting place) for a more processual, expansive, and resonant materialist logic through which we, as embodied subjects, can come to understand (and perhaps actively guide) what passes as our objective historical and cultural existence.

In this way, Ihde employs the autobiographical and familiar as a methodological tactic. He writes: "The use of simple, familiar examples deliberately opens the way to the sense of phenomenology through an 'experiential given'" (*EP* 25). Thus, he may start each of what will turn out to be a set of extremely complex variations on sound with his own "simple" experiences: attuning himself to the ambient sounds of a clock, the radiator, the hum of the light fixture in his home office, that together constitute a "field"; listening with his son to a ballpoint pen roll in a covered box and discovering sound "shapes"; closing his eyes and hearing the material "surfaces" of a concrete wall and a plywood fence resonate quite differently (*LV* 74, 61, 69). Considering the ways our lives are pervasively intertwined with technologies, he may start with a description of the most mundane of academic office artifacts and routines such as telephones, computers, and xeroxing (*ET* 2–3); of watching his children use old-fashioned "dip pens" when they were in elementary school in France and then trying it out himself to discover the embodied meaning of "belles letters" (*TL* 141); or, even more simply, of using a piece of chalk on a blackboard to get in touch literally with reductions and amplifications of his perception of texture (*EP* 139–140). And, as he has in his most sustained autobiographical essay ("The Tall and the Short of It: Male Sports Bodies"), he may compare the generational similarities and differences between himself and his young son of growing up to be an embodied American "male" (*BT* 6–34). (This is the only one of Ihde's essays in which one learns he compensated for his initial lack of height and athletic prowess by becoming drum major of his high school's marching band; it is also the only essay I recall in which Ihde—explicitly proud of his straightforward prose and suspicious of "literariness," word play, and "cuteness"—emphasizes the phenomenological information and power of vernacular language in phrases and words such as "falling short" or "shortcoming."[6])

What is important in the context of the humanities' recent turn to "the body" and the autobiographical is that Ihde's use of the autobiographical is not meant to focus on a particular life—and, even more certainly, not on his life. It is, as he has indicated, a pedagogical and methodological tactic and should not serve as an end in itself—or as an end to (rather than the beginning of) phenomenological variation. Indeed, he explicitly worries that the autobiographical—by virtue of its very concreteness and particularity—can too easily take a literary turn; that, in its telling, "literary devices emerge that possibly belie more mundane actualities" (*BT* 33). And it is in these mundane actualities and their structures, not in a particular life or autobiographical persona, that Ihde is interested. The tactic of autobiographical beginnings to variational method is meant to gently train us within the limits of the familiar in a certain kind of structural description of embodied experience: to foster and practice the recognition of regularities, variations, and multistabilities in "mundane actualities" so as to prepare us to describe (or imagine) experiential "actualities" (or their possibility) that are not so readily graspable as our own. Thus, beginning with familiar (and often simple) autobiographical vignettes, Ihde moves us from the revelation of their multistabilities to alternative perspectives and accommodations to the world to show structural and interpretive differences and similarities to our own, these usually drawn from other times and cultures.

This is to say, Ihde's pedagogical strategy follows the trajectory of phenomenological description, qualified reduction (or thematization), and interpretation in a macro- as well as a micropractice. He begins with microdescription of the familiar (and autobiographical) experiences of the "self," then through variation and reduction moves the "self" into a recognition of "self-alterity" (that is, of the multistability informing its familiar practices and milieu), and then, using further variations, moves the "self" from its now recognized "self- alterity" to an interpretation that is meaningful at both a micro and macro level and allows experiential receptivity to and reciprocity (however unsymmetrical) with the historical and cultural experiences of an "other self."[7]

In this regard, focusing on the autobiographical in connection with Thoreau's Walden (a connection Ihde might well appreciate), Hugh Silverman has pointed to the form's intersubjective and microperceptual grounding as well as to its nonfoundational claims: "The decentering of the autobiographical self is the incorporation of other autobiographical selves who might have approximated the same locale had their autobiographizing been the same. But the difference in the autobiographizing is what writes the difference that distinguishes the selves. Each autobiographical self delineates its own outlines, its own limitations, and its own modalities."[8] Ihde, however, a phenomenologist rather than autobiographer, tests this intersubjectivity not only in relation to his immediate readers but in relation to extensive and concrete empirical research. Thus, as he says, while his style is autobiographical, "the investigations themselves took place over . . . years and involved classroom investigation and much intersubjective research"—which includes research in other than North American contexts (*LV* viii–ix). Beginning at home, Ihde always also takes us perceptually abroad.

Silverman writes: "[A]utobiography must situate itself at the place where metaphoricity meets literality, where the substitution of life is life itself, where the writing of a life is the life, where the activity of translating is living. In this respect, autobiographizing is textualizing, but textualizing is both activity and text."[9] Using autobiographical vignettes in conjunction with variational method, Ihde's pedagogy emphasizes the place where the metaphorical meets the literal. That is, through substitutions and extensions of practice, he translates his textual "writing of a life" into the active life of his readers. Thus, despite the simplicity of his language and his experiential examples, his demand upon his readers is complex in its call for their existential and embodied presence. As he says in *Experimental Phenomenology*, they "must see what is going on, and by that I mean see in its most literal sense" (*EP* 25).

Notes

1. *CT* 123.

2. See John Compton, the back cover blurb of *TL*.

3. Hans Ulrich Gumbrecht, *The Production of Presence: What Meaning Cannot Convey* (Stanford: Stanford University Press, 2004), 141.

4. Thomas J. Csordas, Introduction to *Embodiment and Experience*, ed. Thomas J. Csordas (Cambridge: Cambridge University Press, 1994), 4. Although there is by now an extensive literature on "the body" as distinguished from a focus on "embodiment," the influential work of Judith Butler comes immediately to mind.

5. Reference here to the extreme case is Jane Tompkins, *A Life in School: What the Teacher Learned* (Reading: Addison-Wesley, 1997). I have added the word "equiva-

lent" to Ihde's description here because, in earlier discussion, he has criticized this abstract leveling of differences and ambiguities among various phenomena as they are experienced.

6. Ihde critiques much phenomenological writing: "A third kind of obscurity sometimes occurs which is to be deplored. Essentially, this consists of the language some phenomenologists . . . introduce by inserting unnecessary obscurity and even cuteness into their language. Whatever the motive, any attempt to cover confusion or pretend profundity by means of excess verbiage is naturally distasteful" (*EP* 20). See also *BT* 32–33. (Nobody's perfect and I note here Ihde's uncharacteristic presumption of what is not only "natural" but also naturally "distasteful.")

7. A wonderful "summary" example of this (albeit less overtly autobiographical in style than in practice) is the chapter "Perceptual Teleologies," (*PP* 79–87). Here Ihde reviews perceptual variations on his "pet" Necker cube but then goes on to look at specific perspectival viewing "positions" of the "world" using historical and cultural variants of depictions of gardens; beginning with more familiar perspectival "bird's-eye" images from medieval European and Chinese culture, he moves to less familiar depictions from Australian aboriginal culture, Andean tribal culture, and ancient Egyptian culture.

8. Hugh J. Silverman, "Autobiographical Textuality: The Case of Thoreau's *Walden*," *Semiotica* 41, 1/4 (1982): 273.

9. Ibid., 269.

2

From Phenomenology to Pragmatism: Using Technology as an Instrument

Carl Mitcham

Don Ihde's first book offers an appreciative assessment of the work of herme-neutic phenomenologist Paul Ricoeur, in which he explicitly allies himself with the third (or French) wave in phenomenology (subsequent to the first [Austrian] and second [German] waves led by Edmund Husserl and Martin Heidegger, respectively). But very shortly thereafter Ihde began to contribute to an emerg-ing fourth (North American) wave that he initially termed "experimental phenom-enology," and in which he reaffirmed the importance of Husserl. Although his own sympathies ultimately lay elsewhere, he was equally convinced "that phe-nomenology must begin with [Husserl's] approach [of] rigor and distinction-making" and the appeal to "intuitable" or experienceable evidence.

Phenomenology in each of its European waves exhibited a distinct un-easiness with modern science and technology. Indeed, twentieth-century European phenomenology has often been described as an heir to Friedrich Nietzsche's two-pronged attack on scientism and technological culture—scientism understood as the claim that science is the highest form of knowl-edge and technological culture as one in which massification and consumerism have conspired to reduce the quality of achievements in art, music, and lit-erature while undermining the pursuit of nobility and virtue. Without aban-doning the critical perspective that sought to question scientific abstractions and technological culture, Ihde worked from the beginning to build a bridge between the appeal to concrete experience and that general experimental method that had become a hallmark of American pragmatism, especially in the work of John Dewey. Neither pragmatism nor Dewey are mentioned in Ihde's introduction to *Experimental Phenomenology*, but the very title of the book was, as it were, a promissory note for their future engagement. Ihde's concluding chapter on "interdisciplinary phenomenology," which initiates a phenomenological analysis of machine-human or instrument-human relations, further indicates what will become the vehicle for this future engagement.

As a contribution to recognizing Ihde's unique contribution to American phenomenology, what follows is a brief presentation of the pragmatist tradition and a reflection on Ihde's distinctive and challenging engagement with that tradition, emphasizing his phenomenology of instrumentation.

The Classical Pragmatist Background

As is well known, in its Greek roots, *pragmatikos* is associated with business, political, and even technological affairs; the same goes for the Latin *pragmaticus*. Even when Socrates brought philosophy down from the heavens to dwell in the cities and to reflect on the *anthropina pragmata* or human affairs, he called for placing such *pragmata* in a larger perspective—that of ethics and politics if not metaphysics—and argued against taking the perspective of *pragmata* themselves as a guide about how to think in general. As late as Immanuel Kant the term "pragmatic" continues to designate those laws that have less than fully binding power or are grounded not in philosophical reflection but in practical affairs.

Pragmatism as a philosophical movement arose in the nineteenth-century as an effort to bring philosophy out of the realm of metaphysical speculation—especially in relation to what may be termed the epistemological account of knowledge as justified true belief (a definition that can be traced back to Plato)—and to highlight relations between thought and human affairs, analyzing beliefs in terms of their relationships to human action. Modern epistemologies since René Descartes had begun with doubt concerning the relationship between concepts and reality, and then sought to identify some belief that could be justified so as to escape this challenge, that is, a concept whose representation of the phenomenon was guaranteed by some uniquely trustworthy activity or method. Charles Sanders Peirce, adapting a suggestion from the Scottish philosopher Alexander Bain, argued that beliefs were more properly interpreted as habits of acting than as representations of reality, and thus not so much in need of special foundations as being located in historical and social processes. All the classical American pragmatists—from Peirce through William James to John Dewey—reject the modern foundationalist project in favor of some interpretation of inquiry that unites theoretical and practical knowledge as forms of learning to live more effectively in the world.

Such an approach readily ties knowing into science and technology. Yet one remarkable feature of pragmatism is that despite the clear affinities between science, technology, and pragmatism from Pierce on, it was only in Dewey's mature work that this relationship became a well-articulated theme. Having turned away from Hegelian idealism, and influenced to a significant degree by the Darwinian theory of evolution, Dewey argued that the methods of the sciences broadly construed—including technology—serve as distinctly human tools in a human lifeworld that is continuous with a larger nonhuman lifeworld.

For Dewey logical theory provides the most general description of this tool or method of inquiry and action, which he analyzes into five stages.[1] Stage one involves the recognition of a problematic situation characterized by a disequilibrium between an organism and its environment, in this case human interests and the environment. Stage two is constituted by the explicit formulation of a question concerning this situation as human inquiry comes to bear upon it. In stage three various possible hypotheses, responses, or solutions to the problem are considered. In stage four one or more solutions are played out and tested in action. Dewey is at pains to stress that the initial problematic situation can be cognitive (theoretical) or practical, with responses being able to display the same differential character. But in all cases thought is instrumental for problem solving, and those solutions that test out become, in stage five, part of human life in whatever particular contexts from which they arose. Because of the stress placed on the instrumental character of logic, and indeed of all human inquiry, Dewey's special version of pragmatism is sometimes termed instrumentalism. Dewey nevertheless did not take the step of calling his approach a philosophy of technology.

The first proposal for an explicit philosophy of technology in the classical pragmatist tradition was Joseph W. Cohen's "Technology and Philosophy."[2] Samuel M. Levin's "John Dewey's Evaluation of Technology"[3] and John W. Donohue's "Dewey and the Problem of Technology"[4] likewise recognize the importance of technology in Dewey but are published later and do not draw out the implications as strongly. Cohen, like Dewey, begins by arguing the ontological priority of technology over science. Human beings were "*Homo faber* before [becoming] *Homo sapiens*...Out of technical processes and slowly accumulating skills, out of combinations and recombinations of the tools and expertise of many peoples came the eventual theoretical organization of technology into science."[5] Having defined "technology in a sense broad enough to include science,"[6] Cohen criticizes the views of technology as evil and as neutral for sundering intelligence and value. The former is "tradition-bound, anachronistic" romanticism; the latter is a rationalization that lets scientists and engineers avoid "any disturbing thought that they are also, even as scientists and technicians, concerned with values and as such carry a burden of responsibility for the uses to which their work is put."[7] The truth is that technology is bound up with values, and this insight—which he attributes to Thorstein Veblen, Dewey, and C.E. Ayers—is "the distinctive contribution of American thought to the philosophy of technology."[8]

According to Dewey, Cohen argues, technology is both intelligence and value because "all ideas are intellectual tools employed in experimental operations for the solution of the problems which arise in experience."[9] Dewey's philosophy of technology thus sees technology not as something opposed to value (and hence to democracy, ethics, art, etc.), as anti-technology cultural critics would have it, or as neutral with regard to value, as scientists and engineers think. It is itself valuable, and as such something to be integrated with other values in culture not by monist, technocratic management but through "pluralistic planning." [10] However, although Cohen claims that "Dewey's experimental pluralism"[11] provides a better analysis of the role of technology in culture than do, for instance, Lewis Mumford's historical studies, and that "instrumentalism is a name for competent reflective thinking in every sphere of culture," he also maintains that "technology and science [provide] the clearest pattern of such thinking."[12] In critical commentary on this view—in the context of distinguishing between humanities philosophies that argue for the delimitation of technology and engineering philosophies that defend for its expansion—I have previously suggested that pragmatic instrumentalism could be interpreted as reducing other realms of culture to diminished forms of technology.

Late Twentieth- and Early Twenty-first-Century Pragmatism

A second wave of American pragmatism is manifested in the work of Willard Van Orman Quine, Donald Davidson, Hilary Putnam, and Richard Rorty—all of whom have referred to themselves as pragmatists, but in senses often at odds with early twentieth-century pragmatism. According to Joseph Margolis, this second wave is characterized by two retreats from classical American pragmatism: naturalism and postmodernism.[13]

Quine and colleagues run the danger of retreating from the pragmatic analysis of science as a nonfoundational form of instrumental knowing into a new foundational realism in which cognitive science determines its justified forms. Although Dewey described himself as a naturalist, he never made the scientific study of cognition the foundational basis of knowledge. Instead of defending scientific knowledge as providing a privileged view of the world, Dewey argued instead that the process of science was a privileged means or method for living in the world—but one that could be extended or applied across the spectrum of human activities, from the physical and the social sciences to even politics and the arts. Indeed, Dewey's primary interest was not in epistemology so much as in progressive politics, which he argued was able to learn from the sciences, especially the social sciences.

The postmodernist retreat, by contrast, appears to reject even Dewey's delimited privilege for scientific method as a generalizable way of life. The multicultural, postmodernist, discourse-based pragmatism of Rorty grants science no privileged position and abandons political activism in the name of liberal discourse that is, at most, edifying. In Rorty's words:

> The attempt to edify (ourselves or others) may consist in the herme-
> neutic activity of making connections between our own culture and
> some exotic culture or historical period, or between our own disci-
> pline and another discipline which seems to pursue incommensurable
> aims in an incommensurable vocabulary [or in] the "poetic" activity
> of thinking up . . . new aims, new words, or new disciplines [and] the
> attempt to reinterpret our familiar surroundings in the unfamiliar terms
> of our new inventions.[14]

But surely this is a thin version of the instruction and spiritual improve-ment that the Latin *aedificare*, to construct a temple, once implied. It is even thinner in comparison with the related classical ideal of *paideia* and the modern German notion of *Bildung*—as well as with classical pragmatism, which seeks to edify by means of a circumscribed but substantive reliance on science and expertise as methods of living that must nevertheless be guided by democratic interests and participation. By contrast, Ihde's analysis of the *Consequences of Phenomenology* aims to stake out a *Postphenomenology* that engages the contemporary world in terms of the practical constructions and experiences of its technoscientific instruments in ways that may not be as overtly practical as Dewey but offer more prospects for transformation than talk alone.

Along with his failure to mention Ihde's pragmatic postphenomenology, Margolis overlooks another late twentieth-century pragmatism—that associ-ated with the philosophy of technology. Two primary contributors to pragma-tist philosophy of technology have been Paul T. Durbin and Larry Hickman, both of whom possess their own special links to Ihde. Durbin, as the inspi-ration behind a series of conferences that led to the creation of the Society for Philosophy and Technology (SPT) in 1980, early recognized Ihde's im-portance and made a point to get him engaged in this new organization. Hickman's *John Dewey's Pragmatic Technology* was one of the first three volumes published in the "Indiana Series in the Philosophy of Technology" edited by Ihde, with his *Philosophical Tools for Technological Culture* being a subsequent contribution.

Durbin, inspired more deeply by George Herbert Mead than by Dewey, provides both methodological and substantive developments of Cohen's po-sition.[15] For Durbin a philosophy of technology "amounts to a statement as to what one feels a good technological society *ought* to be like, plus some persuasive arguments aimed at getting influential others to agree."[16] In his attempt to carry forward Mead's pragmatic argument for "the application of

the experimental method to social problems,"[17] Durbin calls for members of
the technical community to become involved in reform movements related to
social problems associated with technological change. In *Social Responsibility in Science, Technology, and Medicine* he provides detailed descriptions of
how progressive social activists in the fields of education, medicine, media,
computers, industry, and public interest groups organized around concern
about nuclear weapons, nuclear power, and the government can in fact me-
liorate problems associated with technology.[18]

But it is Hickman's *John Dewey's Pragmatic Technology* that both re-
trieves the central texts from the Dewey corpus and provides the most extended defense of a pragmatist philosophy of technology.[19] Hickman too sees
the key to Dewey's philosophy of technology in his instrumentalist epistemology and the priority of practice over theory. As he points out, the pivotal
chapter 4 of *The Quest for Certainty*, one of Dewey's most mature and comprehensive works, is a paean to technology. Here Dewey explicitly says that
"there is no difference in logical principle between the method of science and
the method pursued in technologies."[20] Indeed, in a remarkable acknowledgment that Hickman recovers from a text of twenty years later, Dewey says,
"It is probable that I might have avoided a considerable amount of misunderstanding if I had systematically used 'technology' instead of 'instrumentalism' in connection with the view I put forth regarding the distinctive quality
of science as knowledge."[21] Indeed, for Dewey the term "science" already has
such a heavy practical base and problem-solving orientation—as it does for
many heirs of the Enlightenment—that it too is almost interchangeable with
"technology."

This technological theory of knowledge provides the basis for a contrast
between ancient and modern science: "Greek and medieval science formed an
art of accepting things as they are enjoyed and suffered. Modern experimental
science is an art of control."[22] But such a difference is not just to be noted,
it is to be praised:

> The remarkable difference between the attitude which accepts the
> objects of ordinary perception . . . and that which takes them as start-
> ing points . . . is one which . . . marks a revolution in the whole spirit
> of life, in the entire attitude taken toward whatever is found in
> existence . . . . [N]ature as it already exists ceases to be something
> which must be accepted and submitted to, endured or enjoyed, just as
> it is. It is now something to be modified, to be intentionally con-
> trolled. It is material to act upon so as to transform it into new objects
> which better answer our needs.[23]

Although the "art of accepting things" that he attributes to Greek and medieval science may be more complex and subtle than Dewey admits, Hickman

rightly sums up Dewey's position: "What Dewey thought significant about inquiry, and what he thought discloses its technological character, is that *every reflective experience is instrumental to further production of meanings, that is, it is technological.*"[24]

But if virtually all knowing, and indeed all human activity, is or ought to be at its core technological, this raises anew the specter of reductionism. One reviewer of *The Quest for Certainty* even commented on what he saw as Dewey's "reduction of philosophy to technology." As Hickman states the problem, the charge is that "there is a reduction of the function of many tools to the function of one specific type of tool, the extra-organic." Hickman's reply is that the criticism presumes the existence of a sharp line between organism and environment...[B]ut for purposes of inquiry, the skin is not a very good indicator of where the organism stops and the environment begins.[25]

In reality, as Dewey writes in *Art as Experience*:

> There are things inside the body that are foreign to it, and there are things outside of it that belong to it...On the lower scale, air and food materials are such things; in the higher, tools, whether the pen of the writer or the anvil of the blacksmith, utensils and furnishings, property, friends and institutions — all the supports and sustenances without which a civilized life cannot be.[26]

For Dewey all tools remain subservient to human life and its interests and aspirations in the broadest sense. (Note, however, how this passage suggests the idea of tools as extensions of the body, an assumption that Ihde will take up with phenomenological rigor.)

Another possible concern is that if all life is technological then the concept of technology becomes vacuous. Hickman responds at length to this objection in *Philosophical Tools for Technological Culture*, which is perhaps the single best presentation of that pragmatic philosophy of technology he previously attributed to Dewey. In response to the charge of reductionism, Hickman carefully distinguishes four different ways in which human activities can be technological. First, they may use tools or artifacts, or they may not. Second, those that use tools may do so deliberately or merely habitually. Third, those that do not use tools may either be cognitive or noncognitive. As a result, it is possible to distinguish:

(1) The deliberate using of tools/artifacts in *technological* activities—such as engineering, architecture, musical performances, and even cooking a meal or mowing the yard. (Hickman notes that in this category, as in others, it is also possible to distinguish the tools used as tangible or intangible.)

(2) The habitual or nondeliberative use of tools/artifacts in *technical* activities—such as industrial labor, driving a car, writing with a computer, and more.

(3) Cognitive activities that do not employ tools/artifacts—as when, on a hot hike through the mountains, one perceives that snow could be used to cool oneself and does so by rubbing it on one's face. (Hickman admits that such activities are difficult to characterize definitely, but nonetheless argues their importance.)

(4) Noncognitive activities that do not employ tools/artifacts—the best examples being immediate perceptions or unconscious habitual responses such as taking delight in a flower along a mountain path or the smile of someone on the street.

Hickman thus makes a strong case against pragmatism as any reductionism *tout court*—although he appears to allow for reductionism within specific types. As he also observes, while determinate numbers are not available, the move from one to four in his typology involves increasingly large percentages of human activity, with human activities and experiences at the base providing "much of the raw material for technological activity."[27] One might argue further that, historically, the first two categories have been expanded and transformed by changes in technology itself in ways not always beneficial to human well being, points that Hickman would easily take as opportunities for pragmatic assessment and reform.

Indeed, exhibiting such an approach, Hickman proceeds to develop a comprehensive interpretation of Dewey's philosophy of art and his account of the history of technology, then to use a pragmatist philosophy of technology to reassess the fears of technological determinism articulated by Jacques Ellul and others. In an epilogue on "responsible technology" that echoes Durbin, Hickman defines technology as "the sum of concrete activities and products of men and women who engage in inquiry in its manifold forms: in the sciences, in the fine and useful arts, in business, in engineering, and in [politics]." Then he adds:

> Where technology fails to be responsible, it is not because technology as method has failed, but because inquiry and testing have been misdirected, subsumed to nontechnological ends, or aborted. Ends have been dissociated from means. Fixed religious or political ideologies have taken the place of legitimate, testable inquiry. Economic and class interests have intervened where experimentation would have been appropriate.[28]

In short, the problems associated with technologies are caused not by technologies but by nontechnology or failures to bring critical thinking to bear in commercial or public affairs—and are thus to be solved not by less technology, but by more. The problem is what the sociologist William Fielding Ogburn in 1922 first termed "cultural lag," in which culture fails to change so as to take advantage of new opportunities for edification offered by new technologies. But is this really the case? It will depend at least in part on the question of instrumentalization, and how the metaphor of thought as instrument is understood.

Ihde's Phenomenology of Instrumentation

Even before Hickman's articulation of a pragmatic philosophy of technology, Ihde had begun to develop a phenomenological philosophy of technology that can be read as both incorporating and criticizing—if only implicitly—the pragmatic perspective.

Technics and Praxis: A Philosophy of Technology begins by distinguishing between idealist and materialist attitudes toward technology. The former views technology as applied science, the latter sees science as theoretical technology. Siding with the latter (and with classical American pragmatism), Ihde sketches a phenomenology of human-technology-world relations. He then reflects on some experiential implications of modern technology such as computers and electronic music and concludes by examining the pioneering phenomenological approaches to technology found in the work of Martin Heidegger, Hans Jonas, and European existentialists. Phenomenologically, Ihde carefully distinguishes those technologies that extend or embody human experience (e.g., the magnifying glass) and those that call for human interpretations or hermeneutic reflection (the thermometer).

Carrying this phenomenological analysis further, Ihde uncovers a basic amplification/reduction structure in all technology-mediated relations. An embodiment technology such as the magnifying glass, amplifies certain microfeatures of the world, but only by reducing our field of vision.

> With every amplification, there is a simultaneous and necessary reduction. And . . . the amplification tends to stand out, to be dramatic, while the reduction tends to be overlooked. [The result is that] the instrument mediated entity is one which, in comparison with the flesh relations, appears with a different perspective. (*TP* 21)

Based on this amplification/reduction, Ihde argues against any view of technology as neutral or pure transparency with utopian possibilities—a perspective that relies on emphasizing amplification while ignoring reduction. At the same time, he rejects the idea that technology is a "Frankenstein phenomenon" (*TP* 40) opposed to the human—a view that emphasizes only reduction while ignoring amplification. In this, Ihde sides with Cohen (and Dewey). Yet while rejecting "a hard technological determinism" he admits there are often "latent telic *inclinations*" (*TP* 42) in technologies that predispose human beings to develop certain technolife forms over others. In this Ihde asks pragmatism to reconsider more carefully its own progressive interests.

Existential Technics builds on this suggestion by analyzing how technology becomes involved not just in our interpretation of, or theory construction about, the natural world, but also how technology influences our understanding of what it is to be human, that is, our self-image or self-interpretation. As he concludes in the introductory, programmatic chapter: "we end up modeling ourselves on the very 'world' we project and interpret ourselves in terms of technology" (*TP* 22). Part two of *Consequences of Phenomenology*, especially the essay "Technology and the Human: From Progress to Ambiguity," carries forward such existential concerns and concludes that "the deeper question of technics and the human remains one about the variable possibilities or our seeing itself" (*CP* 90)—including the seeing of our selves.

Technology and the Lifeworld: From Garden to Earth and *Instrumental Realism: The Interface between Philosophy of Science and Philosophy of Technology*, originally conceived as one book, constitute the most comprehensive presentation of Ihde's philosophy of technology. *Technology and the Lifeworld* rests on the argument that human beings are not able to lead nontechnological lives in some garden state, because on the Earth they are inherently technological organisms. Having made his special argument to this effect, Ihde reviews the relevant insights of others in the phenomenological tradition (Heidegger, Husserl, and Merleau-Ponty) and describes the pivotal historical importance of technology to the rise of modern science (e.g., Galileo and the telescope).

Then following a reprise and extension of the human-technology-world analysis from previous works, in the latter half of the book Ihde extends his reflections on the existential import of technology and examines these in cross-cultural perspective. As he emphasizes in *Philosophy of Technology: An Introduction*, he "*celebrates* a certain disappearance of a 'core,' or a 'foundation'" to culture in the technological world, but admits the need to find "post-enlightenment means of securing inter-cultural ... modes of tolerance and cultural pluralism" (*PT* 115). *Instrumental Realism* constitutes an extended dialogue, especially related to the phenomenological interpretation of technoscience, with the work of such contemporary authors as Thomas Kuhn, Michel Foucault, Heidegger, Hubert Dreyfus, Patrick Heelan, Ian Hacking, Robert Ackerman, Peter Galison, and Bruno Latour.

Ihde not only wrote the first monograph on the philosophy of technology in English, he has produced the most extensive corpus devoted to the subject yet. Indeed, he emphasizes that his vision of philosophy *of* technology is distinct from other studies in philosophy *and* technology (which he sometimes criticizes as anti-technology). But in regard to the pragmatic relation between philosophy and technology, there are both challenges to and from pragmatism. The challenge to pragmatism is to consider what Ihde's phenomenology of human-instrument relations might imply for pragmatist instrumentalism. The challenge from pragmatism is to consider in what ways Ihde's phenomenology might be a basis for societal, political, and technological reform.

Unlike many phenomenologists, Ihde has been in regular dialogue with pragmatism, and has on more than one occasion challenged its late twentieth-century manifestations. By weaning phenomenology from any residual foundationalist pretensions, as well as bringing it out of the more purely philosophical traditions and introducing it into the scientific laboratories and their heavily instrumented practices, Ihde has created a postphenomenology that is, in effect, a pragmatic phenomenology. Ihde has been a model of philosophical receptivity, willing repeatedly to learn from pragmatism. But has pragmatism been equally willing to benefit from Ihde's postphenomenology? Other than Durbin and Hickman, themselves exemplars of philosophical receptivity, few pragmatists even cite Ihde's work, much less seek to bring his phenomenology of instrumentation to bear in the self-understanding of instrumental pragmatism.

At the same time Ihde's interest in social-cultural reform has been less than what is typical of classical pragmatism, at least as exemplified by Dewey and promoted again by Durbin and Hickman. Although Ihde admits to siding with Enlightenment modernism in promoting the development of "a secular world [with] principles of relations between religions and ethnic groups that allow them to function within a spirit of toleration and mutual respect," there is perhaps more that could be done to draw out the "stewardship recommendations" that constitute the final chapter of *Technology and the Lifeworld* (CT 120).[29]

Notes

1. See John Dewey, *Logic: The Theory of Inquiry*, in *John Dewey: The Later Works, 1925–1953, vol. 12 1938*, ed. Jo Ann Boydston (Carbondale: Southern Illinois University Press, 1986).

2. Joseph Cohen, "Technology and Philosophy," *Colorado Quarterly* 3, 4 (Spring 1955): 409–420.

3. Samuel Levin, "John Dewey's Evaluation of Technology," *American Journal of Economics and Sociology* 15, 2 (January 1956): 123–136.

4. John Donohue, "Dewey and the Problem of Technology," in *John Dewey: His Thought and Influence*, ed. John Blewett (New York: Fordham University Press, 1960): 117–144.

5. Cohen, "Technology and Philosophy," 409.

6. Ibid.

7. Ibid., 413.

8. Ibid.

9. Ibid., 416.

10. Ibid., 418.

11. Ibid., 417.

12. Ibid., 416.

13. Joseph Margolis, *Reinventing Pragmatism: American Philosophy and the End of the Twentieth Century* (Ithaca, NY: Cornell University Press, 2003).

14. Richard Rorty, *Philosophy and the Mirror of Nature* (Princeton: Princeton University Press, 1979), 160.

15. Paul Durbin, "Technology and Values: A Philosopher's Perspective," *Technology and Culture* 13, 4 (October 1972): 556–576. Also, see Paul Durbin, "Toward a Social Philosophy of Technology," *Research in Philosophy and Technology* 1 (1978): 67–68.

16. Durbin, "Toward a Social Philosophy of Technology," 67–68.

17. Ibid, 71.

18. Paul Durbin, *Social Responsibilty in Science, Technology, and Medicine* (Bethlehem, PA: Lehigh University Press, 1992).

19. Larry Hickman, *John Dewey's Pragmatic Technology* (Bloomington: Indiana University Press, 1990).

20. John Dewey, *The Quest for Certainty*, in *John Dewey: The Later Works, 1925–1953, vol. 4: 1929*, ed. Jo Ann Boydston (Carbondale: Southern Illinois University Press, 1984), 68.

21. John Dewey, *Problems of Men*, in *John Dewey: The Later Works, 1925–1953, vol. 15: 1942-1948*, ed. Jo Ann Boydston (Carbondale: Southern Illinois University Press, 1986), 291 n3.

22. Ibid., 80.

23. Ibid., 80–81.

24. Hickman, *John Dewey's Pragmatic Technology*, 40–41. Emphasis in original.

25. Ibid., 43.

26. John Dewey, *Art as Experience*, in *John Dewey: The Later Works, 1925–1953, vol. 10: 1934*, ed. Jo Ann Boydston (Carbondale: Southern Illinois University Press, 1987).

27. Larry Hickman, *Philosophical Tools for Technological Culture: Putting Pragmatism to Work* (Bloomington: Indiana University Press, 2001), 20.

28. Ibid., 202.

29. Acknowledgment: Portions of this text have been adapted and reprinted with permission from *Thinking Through Technology* © 1994 by *The University of Chicago Press*.

Part II

Listening to Ihde:
Phenomenology and Sound

3

The Primacy of Listening: Toward a Metaphysics of Communicative Interaction

Lenore Langsdorf

The first and most basic rule is to consider social facts as things.

—Emile Durkheim

... to judge rationally or scientifically about things signifies to
conform to the things themselves or to go from words and
opinions back to the things themselves, to consult them in their
self-givenness and to set aside all prejudices alien to them.

—Edmund Husserl

... the old High German word *thing* means a gathering, and
specifically a gathering to deliberate on a matter under
discussion ... that in any way bears upon men, concerns them, and
that accordingly is a matter for discourse.

—Martin Heidegger

Emile Durkheim urged us to "consider social facts as things"[1] and Edmund
Husserl urged us to attend "to the things themselves."[2] In contrast to this
ontological focus, the social sciences are marked by a focus on competing
methodologies that (their advocates claim) enable us to gain knowledge of
social things—a focus that's encouraged by traditions in Euro-American scholarship as well as institutional exigencies. The result is an emphasis on epistemology and methodology at the expense of ontological inquiry. The
meliorative efforts of much social scientific research are hampered, I suspect,
by investigation of the phenomena of the social world that begins with

unexamined conceptions of the nature of social things and incorporates (rather than investigating the validity of) commonsensical as well as traditional metaphysical conceptions of "things." These preconceptions obscure the potential value of Durkheim's and Husserl's injunctions for social scientific research, and especially for research seeking "practical" knowledge that serves meliorative goals.

Don Ihde's use of "second phenomenology" in analyzing auditory and "multistable" visual phenomena enables ontological investigation of social things that challenges those preconceptions, suggests an alternative ontology, and enables us to interpret Durkheim's and Husserl's injunctions as supporting interpretive modes of inquiry, rather than (as critics have done) as requiring empiricistic and even positivistic methodologies. In the early work that informs this chapter, Ihde explicates phenomenology as a two-stage mode of analysis. He uses that explication, grounded in the work of Husserl and Martin Heidegger, for an analysis that's "intended as a prolegomena to an ontology of listening" (*LV* ix). Throughout his teaching and writing career, Ihde has emphasized the primacy of *doing* phenomenology, in contrast to and conjunction with tendencies to dwell in textual exegesis or in talk about phenomenology as an epistemological method. In other words, he follows phenomenological tradition in holding text and talk as secondary to investigating "the things themselves." In what follows I sketch Ihde's phenomenological ontology and suggest its value for investigating the nature of social things.

Toward a Phenomenological Ontology

> . . . as a radical philosophy, phenomenology necessarily departs
> from familiar ways of doing things and accepted ways of thinking.
> It overturns many presuppositions ordinarily taken for granted and
> seeks to establish a new perspective from which to view things.
>
> —Don Ihde (*EP* 17)

> Only as phenomenology is ontology possible.
>
> —Martin Heidegger

Ihde distinguishes a "first phenomenology"—a "method and field of study" for which Husserl is the guide—from a "second phenomenology," which, with Heidegger as the guide, builds from the first "toward a fundamental ontology of Being," and so evolves into "a hermeneutic and existential philosophy" (*LV* 17–18). "The things which are intended and the acts by which their meanings are constituted occupy first phenomenology centrally," Ihde tells us; thus, first phenomenology "operated like a science and is . . . a statics of experience" (*LV* 18–19). Husserl's early attunement toward stasis was even more thoroughgoing than Durkheim's, perhaps because his initial subject matter was the formal objects of arithmetic and logic. Durkheim took the "natural" or physical sciences of his day—physics and chemistry, focused on the stable structures of diverse particulars—as the appropriate models for sociology. Thus both were concerned with developing a methodology for identifying and describing, in isolation from the particularities of their contexts, stable elements that justify descriptions (Husserl) or explanations (Durkheim) of "the same phenomenon" despite the observed diversity of multiple instances.

Durkheim's third rule for sociological method, "investigate . . . social facts . . . in isolation from their individual manifestations" was joined to his advocacy of statistical analysis as the means for "isolating" "beliefs, tendencies, and practices of the group taken collectively" from "individual circumstances which may have played some part in producing" particular manifestations of those forms.[5] Husserl's method—the much-misunderstood eidetic intuition—was radically different, but also sought a stable subject matter within the flux of experience. Thus despite Husserl's insistence that phenomenologists must identify and justify presumptions—reminiscent of Durkheim's second rule, "One must systematically discard all preconceptions"—they both assumed that investigation of a stable subject matter is required for (respectively) a phenomenology that would be "a rigorous science," or a sociology that would "pass from the subjective stage . . . to the objective stage." In other words, Husserl, in his radical turn from the "natural" to the "phenomenological" attitude in order to achieve a scientific phenomenology, as well as Durkheim, in his radical turn from individual to social explanation in order to achieve a scientific sociology, neglected ontological inquiry that would challenge the extent to which their subject matter could be stable and isolable from its context.

Second phenomenology does not share the predominant epistemological and methodological orientations preconceptions of the Euro-American intellectual tradition. Ihde explicates second phenomenology as "an extension and a deepening" of first phenomenology by virtue of being "opened 'outwards' towards limits and horizons" as it expands analysis from the static to the active (*LV* 18). That expansion requires a more extensive application of phenomenology's epoché of the natural attitude; an expansion that suspends acceptance of the Platonic heritage that's sedimented in both mundane and disciplinary assumptions about the nature of things. Ihde (quoting Heidegger) characterizes this application as responding to a need for "'destruction of the history of ontology'" if experience is to be "understood ultimately in relation to its historical and cultural imbeddedness" (*LV* 20).

This shift from Husserlian first phenomenology to Heideggerian second phenomenology complements Husserl's attention to "essence, structure, and presence" with Heidegger's primary interest in "existence, history, and the hermeneutical" (*LV* 20). In contrast to Durkheim's third rule, second phenomenology requires a turn from treating social facts in isolation from their contexts and presented as static, relatively fixed entities to treating social facts as persistently informing and informed by history, and thus, as active processes (feeling, listening, seeing, thinking, valuing, etc.) relating to objects (emotions, voices, bodies, thoughts, values), and within contexts (abstract/formal or spatiotemporal fields). The contextual and processual analysis of second phenomenology engages and builds from, rather than dismisses, static analysis; it insists upon inclusive investigation of both essence and existence, structure and history, the horizonal absence (persistent incompleteness) of meaning as well as the complex presence of sensory experience in which and through which things are manifested.

Expanding analysis to description of "the things themselves" within—rather than in abstraction or isolation from—their experiential context requires that we "begin with the 'objects,' or things which are 'out there,'" now named as "the noema, or 'object-correlates' of the experience process" in order to discern the "eidetic or structural components of the experience in question" (*LV* 29). This aspect of experience is "not immediately apparent," but can be discerned in "patterns" that persist through perceptual and imaginative variations. By attending to actual or imagined manifestations (variations on the phenomena), then, we go about a "gathering of descriptive characteristics," the telling of which "functions like an argument" for "locating and determining existential possibilities"—that is, possibilities for how the things of experience might present themselves (*LV* 32, 34). Claims about which structural components are necessary to a particular phenomenon's presence as one thing, rather than another, are in Husserl's terminology "eidetic" claims. But interest in what is possible for particular social things calls for ontological inquiry that seeks out contingent as well as necessary characteristics. Second phenomenology's primary interest in contextualized historical processes enables social research that's attuned to the functioning of change, contingency, and correlation in actualizing possibilities—without neglecting what is necessary for a particular social thing to be that thing.

Ihde demonstrates second phenomenology at work in analyzing auditory phenomena in *Listening and Voice* and in analyzing visual phenomena in *Experimental Phenomenology*. His examples are simple—the sounds of things (*LV*) and line drawings of "multistable objects" (*EP*). Yet those demonstrations display the function of communicative interaction in making both auditory and visual things present and in enabling, as well as revealing limits to, their variation. Despite their simplicity, these examples meet Durkheim's criteria for being social things: they are external to us, constructed (brought into being) and constituted (becoming meaningful) in sounds that are heard and drawings that are seen; they allow of variation while resisting our will that they exist in particular ways, and they impose themselves upon us by disallowing variations that seem to exceed their limits and by pressing other variations upon us. Although they are rudimentary social things, studying our interaction with them suggests much about the nature and possible variations of more complex social things. Although no summary can do any justice to the richness of Ihde's comparative analysis of auditory and visual phenomena, I need to sketch some descriptive findings from Ihde's phenomenology of the auditory dimension before turning to consideration of second phenomenology's usefulness for investigating communicative interaction.

Even a "prolegomena to an ontology of listening"—that is, initial steps toward a phenomenological ontology of auditory phenomena—calls our attention to the dominant concern with visual phenomena within Euro-American philosophy, science, and theory. We can then recognize, within communicative experience, "vast differences between hearing voices and reading words" (*LV* x) and, more generally, between auditory in contrast to visual experience. An early finding is that visual phenomena—especially a written text, and to a somewhat lesser extent, a pictorial display—can be present in abstraction from time and circumstance. A sentence focally presents itself in front of me as a static thing. Typically, I see it without attending to features of the immediate or encompassing contexts ("field" and "horizon") that must also be present: the page on which it's written, much less the typography or binding of the book containing it, the personality of its author, or the economics and politics governing its publication and distribution. Correlatively (noetically) my bodily placement, prior and future activities, or reasons for reading this sentence, now, are tangential to the actual seeing of the page. In terms of Ihde's tripartite analysis: my seeing can be relatively limited to the focal thing directly in front of me, without intrusion from the field that is its context ("fringe") or the world ("horizon") implicated by both thing and context.

Reflecting on the "shape" of the auditory field reveals those same three structural elements, but all of them offer more resistance to my will. I cannot limit the auditory field to a focus (and minimal periphery) that's directly in front of me. Rather, the auditory field "surrounds" me: I hear what is behind me and what is within my body, although both are hidden from me visually (*LV* 75).[3] The auditory field "penetrates" me: I hear "from bones ["fringe"] to ears ["focus"]" while the "deaf person . . . 'hears' from only the fringe" (*LV* 81, 138). It more successfully resists my will to efface it than the visual field does: "ears have no flaps" (*LV* 81). Its "temporality is not a matter of 'subjectivity' . . . I cannot 'fix' the [musical] note . . . there is an objectivelike recalcitrance to its 'motion'" (*LV* 94). It refuses to accommodate itself to being a static thing: "Sound embodies the sense of time" by persistently fading out of temporal immediacy (*LV* 84). It also refuses to be a uniform absence: By closing my eyes, I can efface the multiplicity given in any visual focus and its horizon by diminishing the visual field to a uniform redness or darkness. But any attempt to cease listening only magnifies the multiplicity of auditory phenomena (both within the body and in the surrounding environment) that remain in the background (field or horizon) of focused listening. Despite this omnipresence, sound resists our epistemic demands and exercises our methodological strategies: science—"an instrumental context in which instruments extend and embody experience"—must translate auditory phenomena into visual display in order to study it (*LV* 97). Little wonder, then, that Euro-American philosophy, science, and theory privileges the visual (including the written word), over the auditory. Furthermore, research implicitly takes visual phenomena in static immediacy, rather than as emergent "multistable objects."

Ihde prefaces his phenomenological analysis of visual phenomena with the observation that "despite much philosophical and psychological tradition, dealing with vision in isolation is phenomenologically suspect" (*EP* 55). Although even initial reflection reveals that any "span of experience is one of vast complexity and multiplicity," he continues, "I am able to concentrate my attention upon the visual dimension": "other phenomena do not disappear . . . but recede to the fringe of awareness" while remaining a "recalcitrant presence" (*EP* 56). Ihde's use of line drawings mimics the characteristics of words on a page that I mentioned earlier, in that I can focus on them to the exclusion of their "historical and cultural imbeddedness"—although the variations that I'm able to make, thanks to the stories that he tells about them and the stories that gather as I see/read, rely on just that history and culture (*LV* 20). The invariant figure-and-(back)ground structure of visual experience, then, retains the focus-fringe-field structure of auditory phenomena. Even more insistently than in auditory experience, "what appears most clearly is at the core of the field and is centrally located . . . phenomena located nearer the fringe are barely noticed, vague, or difficult to discriminate" (*EP* 60). Along with aspects of what I see that I know must be present but are visually absent (such as the reverse of this page, the desk underneath it, and the legs and floor that support it), they are easily ignored or forgotten. There is always "this sense of absence-within-presence," which supplies a "latent sense along with what is manifest . . . an inner horizon" correlative to the horizon that gives the "shape of the visual field" and that is a necessary condition for the possibility of the "manifest profile" that I do see (*EP* 59–60). "Variations can establish this sense," Ihde notes, and so enable more adequate description—since "I do not see the world without 'thickness' nor do I see it as a mere façade. What appears does so as a play of presence and a specific absence-within-presence" (*EP* 62–63).

My sketch of Ihde's analysis of auditory phenomena has taken up far more of the limited space in this chapter than his analysis of visual phenomena, for two reasons. First, the latter have been privileged throughout Euro-American philosophy, science, and theory. Although the everyday world within which we find social things is, arguably, even more dependent upon the auditory than the visual, social research has focused on what has been done by social actors, and thus can be studied as (relatively) stable visible products—rather than on their actual doing, and in particular, their oral/aural interaction. Despite recent emphasis within the field of communication studies on communication as a process, research continues to be dominated by epistemologies and methodologies that incorporate this traditional social scientific starting point. Thus, typically, "communication as a process" is conceptualized as beginning with (speaking) subjects and (represented) objects, and research has a meliorative concern that presumes the value of unambiguous and accurate representation as the goal of communication.[4] Ihde's experiments in second phenomenology provide an ontology that problematize that conception without dissolving its elements into language or rejecting melioration as a goal of research. We need to look briefly at some contemporary alternates to traditional social scientific communication research in order to identify the relevance of Ihde's ontologically oriented experiments to those alternatives.

Toward a Metaphysics of Communicative Interaction

... the things of the world become material exemplars of the values which the tribal idiom has placed upon them. Thus, in mediating between the social realm and the realm of nonverbal nature, words communicate to things the spirit that the society imposes ... The things are in effect the visible tangible material embodiments of the spirit that infuses them through the medium of words. And in this sense, things become the signs of the genius that resides in words.

—Kenneth Burke

... paradoxically, the linguistic turn, despite the referential twist of philosophical semantics, has often signified a refusal to 'go outside' of language and a mistrust equal to that of French structuralism with respect to any extra-linguistic order ... the implicit axiom that 'everything is language' has often led to a closed semanticism, incapable of accounting for human action as actually happening in the world ... a phenomenology like Husserl's, according to which the stratum of language is 'ineffectual' in relation to the life of intentional consciousness, has a corrective value, just because it proposes the opposite extreme.

— Paul Ricoeur

First phenomenology follows Husserl to "the things themselves" and second phenomenology follows Heidegger in listening to the insistent givenness of those things: "Listening 'lets be,' lets come into presence the unbidden giving of sound. In listening humankind belongs within the event" (*LV* 110). The recalcitrance of sound to our will—its "unbidden giving" of itself—reinforces its claim to be a social thing. Ihde's experiments also demonstrate the social nature of vision: The amenability of "multistable" visual phenomena to displaying alternative meanings, especially when suggested by a "story device" or through "direct instructions" but without alteration in their physical gestalt (*EP* 86–88), reinforces the ontological status of vision as a social thing.

We are apt to valorize our own sounding—and especially our speaking and the (visible) record of that speaking on the page—more than our hearing of others' sounds, and especially, the sounding of nonspeaking bodies. Thus it's not surprising that much communication research emphasizes verbality and takes much of its vocabulary and theoretical framework from linguistics and (individual, rather than social) psychology. That practice incorporates an insistence upon stable and isolated subject matter, ratified for linguistics-based research by Saussure's separation of language and speech and for psychology-based research by a tradition of separation between mind and body, thought and communication, reason and emotion. Studying language in isolation from speech (auditory experience) and bodily communication (visual and visceral experience) that abjures or exceeds verbal formulation, however, is studying language as an abstraction from one component of the event that is listening in the Heideggerian sense of that term.

Along with its focus on verbality, mainstream social scientific communication research has assumed a dualistic ontology of messages and persons quite in keeping with traditional internal/mind and external/body dualism. Correlatively, the philosophy of language has extended linguistics' reduction of its subject matter from social to abstract things by privileging propositional language, amenable to rules for determining truth or falsity, in preference to forms of language typically characterized as dramaturgical, metaphorical, poetic, rhetorical, or ritual. "Philosophy," as Ihde reminds us, "has often harbored a suspicion of dramaturgical voice . . . Rhetoric, theater, religion, poetry . . . persuades, transforms, and arouses humankind"; these auditory forms exercise a "potential power" at odds with any conception of "Reason," which "carries hidden within it a temptation to create a type of disembodiment which becomes a special kind of tyranny forgetful of . . . the existential position of humankind" (*LV* 171).

An ontology of abstract rather than actual (and social) things, along with a metaphysics of presence, stasis, and transmission, thus pervades communication research.[5] Jürgen Habermas's analysis in *The Theory of Communicative Action* may be the most thoroughly worked out instance of research incorporating that ontology and metaphysics.[6] In contrast to Habermas's analyses, an ontology of listening and speaking that takes its direction from Ihde's "ontology of the auditory" (*LV* 15) demands an ontology derived from attending "to the things themselves" in their actual (social) being—in Husserl's terms, as emergent within the lifeworld—and implies a processual and relational metaphysics There are several trajectories in the philosophy of communication that could benefit from, and extend, Ihde's phenomenology of auditory and visual phenomena. I'll note only three that suggest the cross-disciplinary practice of that endeavor.

Kenneth Burke's inversion of everyday assumptions is evident in the first epigraph for this section: Things embody a socially imposed "spirit" by way of the medium of "words," rather than words representing things. He goes on to say (after the quoted epigraph) that his "plan is experimentally to reverse the usual realistic view of the relation between words and things." Calvin Schrag challenges conceptions of communication as transmission between speakers and audiences by portraying communicative praxis as an "amalgam of discourse and action" in which "a display of a social semantics [is] borne by the public language that is spoken."[7] Here again is an inversion of everyday assumptions, for Schrag argues that the subject is implicated in, rather than the source of, communicative interaction: "One has discourse only in the performance of a saying, in which the act of speaking and the system of language conspire as a unitary event. It is in and through this unitary event that the speaking subject is implicated."[8] Harold Garfinkel, reflecting about an exercise in "practical sociological understanding" that required students to "report on common conversations by writing . . . what the parties actually said" as distinct from "what they and their partners understood they were talking about," concludes that the latter "task was, in principle, unaccomplishable."[9] "An alternate conception of the task may do better," he proposes: "suppose we drop the . . . theory of signs, according to which a "sign" and 'referent' are respectively properties of something said and something talked about . . . then what the parties talked about could not be distinguished from *how* the parties were speaking. An explanation . . . would then consist entirely of describing how the parties had been speaking . . . "[10]

These trajectories from rhetoric, philosophy, and sociology extend the "ontology of the auditory" and hermeneutic phenomenology of the visual field that Ihde began in his early work. They understand communicative interaction as a social thing, rather than as a facet of (individual) psychology, a transient manifestation of linguistic structure, or a representation of created entities independent of their socially constituted nature. That ontology recommends a processual and relational metaphysics grounded in listening to "the things themselves" as the matrix for discovering how communicative interaction enacts its being as a social thing and how it accomplishes a "community of understandings"—constituting a diverse multiplicity of social things that (as Heidegger reminds us in the epigraph with which we began) bear upon us, concern us, and so are given to us as matters for discourse.

Notes

1. Emile Durkheim, *The Rules of Sociological Method*, ed. Steven Lukes, trans. W.D. Halls (New York: Free Press, 1982), 60. Cf. 54–55, 82.

2. Edmund Husserl, *Ideas Pertaining to a Pure Phenomenology and to a Phenomenological Philosophy, First Book*, trans. F. Kersten (The Hague: Martinus Nijhoff, 1982), 35. The earliest formulation of Husserl's well-known injunction is in *Logical Investigations*: "Meanings inspired only by remote, confused, inauthentic intuitions— if by any intuitions at all—are not enough: we must go back to the 'things themselves'." Edmund Husserl, *Logical Investigations*, 2 vols., trans. J.N. Findlay (New York: Humanities Press, 1970), 252. In the *Cartesian Meditations* Husserl claims: " . . . science looks for truths that are valid, and remain so, once for all and for everyone; accordingly it seeks verifications of a new kind. . . . the idea of science and philosophy involves an order of cognition, proceeding from intrinsically earlier to intrinsically later cognitions . . . that are not to be chosen arbitrarily but have their basis 'in the nature of things themselves'." Edmund Husserl, *Cartesian Meditations: An Introduction to Phenomenology*, trans. Dorian Cairns (The Hague: Martinus Nijhoff, 1960), 12.

3. Instrumentation—e.g., mirrors and stethoscopes—can reveal what's hidden, and thus extend the "limits and horizons" of the visual and auditory fields. Ihde's later work focuses on the instrumental expansions of the "limits and horizons" of the human body's capacities.

4. Aesthetic (i.e., poetic) speech is exempted from that goal, and typically is considered as a distinct genre outside the purview of mainstream research.

5. These two terms (ontology and metaphysics) are used in diverse ways within scholarly writing. I use them to designate the task of describing the items presumed and/or found to be within a domain (ontology) in contrastive conjunction with a systematic exposition of how being shows itself within any domain, and possibly across diverse domains (metaphysics). I engage both as yielding descriptive/interpretive claims seeking apodicticity (certainly as to what is present to the investigator, while affirming the openness of any phenomenon's horizons)—rather than prescriptive/definitive assertions of adequacy (completeness, which implies exhaustive comprehension of a phenomenon's horizons).

6. Jürgen Habermas, *The Theory of Communicative Action*, 2 vols. (Boston: Beacon Press, 1984, 1987). Although venerable, that analysis continues to influence contemporary philosophy of communication and to inform Habermas's current work. I've argued elsewhere ("The Real Conditions for the Possibility of Communicative

Action," in *Perspectives on Habermas*, ed. Lewis Edwin Hahn [Chicago: Open Court, 2000] and "Reconstructing the Fourth Dimension: A Deweyean Critique of Habermas's Conception of Communicative Action," in *Habermas and Pragmatism*, ed. Mitchell Aboulafia et al. [London: Routledge, 2002]) that Habermas gives us a theory of propositional language use, rather than a theory of communicative action.

7. Calvin O. Schrag, *Communicative Praxis and the Space of Subjectivity* (Bloomington: Indiana University Press, 1986), 33, 36; cf. viii.

8. Ibid., 125. Schrag's focus is on the constitution of self or subject; I propose (in "In Defense of Poiesis: The Performance of Self in Communicative Poiesis," in *Calvin O. Schrag and the Task of Philosophy after Postmodernity*, ed. Martin Beck Matustík and William L. McBride [Evanston: Northwestern University Press, 2002], Endnote 18 re: constitution) that communicative praxis constitutes both other (object) and self. Burke's conception of things as "tangible material embodiments" of social values has provocative implications for theories of human beings' liberation from oppression. (See Endnote 8 reference to hooks on values.)

9. Harold Garfinkel, *Studies in Ethnomethodology* (Englewood Cliffs: Prentice Hall, 1967), 25, 28.

10. Ibid., 28.

4

Voices in the Electronic Music Synthesizer: An Essay in Honor of Don Ihde[1]

Trevor Pinch

Introduction

Reading Don Ihde's inspirational *Listening and Voice: a Phenomenology of Sound* is like returning to a familiar friend. This should not be surprising as the roots of my own field— Science and Technology Studies—are to be found in the traditions of phenomenology, particularly the philosophy of Alfred Schutz as rendered through the influential writings of Berger and Luckmann, ethnomethodology, and Wittgenstein. Although Ihde's theoretical background (Husserl, Heidegger, and Merleau-Ponty) and agenda as a phenomenologist are somewhat different to my own, there are many resonances. *Listening and Voice* offers a wide-reaching survey of the territory that the auditory field presents and is a siren call in what, back then, was a wilderness.

In *Listening and Voice* Ihde firmly rejects the Cartesian perspective— listening and voice are always part of our world. Sound is inseparable from language and culture. As Ihde puts it:

> Listening to the sounds of the World, listening to the "inner" sounds of the imaginative mode, spans a wide range of auditory phenomena. Yet all sounds are in a broad sense "voices," the voices of things, of others, of the gods, and of myself. In this broad sense one may speak of the voices of significant sound as the "voices of language." At least this broad sense may be suggestive in contrast to those philosophies and forms of thought which seek to reduce sounds to bare sounds or to mere acoustic tokens of an abstract listening. . . . (*LV* 149)

Ihde teaches us to pay attention to the meaning given to sound in particular contexts—there is no meaning outside of context or use. The focus upon sound within science studies owes an inescapable debt to Ihde.[2] Recent work is concerned with how we come to recognize and characterize sound and how the meanings given to sounds change with the entry of new material and technical practices—in other words new ways to produce, transmit, and consume sound. The entry of new machines, such as synthesizers, into the world of sound, music, and noise is my own particular area of interest.[3] The synthesizer is arguably one of the few new instruments to enter mainstream musical culture. How does this new machine evolve in a world where sound already has meaning? My topic, in terms of Ihde's phenomenological approach of Don Ihde, is: how do we give voice to the synthesizer?

Listening and Voice is a phenomenological exploration of sound. Ihde draws to good effect on his own experiences of sound and that of his students; he introspects and analyzes how he experiences sound. The setting is nearly always mundane—sitting in his study at his desk, walking in a park in North London, or listening to a concert. Also, he does not limit sound to music, and when it comes to music he considers all genres: the Indian raga, Beethoven, and the Rolling Stones are all mined for examples. He ranges across a huge range of problems—as he himself says, he is staking out the territory of auditory experience for phenomenology. He also draws usefully upon research on the deaf and blind and their own experiences, for instance, how the visual field is experienced by a blind person when it is partly restored. We learn how the auditory field contrasts with and is similar to the visual field, how different sorts of sounds are experienced and imagined, what it is to hear voices and to introspect as to what the inner voice is, what the meaning of silence is, and so on.

I admire the ambition of Ihde's work; he tackles big issues and raises some of the most important problems. That he is prepared to use everyday examples from a range of different sort of musical and sound experiences means his work has enormous relevance. Just compare what Ihde was doing back then with what philosophers of science were doing. Most were focused on the "high church" of physics. The beauty of sound and Ihde's approach to it is that there is no "high church."

The specific empirical focus on technology and voice and hence upon specific groups of actors in a specific temporal context, which I describe in this chapter, seems a natural extension of *Listening and Voice*. Rather than relying upon the phenomenological tool of introspection I draw upon interviews with participants in the synthesizer culture. Some small part of the phenomenology of sound is amplified so we hear all the nuances generated in the new meanings and practices associated with new sounds and instruments. I listen to and amplify not only the voices of the machines but also the people who work with the machines—the musicians and engineers.

The Synthesizer

There is something unique about the synthesizer. Unlike almost any other instrument it can be used to emulate or imitate other instruments. Although with imagination and dexterity some instruments can be made to sound like others, the modern synthesizer, at the push of a button, can be made to sound like almost any other instrument (including other synthesizers). It is this property of emulation that is of interest to me here. The process of designing an instrument to emulate another is described technically as "voicing" the synthesizer. There is a history here: synthesizers have not always had voices and indeed as we shall see, in the early days of their development synthesists decried the whole process of trying to imitate other instruments. They, in short, wanted the synthesizer to have its own voice.

My research has focused on the period 1964–1975 when the best known early synthesizer, the Moog Synthesizer, was developed and manufactured. This modular, transistorized, voltage-controlled device was much smaller than the existing room-sized tube synthesizers such as the RCA Mark II (built in 1958) housed at the Columbia-Princeton Electronic Music Studio.

The synthesizer is one of the few successful innovations in the history of musical instruments. Indeed arguably the synthesizer presents us with more than just a case of a successful musical innovation, it is also a crucial point in the revolution in the very way that music is produced and consumed—a revolution that is still underway. The synthesizer and closely aligned technologies like the digital sampler when coupled with the digital computer and Internet allow all sorts of new possibilities for making, manipulating, storing, and moving music around the world. It is now possible to bypass the recording studio completely and music can be made as a process of distributed cognition across space and time. Synthesizers now built into sound chips are everywhere. Indeed for many years Stanford University's biggest earning patent was one held on a form of synthesis, FM synthesis, which formed the guts of the Yamaha DX-7 synthesizer (the first commercially successful digital synthesizer), and later generations of computer sound cards such as "Sound Blaster." Today the Japanese Multinational Corporations Roland, Yamaha, Korg, and Casio dominate the market for synthesizers. They are used in every genre of music and can be found in games, children's books, and in novelty children instruments.

Modern synthesizers are digital in form. They invariably are portable keyboard instruments (although drum synthesizers are also important) with a menu of "stored sounds," "sound effects," or "factory sounds," and many of these sounds include acoustic instruments like marimba, harpsichord, and clarinet; they also include sounds of earlier electronic instruments such as the Hammond B3 organ, or the Moog Synthesizer (often referred to as the M sound) and they

include "natural" sound effects such as "handclaps" or "thunder," and "synthetic" "made-up sounds" with evocative names such as: "Mr Analog" or
"Laser Synth." In addition to sounds, there are often whole accompaniments
with different combinations of instruments in different beats. One of the latest
developments is software synths, which include digital emulations of old
analog synthesizers. These attempt to not only emulate the sounds of old
synthesizers but also the interface (knobs and wires are shown on screen and
are controlled by mouse clicks and movements).

Some Important Changes in Synthesizers

The modular synthesizers sold by Moog numbered a few hundred. The 1970
Minimoog, which is essentially a portable keyboard instrument with
"hardwired" modules, sold around 12,000 units in its lifetime. The Yamaha
DX-7 sold around 200,000 units between 1983 and 1986. And Casio sold
more than 15 million of their keyboard devices between 1980 and 1990. The
synthesizer market has expanded rapidly from 1963 to the present. The price
of the instruments has also fallen dramatically. Modular Moogs cost about
$15,000 in 1968—the price of a small house. Today you can buy a Casio for
less than $100. Also as the market expanded the method of selling synthesiz-
ers changed. Moog sold his modular equipment to wealthy individuals and
academic studios. With the development of the Minimoog, synthesizers were
sold in retail music stores for the first time. Today the top-end instruments are
still sold that way, although many of the cheaper Casio instruments are sold
through electrical and electronic retailers and even through toy stores. Synthesizers like almost anything else can, of course, be purchased via the Internet.
    It is difficult to comprehend now, but back in 1963 people were hardly
ever exposed to electronic sounds. The main electronic sounds available were
the Theremin (and Trautonium and Ondes Martenot) used in Hollywood movies (and a very few classical performances), and the experimental and avant-
garde music of composers like Cage and Stockhausen. But today we are saturated
with electronic sounds (from films, TV, popular and dance music, and electronic devices). Electronic sound is almost impossible to escape, although listeners are often unaware of the ubiquitous nature of the electronic soundscape.
    The way that sounds are produced by synthesizers has changed over
time. Modular Moogs had an open architecture—you could connect up the
wires that linked different modules (known as patch wires) in infinitely flexible
ways to make myriad different sorts of sounds. Emulation of acoustic instruments was difficult to do, not very convincing, and rarely attempted. Today,
as noted above, most keyboard synthesizers play prepackaged sounds. The
1970 Minimoog is an important juncture in all these changes: it was the first

hardwired instrument with "standard sounds" that could be reproduced with the aid of "sound charts." Reproducible voices of many acoustic instruments at the touch of a button came with the 1983 DX-7. But the DX-7 was so hard to program that a cottage industry programming sounds soon arose.[4]

Today there is an analog revival: old analog machine, known as "Vintage Synthesizers," command top prices, companies are still manufacturing and selling some old analog machines, and these analog machines are used in a variety of genres, like pop, rock, rap, and rave.[5] Part of the Analog Revival is nostalgia but also there is something else going on—some musicians prefer the old interface of "knobs and wires" (most modern digital synthesizers use digital menus and LEDs); also they feel that modern synthesizers don't have such an interesting range of sounds.[6] They miss the sounds "between the knobs" as it were. They often use digital samplers to sample the sound of old analog synthesizers.

In order to understand these changes and how the synthesizer became a very special sort of instrument, one that could *emulate or imitate* other instruments, we need to delve a little more into the design of Moog's synthesizer.

Moog and Music

The spur to Moog's invention of the synthesizer was a 1963 chance meeting with Herb Deutsch, an avant-garde electronic music composer. Deutsch worked in the standard way at the time with oscillators and tape recorders—the oscillators were used as sources of sound and Deutsch laboriously assembled electronic music by recording such sounds and splicing the tapes together. Deutsch told Moog that he and other composers wanted a more portable and affordable studio on which to make such compositions. Also making electronic music was a time-consuming business and it would be great if there was some way to make the process more dynamic—as Deutsch put it, a way "so sounds could move."[7] Moog set to work to help Deutsch.

Moog's goal in developing the synthesizer was not just to produce an electronic box that produced sounds—he wanted to make a musical instrument. He had learned piano as a kid and built Theremins; he came out of the radio hobbyist tradition working in his father's basement workshop (his father was an engineer for Con Edison). With a degree in electrical engineering at Columbia, he also knew about developments in transistors. When he encountered Deutsch in 1963, he knew how to make certain sorts of sounds and how to control them. He had worked with sound and knew the shapes of different waveforms and the sounds they made. He was an inveterate tinkerer. The musicians played the instruments, but the engineers played the circuits. To play them well they needed to have good eyes, ears, and hands. Different instruments and senses combined in the way Moog worked. With the aid of an oscilloscope he used his *eyes* to *see* the shape of the waveform, with the aid of a loudspeaker he used his *ears* to *hear* the sound of the waveform, and with the aid of a voltmeter he used his *hands* to *tinker* with the circuit producing the waveform.

Moog knew that cheap silicon transistors had become widely available, replacing the bulky and expensive vacuum tubes. One newly introduced form of the silicon transistor was of particular interest to him. It had an exponential (logarithmic) relationship between its input voltage and output current over the frequency range of musical interest (several octaves). Exponentially varying properties are common in music; for instance, the frequency of the tones in a scale in the lower range increases exponentially in the higher registers (an octave increase is a doubling of pitch), as does loudness, which is measured by the exponential decibel scale. So Moog thought that he might be able to make something *musically* useful if he used these new transistors.

Moog now had a key insight—voltage control. He built oscillators and rather than varying the pitch of an oscillator manually by turning a knob— or, as in the case of the Theremin, by moving a hand—he could make the pitch change electrically by using a "control voltage" to vary it. A larger voltage fed into the oscillator as a "control" would produce a higher pitch. This meant that an oscillator could be swept through its total pitch range (several octaves) simply by increasing the voltage. Similarly a voltage-controlled amplifier could be swept through the complete dynamic range of human hearing. By building "exponential converter" circuits into his devices— circuits that converted a linearly varying parameter like a voltage into an exponentially varying parameter like frequency or intensity—Moog made these control voltages musically useful. It enabled him to design all his modules around a single standard—the volt-per-octave standard—such that a change of a control input of one volt produced a change in the output pitch of one octave. Some form of the volt-per-octave standard was adopted by other synthesizer manufactures in the 1970s like ARP and EMS.[8]

At this stage what Moog had built didn't look very impressive—a few transistors wired together, along with a couple of potentiometers. Moog:

> I had this little breadboard with three different circuits on it: two voltage control oscillators and a voltage control amplifier. They weren't accurate and they weren't a lot of things, but they had the advantage of voltage control. You could change the pitch of one oscillator with the other oscillator. You could change the loudness.[9]

Moog compared that breadboard to a hot rod, "It's an electronic circuit that's all hanging out so you can get in and change things quickly. So it's like a hot rod without any body on—everything is sticking out."[10]

Having two voltage-controlled oscillators as opposed to one doesn't sound like very much, but it was the breakthrough. The two oscillators were designed such that the output from one (itself a varying voltage) could be used to control the pitch of the other or the loudness of the signals via the voltage-controlled amplifier. By adding a slowly varying sine wave as an input to an oscillator a vibrato effect could be obtained. Feeding the same input into a voltage-controlled amplifier could produce a tremolo effect. But this was only the start. Many, many more interesting sonic effects could be obtained by experimenting and feeding back signals, which in turn could be used as new controls. This was the secret to making sounds move. The hot rod now was ready to roar. Moog describes what happen when Deutsch came to visit him in remote Trumansburg where he had his first shop:

> Herb, when he saw these things sorta went through the roof. I mean he took this and he went down in the basement where we had a little table set up and he started putting music together. Then it was my turn for my head to blow. I still remember, the door was open, we didn't have air-conditioning or anything like that, it was late spring and people would walk by, you know, if they would hear something, they would stand there, they'd listen and they'd shake their heads. You know they'd listen again—what is this weird shit coming out of the basement? [11]

The "weird shit" was historic. It was the first sounds from the very first Moog synthesizer.

In terms of making a musical instrument Moog had embedded a key design concept into his instrument. By thinking in terms of octaves Moog had embedded an element of conventional musical culture into his machine: music was to be thought of in terms of intervals and octaves. Even more crucially, Moog and Deutsch soon wired up an organ keyboard as a controller—with the exponential converter circuits in his oscillators the linear varying voltage output from a chain of resistors and switches could be converted into a useful musical control—a monophonic keyboard.

This was a much more immediate way of working with electronic music than in a classical studio—the potentiometers and patch wires provided immediate changes in the timbre of the sound in *real time* in dynamic ways. With just a twist of the knob or the plugging in of a wire you could cover the full frequency of human hearing and the timbral qualities of these sounds could be varied at a much faster rate and with much more dramatic effects than had proved possible before.

The Moog instrument was based on a process known as *subtractive synthesis*. Moog's sources of sound, for instance, oscillators, produced complex waveforms, such as saw tooth, and square wave, which had many overtones.

By using devices like filters (which could remove a certain range of frequencies) you could filter these overtones to make the sounds even more sonically interesting. Most classical studios worked with *additive synthesis*—since any sound can by Fourier analysis be broken down into sine waves of different frequencies (a fundamental and overtones), it should be possible to assemble any sound by adding together sine waves.

It was noted early on that some of the waveforms the Moog synthesizer produced sounded a bit like acoustic instruments. For instance, the sawtooth waveform makes a bright, full, brassy sound; a triangle waveform sounds much thinner and purer, like a flute; and the pulse wave produces a nasal, "reedy" sound. However, the early composers and musicians who used Moog's instrument were reluctant to attempt to emulate conventional instruments with this new instrument. Many electronic music composers (like Stockhausen, Ussachevsky, and Cage) thought that electronic music should develop its own aesthetics working with this radical new source of sound.

Buchla's Radical Vision

Don Buchla was another pioneer electronic music inventor who worked on the West Coast at the same time as Moog. Buchla was much more influenced by the avant-garde tradition. Buchla, like Moog, came from the hobbyist tradition and like Moog also shared a background in electronic engineering (at Berkeley). He met avant-garde music composers Mort Subotnick and Ramon Sender at precisely the same time that Moog met Deutsch. Sender and Subotnick had just founded the San Francisco Tape Music Center and wanted to use electronics to make a more portable and affordable electronic music studio. The design that Buchla came up with independently from Moog's was very similar: it was modular, used patch wires and voltage control—but there was one crucial difference—Buchla rejected the standard keyboard altogether and did not build oscillators that followed the volt-per-octave standard. Buchla also invented a new device, which became known as the "sequencer," which was a means of repeatedly generating a sequence of different voltages, and thus a way of avoiding tape-splicing altogether.[12]

Buchla reasoned that here was a new source of sound—electronics—but why be stymied by an old technology based upon hammers and wires. He wanted something more imaginative as a controller that would better enable the performer to connect to the new source of sound. He designed arrays of touch-sensitive metal pads housed in wooden boxes that he called the "Kinesthetic Input Ports." Although these pads could, with extreme difficulty, be tuned to play the twelve-note chromatic scale, Buchla's whole design philosophy was to get away from the standard keyboard.

His attitude was shaped by the avant-garde composers, like John Cage and David Tudor, whom he met at the Tape Center. Cage used Buchla's touch pads to control one of his favorite pieces of equipment, the voltage controlled FM radio receiver (which he used as a source of electronic sound for musical performance). Each pad was used to control a different station. Buchla's first ever sale was to David Tudor for whom he designed a set of five circular pads that when coupled with the appropriate module could move sound around a space, from speaker to speaker.

In Buchla's vision of a keyboardless synthesizer the operator would be stimulated to explore the new sounds of which the new instrument was capable:

> A keyboard is dictatorial. When you've got a black and white keyboard there it's hard to play anything but keyboard music. And when's there not a black and white keyboard you get into the knobs and the wires and the interconnections and the timbres, and you get involved in many other aspects of the music, and it's a far more experimental way. It's appealing to fewer people but it's more exciting.[13]

Electronic music composers like Vladimir Ussachevsky found Buchla's way of working more appealing than Moog's, and another of Buchla's earliest orders was for three identical systems for each of the three studios that Ussachevsky ran at the Columbia-Princeton electronic music studio. Interestingly enough at this time the only module that Ussachevsky bought from Moog was his envelope generator. But Ussachevsky did not want this module to work in real time with a keyboard. Instead he got Moog to redesign it so with a push of a button it could be used to add dynamic contours to taped sounds in the studio.

The argument I am building here is that the different design choices made by Moog and Buchla gave affordance to different sorts of musical usages.[14] Moog's design was much more attuned to conventional musical use—the sort of music that could be played on keyboards—while Buchla's designs gave affordance to the sort of experimental electronic music compositions favored by the avant-garde. Moog did not know it yet, but he was on the path toward an instrument that could emulate other instruments.

I want to stress here that one should not essentialize the technology and the sort of music it could make. In terms of the sociology of technology there was "interpretative flexibility."[15] Buchla's keyboardless synthesizers could with a degree of effort be used to make conventional melodic music and Moog's keyboard synthesizers could be used to make unconventional music. Indeed, it is worth pointing out that as well as the keyboard, Moog developed a new form of controller the "stringer" or "ribbon controller"—a taut metal resistance strip, which produced a continuously varying voltage depending on where it was pressed down.

Keyboards Mean Music

But there is no doubt that over time Moog's synthesizer became a keyboard device. There were several reasons for this—primarily the answer is to be found in the "context of use." Just as Wittgenstein famously argued that the meaning of language comes from use—so too the meaning of musical instruments is to be found in their use. Moog's explicit design philosophy was to learn from his customers and from the very start he wanted to mass produce for many different sorts of customer—not just avant-garde musicians. His second ever sale was to Eric Siday, a classically trained musician who had turned to making commercial music and in particular "sound signatures" (such as the CBS logo and a Maxwell House coffee advert). The synthesizer Moog delivered to Siday was his first ever complete system and had a fully tunable keyboard (with each separate note tunable).

Promotional photographs of the synthesizer from around this period show keyboards clearly displayed. We asked Moog about this. He told us:

> The keyboards were always there, and whenever someone wanted to take a picture, for some reason or other it looks good if you're play- ing a keyboard. People understand that then you're making music. You know [without it] you could be tuning in Russia! This pose here [acts out the pose of the left arm extended] graphically ties in the music and the technology. So there are probably a zillion pictures like that. [16]

The keyboard through its association with the piano carried one of the most symbolic meanings in music. It was also what many musicians were most familiar with. In order to reach more users and sell more products Moog adapted to what most users wanted—keyboards.

How Musicians Used the Synthesizer

Despite the use of keyboards and waveforms conducive to imitating some acoustic instruments the early Moog synthesizers were not used much to emulate or imitate other instruments. The vast range of sounds and new sonic effects found in the Moog encouraged the genre of exploration. Many of the early users were interested in producing sounds that had never been heard before and, in general, it was much easier to produce new sounds than to produce recognizable instrumental sounds. The instrument was also complex to use and rather unstable. Different modules could be patched together in a bewildering number of combinations and there were a vast number of different parameters that could be adjusted—change a knob setting by only a minute amount and you would get a totally different sound. Often analog synthesists reported getting the most fantastic sounds on their instruments, which were "lost" when they returned the next day and tried to set everything up the same way—the early instruments were notoriously unstable with oscillators going out of tune and being highly temperature sensitive. Your "best friend" in those early days was your tape recorder. If you got a sound you liked you would try and capture it on tape as soon as possible before you lost it.

Many early synthesists were rather disparaging of any attempt to imitate other instruments. Here is Jon Weiss a Moog studio musician who was trained as a violinist:

> I had no interest in using the synthesizer to create instrumental sounds. Because as far as I'm concerned even when you are using the modern digital generation stuff, the sounds are never as good as the original acoustic sounds, they are so many degrees more complex. I figured what's the point of that—if you wanted something to sound like a French horn then play a French horn . . . Why use this machine to do just that? [17]

Others saw the use for imitation as simply the wrong use of the instrument. For them the synthesizer is an "independent" instrument with its own sound, as David Borden, an early pioneer in electronic minimalism who used the Moog for live performance, told us, "I wanted the Moog to be Moog."[18]

Contributing to this use of the Moog for exploring new sounds and sound washes was the whole development of psychedelic rock of which the synthesizer was an integral part. New instruments like the mellotron, unusual instruments like the sitar, and new effects like feedback, distortion, phasing, and echo were all part of the psychedelic exploration. One of the first uses of the Moog was by The Doors on their *Strange Days* (1967) album where synthesist Paul Beaver treated Jim Morrison's voice through the Moog filter for the title track.

Despite the disdain and the practical difficulties, early synthesists found ways to emulate some of the sounds of conventional instruments. Bernie Krause and Paul Beaver were two of the best known early users of the synthesizer. They were commercial musicians who did countless studio sessions with their Moog for West Coast musicians like The Byrds and The Doors and used the Moog on dozens of Hollywood movies. They made new sounds as well as doing imitative synthesis. Here is how Bernie Krause described their approach toward emulation:

> Now, if you were to create a trumpet, what of the four available wave forms that Moog has on the synthesizer would you use? . . . If you

could hear it in your mind and could hear what it would do, and then you had to filter it in such a way so that you got the feeling of the tone. Flute sounds, and woodwind sounds were some of the easiest acoustic sounds to make because the standard waveforms produced had these sorts of sounds. Strings were much harder because of subtleties in the white noise component which the bow produces and Beaver and Krause would struggle to produce a credible string sound. [19]

Even artists wedded to the idea of using the synthesizer for making new sorts of sound were known to derive pleasure from successfully imitating an acoustic instrument or sound. Here is Malcolm Cecil of the early 1970's cult synthesizer group Tonto's Expanding Head Band talking about how he made his first gong sound used on a track called "River Song" on their album *Zero Time* (1971). It was unusual for Tonto to make a sound like a conventional instrument because they rejected "imitative synthesis" and their goal was to try and capture the instrument for its own sounds. They were also purists and did not want to use conventional instruments on their all-synthesizer recording:

> ... [W]e wanted this bell sound. And we figured out the envelope okay, that wasn't hard, you know, the strike and all that. But nothing sounded like a bell when we did it. So I said, "You know what, I've got this book, Helmholtz [*Sensations of Tones*], that I've been reading for years." I said, "I seem to remember . . . he analyzed the sound of the big bell in Kiev, the harmonics, and he wrote them down. . . . " So we dialed up the harmonics from the great bell of Kiev, exactly as Helmholtz had written . . . fed them into the mixer, put them through the filter, put the envelope on there that we'd already figured out, pressed the key, and out came this bell. I'm telling you, it happened! It was unbelievable! We were hugging each other, dancing around the studio. "We did it, we did it, we did it, we did it!"[20]

Another early success was the use of the synthesizer by the Beatles on *Abbey Road* (1969), in particular on tracks like "Here Comes the Sun," where the increasing brightening in timbre of the Moog reflects the brightening of the sun as the song progresses. On another *Abbey Road* track, "Because," George Harrison uses a Moog emulation of a horn sound (made by noise added to a sawtooth waveform passed through a low-pass filter with envelope generator).

In terms of the history of the Moog the best known record is Wendy Carlos's *Switched-On Bach* (1968). This album went platinum and is one of the best-selling classical records of all time. Carlos started off as a studio engineer and was very adept at over-dubbing and tape splicing. She used the Moog to make Bach keyboard music but she added in many new timbres. It is Bach, but sounds very different to Bach played on conventional instruments.

The success of *Switched-On Bach* made Carlos and Moog famous and further reinforced the synthesizer as a keyboard instrument on which to play conventional music albeit with unconventional timbres. It also led the record industry to try all sorts of Moog gimmick albums. A whole genre of "Switched-On" records appeared, such as *Switched-On Baccarach, Switched-On Beatles, Switched-On Santa*. None of these had the artistry of Carlos and often used the Moog to play a solo line from a standard pop tune. None were hits.

The use of the synthesizer for emulation was, as I have said, rejected by many early synthesists. Certainly for those who worked in the experimental tradition or who used the keyboardless Buchla synthesizer, emulation or imitation was seen as missing the point. An example here would be Mort Subotnick's use of the Buchla on his album *Silver Apples of the Moon* (1967)— a minor underground hit with some significant classical sales.

Many early synthesists like Carlos strove to produce sounds that were somehow familiar but which were different enough to be interesting. Here is Edgar Froese of Tangerine Dream: "the idea is not to use this machine to duplicate a flute or a violin...What you do is use those characteristics . . . which will give you a flute or a violin that hasn't been heard before." [21]

One of the characteristic sounds of the Moog is the low-pass filter that produces the fat, "squelchy" sound (it is the only module that Moog actually patented). When the filter is used with an envelope generator in the bass range, the resonant deep sound is particularly appealing and was soon discovered by synthesists.[22] Over the years it has become a staple of pop and rock music, as has the bass sound of the Minimoog (which uses a similar filter). Moog was himself a witness to the power of his bass sound when he was invited to bring his synthesizer to a New York studio session where Simon and Garfunkel were recording their album, *Bookends* (1968). Moog set up the bass sound himself for the track "Save the Life of a Child," which opens with the sound: "One sound I remember distinctly was a plucked string, like a bass sound. Then it would slide down—it was something you could not do on an acoustic bass or an electric bass . . . a couple of session musicians came through. One guy was playing a bass and he stops and he listens, and listens. He turned white as a sheet."[23] The significance of the Moog bass sound was not lost on this session musician. The Moog not only sounded like an acoustic or electric bass, but it also sounded *better*. Moog liked to repeat this story, he felt that at last he was "getting somewhere." Where he was getting was that at last the Moog was finding a home among musicians at large, rather than being merely an instrument for the avant-garde. Session musicians were some of the first to see the writing on the wall; their livelihoods were under threat. This threat was something that the powerful musicians' union (the AFM) eventually took up but they failed in their attempts to limit the spread of the synthesizer.[24]

There is no doubt that over time there was a change in the way the Moog synthesizer was used. Bernie Krause was in a position to see this change over time. Rather than explore sounds, he was asked at recording sessions to get particular sounds:

> Well, can you get us the sound that you got on the Stevie Wonder album? Can you get us the sound you did on the Byrds? . . . So it's usually they would dig a little bit, but not terribly deep, and so we found ourselves with this limited repertoire of 20 or 30 sounds that we got, that were very easy to patch and do.[25]

Over time a series of sounds were becoming associated with the synthesizer. Furthermore the technology was itself evolving. The Minimoog hardwired in sounds and made them available to the operator through sound charts (the sound chart consisted of a cardboard template of all the knob and switch settings necessary to reproduce a particular sound). The use of the Minimoog for live performance further stabilized certain sorts of sounds. Sound charts enabled the users to reproduce those sounds. Well-known progressive rock keyboardists like Rick Wakeman and Keith Emerson had their own sounds inscribed in sound charts (for instance, the "Lucky Man" sound—named after the ELP hit "Lucky Man").[26]

As the technology became more miniaturized with ICs and microprocessors facilitating the use of polyphonic keyboards, the sound charts were eventually replaced on later generations of synthesizers with presets and factory sounds. By 1983, with digital synthesizers like the DX-7, the programming of sound was so complex that users found they could not program new sounds themselves and came to rely only on factory sounds and sounds provided by the new cottage industry that arose in sound programming.

Discussion

What I hope to have begun to explore in this chapter is how the process of emulation of sound in the synthesizer is one that slowly evolves in a complex sociotechnical environment. The story is one of the interweaving of this technology with different "contexts of use" in the social construction of sound. Certain sounds predominate, they are recognizable sounds, sounds that are materially built into the technology and that can be reproduced. Over time the *meaning* of these sounds stabilize—in this way the synthesizer slowly gained its voices. The success of the synthesizer as a special instrument that can imitate other instruments can be traced back to Moog's early design decisions. By attending to what most users wanted, Moog made his instrument musically useful and this eventually (sometimes against the wishes of the users) made the instrument into one that could imitate the sounds of other instruments.

But the voices given to the synthesizer are only an echo of the voices of real instruments. In the process of electronically rendering a sound, that sound must be torn away from its local situatedness. Something is lost in the process of making the sound generalizable and transportable in the electronic media. The clue to what is lost is to be found in the naming of the voices on synthesizers. Sometimes a whole class of instruments is named, such as "brass," or "strings"; sometimes it gets more specific and refers to a particular instrument like a trumpet or violin. But a "brass" sound is not the same as a trumpet anymore than a violin is the same as "strings." The emulated instrument is always stripped of its context—it is rather like an "ideal type" in social science. Even when it is a violin sound that is emulated it is not a particular violin such as a Stradivarius violin, or a particular Stradivarius instrument. All the little resonances and peculiarities that make an instrument unique are effaced. Of course, new peculiarities may be added in the synthesized sound, but this just points again to the problems of thinking of emulation as copying or imitation. All the peculiarities of a particular performer and place of performance also vanish—there is no "Charlie Parker saxophone" emulation, or "Charlie Parker in a smoky club" as opposed to "Charlie Parker in a concert hall" emulation. Emulation in synthesizers seems to always involve this process of simplification of stripping. This can be most clearly seen when it comes to the emulation of other synthesizers. The Moog synthesizer, which as we have seen is capable of emulating other instruments, can itself be emulated in more modern synthesizers. It is usually only one Moog sound (typically the sound of the filter in the base region), which is chosen to characterize the sound of the whole synthesizer—the M sound on a Roland synthesizer.

Emulation of the analog world is best described as a process where a new voice rather than a copy is made. The new voice may be heard to all intents and purposes as a perfect copy or imitation but that depends on the listener and what is heard. Even in the digital world sounds must be reproduced in an analog media to be heard. This raises another whole set of fascinating issues beyond the purview of the present chapter. But the hearing of any sound as being "the same" must always rest upon sets of sociotechnical processes as well as cultural assumptions.[27]

Emulation in synthesizers seems most successful in areas where listening practices are furthest removed from the demands of a performance with real instruments. Thus synthesized emulations work well for film music (where typically a synthesist and one orchestral soloist will be used); for TV music (shows like the X-files use synthesized music to add mood); for instructional uses (to help learn to play keyboards); for play (whether children's toys or video games) and in some studio genres or pop and dance music. And, of course, listening practices themselves change. Sitting round a scratchy Edison phonograph with poor fidelity in a drawing room has been replaced by the anonymity of the Sony Discman or Apple I-Pod. To give a full account of emulation in sound would also involve inquiring more into these listener practices and that would bring us back once more to where we started—to *Listening and Voice*.

Notes

1. An earlier version of this paper was presented at the Vienna Social Studies of Science meeting in 2000.

2. For examples of recent science studies work on sound see, *Music and Technology in the 20th Century*, ed. Hans-Joachim Braun (Baltimore: Johns Hopkins University Press, 2002); Trevor Pinch and Frank Trocco, "The Social Construction of the Electronic Music Synthesizer," *ICON Journal of the International Committee for the History of Technology*, 4 (1998) 9–31; Trevor Pinch and Frank Trocco, *Analog Days: The Invention and Impact of the Moog Synthesizer* (Cambridge, MA: Harvard University Press, 2002); Emily Thompson, *The Soundscape of Modernity: Architectural Acoustics and the Culture of Listening in America, 1900-1933* (Boston: MIT Press, 2002); Jonathan Sterne, *The Audible Past: Cultural Origins of Sound Reproductions* (Durham: Duke University Press, 2003) and "Sound Matters: New Technologies and Music," ed. Karin Bijsterveld and Trevor Pinch, Special Issue *Social Studies of Science*, 34 (October 2004): 635–817.

3. Trevor Pinch and Karin Bijsterveld, "Should One Applaud? Breaches and Boundaries in the Reception of New Technology in Music," *Technology and Culture* 44 (2003): 536–559; and Pinch and Trocco, *Analog Days: The Invention and Impact of the Moog Synthesizer*, note 3.

4. Paul Therberge, *Any Sound You Can Imagine: Making Music/Consuming Technology* (Connecticut: Wesleyian University Press, 1997) and Pinch and Trocco, *Analog Days*.

5. *Vintage Synthesizers*, ed. Mark Vail (San Francisco: Miller Freeman, 2nd Edition, 2000).

6. See Pinch and Trocco, *Analog Days* for more details.

7. See Pinch and Trocco, *Analog Days* for more details.

8. On the importance of standardization in technology in general and the social, cultural, and economic assumptions built into standardization see Ken Alder, *Engineering the Revolution: Arms and Enlightenment in France, 1763–1815* (Princeton: Princeton University Press, 1997). In the adoption of the player piano developing a

standard roll was crucial, see Theberge, *Any Sound You Can Imagine*, 29. For later digital instruments the development of the MIDI standard was also crucially important see ibid., 145–153.

9. Interview with Bob Moog, June 5, 1997.

10. Interview with Bob Moog by Joan Thomson, February 2, 1979, Yale Archive for the History of American Music.

11. Interview with Bob Moog, June 5, 1997.

12. There are other subtle differences between the Moog and Buchla synthesizers, see   Pinch and Trocco, *Analog Days* for full details.

13. Interview with Don Buchla, April 4, 1997.

14. The notion of affordance is developed by Pablo Boczkowski, *Digitizing the News: Innovation in Online Newspapers* (Cambridge, MA: MIT Press, 2004)

15. For "interpretative flexibility" see Trevor Pinch and Wiebe Bijker, "The Social Construction of Facts and Artifacts," *Social Studies of Science* 14 (1984): 339–441. See also the essays in *The Social Construction of Technological Systems*, ed. Wiebe Bijker, Thomas Hughes, and Trevor Pinch (Boston: MIT Press, 1987).

16. Interview with Bob Moog, June 5, 1997.

17. Interview with Jon Weiss, May 8, 1996.

18. Interview with David Borden, May 3, 1966.

19. Interview with Bernie Krause, August 24, 1998; indeed, throughout the 1970s the quality of a synthesizer's string sound would be the benchmark for its emulation capabilities.

20. Interview with Malcolm Cecil, March 31, 2000.

21. Interview with Edgar Froese in *Art of Electronic Music*, ed. Tom Darter and Greg Armbruster (New York: William Morrow & Co 1985), 173.

22. A good example is the Tonto track "Cybernaut" on *Zero Time* (1971).

23. Interview with Bob Moog, June 5, 1996.

24. For more details see Pinch and Trocco, *Analog Days*.

25. Interview with Bernie Krause, August 24, 1998.

26. The Emerson, Lake and Palmer hit single "Lucky Man" (1970) with its Moog solo at the end is one of the best-known uses of Moog in rock during this period.

27. This provides a new take on issues around the notion of an "aura" developed in Walter Benjamin's famous 1937 essay, "The Work of Art in the Age of Mechanical Reproduction." Perfect reproduction or emulation of a work of art assumes that the material and social context for the reproduction of sound can be ignored—the argument here is that they cannot be.

5

Visualizing the Musical Object

Judy Lochhead

Introduction

To make sound "visible"—this sounds like a dubious, or perhaps undesirable, task for a music scholar devoted to phenomenological approaches to understanding music. Don Ihde, however, has reminded us that sound plays an important role in defining the world we see. In his ground-breaking *Listening and Voice: A Phenomenology of Sound*, Ihde demonstrates how our aural sensibilities help to define aspects of human experience that are typically associated with things we see—such things as the shape of an object, the height of a room, the speed of a train. Ihde argues that the Western philosophical inattention to the sounding world grows out of a general "visual" bias that values seeing over hearing as a source of credible information about the world.

Following in the footsteps of Maurice Merleau-Ponty, Ihde draws attention to the bodily nature of perceptual experience generally and of aurality in particular—as he writes "I hear with my whole body" (*LV* 45). Through the body hearing intercommunicates with the other senses of sight, touch, smell, and taste, woven together in the totality of lived experience. From this bodily based sensory holism we may understand sonic meaning as informed by sight, as well as the other senses. Such sensual intercommunication is confirmed when we observe that a sound is "high," that a sonority is "bright," or that melody is "angular." Thus, the project of visualizing music recognizes that sight plays an important role in defining sonic meaning.

The recognition that vision informs hearing does not directly justify the project of making sound visible. If sound is inherently meaningful, then listening should be sufficient to our understanding. But our engagement with music has historically been attended by other forms of address. If someone asks "why do you like those Rags by William Bolcom?" I need some way to characterize aspects of their sound and explain their appeal.[1] My answer to such a question could be to "talk" about the Rags, using linguistic concepts that refer to sound. But historically people have used other means to address sound. For instance, numbers have been used to characterize intervallic qualities, sometimes people use physical gestures to characterize a melody, and visual models of various sorts have been used to represent sound features. In other words, we use various tools to grasp musical sound—sometimes for practical reasons of communication and sometimes for the purposes of knowledge building. So, while one might assume that hearing is sufficient for musical understanding, attempts to "grasp" musical sound with some other tools seem always to have accompanied music making itself. My project here is focused on visualizing, because it opens up some conceptual avenues that these other tools do not.

Visualizing the Musical Object

To "visualize" implies more than simply seeing, it implies "making" something that can be seen—a bringing to visibility. As such it implies a certain kind of comprehension through conceptualization and it affords a kind of "sharability." Practically, visualizing allows us to point—literally or figuratively—to the thing and share thought about that thing with others. And, in the case of music, it means engaging the object in a way different from the way it is primarily apprehended—a visible thing is used to take account of a heard thing. For music, I am interested in how visualizing has the effect of "making visible" some aspect of sound, allowing for communication and exchange, and then how this process can influence what is hearable.

By the term musical object I simply mean some "thing" of a sounding musical instance, which may become the focus of experience. This sense of "object" is based in principles of phenomenological philosophy that hold that "things" arise as a result of intentional acts within experience.[2] In a musical context, an object or musical thing has some kind of "shape" and meaning in our musical experience. While the musical object could be an entire piece, my primary interest here is with shorter, constitutive things that emerge from the moment-to-moment progress of a musical instance. The range of possible musical objects is wide: a melody, a "pastoral" character, a metallic timbre, a "blue" color, and so on.

The attempt to visualize music is long-standing. The earliest records of human writing also include some sort of representation of musical activity. And since these earliest attempts, there have been a great variety of different notational systems both within and across various world cultures. The encyclopedia *Grove Music Online* gives the following definition of notation: "A visual analogue of musical sound, either as a record of sound heard or imagined, or as a set of visual instructions for performers."[3] The authors don't clarify in what senses musical notation is analogous to sound, but they do articulate two different purposes that notation serves. On one hand, notation provides a way of "preserving" a sound that is held in imagination or in memory: from sound to visual representation. On the other hand, notation is read by a musician for the purposes of performance: from visual representation to sound. It is widely believed that notation within the European tradition developed as an aide to memory, initially indicating only the contour of pitch sequences. It was primarily a tool for performers, and secondarily a way to preserve a repertoire or piece. Over time, notation became more specific, representing more features of sound such as rhythm, timbre, dynamics, and articulation; and in conjunction with such growing specificity, it began to serve in the nineteenth century the function of preserving a composer's intentions.

Despite its increasing specificity and its role in defining the "musical work," notation does not completely determine a performance or a work. As an analog, the notation is not identical to the "music." For instance, consider this notational figure from the beginning of William Bolcom's *Incineratorag*.[4] The notation is symbolic in the sense that the physical marks stand for some "thing"—say, a pitch or a duration. The musician must learn not only the general system by which visual marks refer to sound but also the specific ways the notated sounds are realized on an instrument or voice. In this particular instance, the musician must have acquired an advanced technique on the piano. From this background knowledge, the performer makes the notation "sound" by "reading" the notation in two senses. One is the simple correlation between mark and sound: for instance, in the Bolcom passage I must know that the first pitch in both the left and right hands is an E♭ at a

3. INCINERATORAG

WILLIAM BOLCOM (1967)

Figure 5.1   Bolcom, *Incineratorag,* measures 1–3

soft (*piano*) dynamic and that I should play the music at roughly the speed in which the quarter-note beat occurs 66 times per minute. Second, in order to make the "music" of this rag I must know something about the history of rags in the early twentieth century in order to project its proper expressive character, to play the syncopated rhythms with the appropriate amount of accent, and so on. In other words, to make the visual representations of the notation "come alive" the performer must interpret the music from the notation. Thus we might more properly characterize the person who interprets as the "musician-performer"—that is, the performer must bring to bear a considerable and deep knowledge of "the music." [5]

European notational practice provides a kind of recipe for the music. It symbolizes directly what we might think of as the "basic ingredients" of the piece—its pitches, dynamics, durations, instrumentation—which must be "cooked up" so to speak. And while it facilitates communication between composer and performer about the sounds of a particular piece, notation does not directly visualize the music. Following Charles Seeger, we may observe that the primary function of notation is prescriptive, not descriptive.[6] It tells the performer what to do, and does not directly establish a visual analog of the musical object in descriptive terms.

Besides its function as a kind of "recipe" for performance, notation serves other kinds of purposes. In giving a kind of permanence to musical ideas, it serves to define a work apart from its performances. Further, notation is used for the purposes of study or other such investigation. For instance, we draw on scores for study of the historical development of musical style, of musical organization from the perspectives of theory and analysis, and of musical aesthetics. Thus thinking about music is generated in part from the same graphic symbols that are primarily intended as a kind of communication to performers. The people who engage in such study, who I'll refer to as "scholars," must interpret the notation in ways similar to that of performers. These scholars must read the music into the notation and hence must engage their abilities as musicians. In other words, they must operate as "musician-scholars" in order to engage the music.

While its function is primarily prescriptive not descriptive, traditional musical notation has provided access to the music of a work for the purposes of performance and study, and it has defined a work apart from its performances. However, in the twentieth and now twenty-first centuries various musical, technological, and cultural changes have challenged this role of notation and have drawn attention to the function of "visualizing" generally. I briefly mention only some of these changes here and suggest how they have challenged both how music is performed and how we take account of it through verbal or visual means. I consider three types of challenge.

Challenges

First, the advent of electronic music in the concert tradition has changed the way works in that medium are defined and preserved. Some works utilize only electronic sounds; they typically have no score and are preserved in sound recordings (tapes, CDs, digital files). For instance, classic works of this sort include Mario Davidovsky's *Electronic Study #1* and Edgard Varèse's *Poème Èlectronique*, the latter including instances of musical borrowing from pre-existing recorded music or naturally occurring sounds.[7] The performance of these works is enacted when someone—usually referred to as the "technician"—pushes the play button. Thus, with no score, study and discussion of the music is obviously affected.[8] Second, the rapidly growing prevalence of sound recordings in our daily lives has had a significant impact on musical practices—an impact felt in performance, scholarship, and listening itself. For instance, Terry Teachout has demonstrated that performance styles have lost their "regional" accents, replaced by an "international" style that arose as a consequence of young performers emulating the style of a few recorded performers.[9] Scholars such as Jose Bowen now study recordings for evidence of the history of changing performance styles.[10] And others link styles of performance to the needs of recording and broadcast technologies.[11] Third, the expansion of professional scholarship to include music of the jazz and popular traditions requires that some methodology be devised for the study of genres for which a score is not understood as the defining mark of a work.

These challenges have implications for not only the ways that we address but also how we comprehend the musical object. They illuminate the reliance of such comprehension on the notated score as a kind of visualization and suggest that other types of visualizing be used to assist our efforts toward comprehension. The remainder of my presentation here first examines in more detail the various ways that music has been visualized in both prescriptive and descriptive terms and then demonstrates some other models based on principles of mapping.

Visualizing Music: Prescriptive and Descriptive Approaches

The excerpt of Bolcom's *Incineratorag* in Figure 5.1 exemplifies a prescriptive visualization: the composer writes symbols, whose references are predetermined by an interpretive community, that prescribes what sounds should be played. Typically such visualizing provides the means for performing the sounds—both for the purposes of public performance or scholarly engagement with a work. Sometimes composers use other graphic models, which,

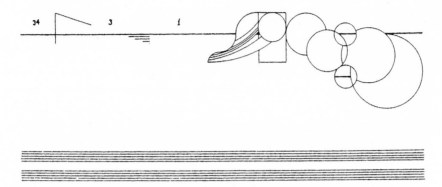

Figure 5.2   Cardew, *Treatise,* page 1

though they symbolize sound in other ways, are still prescriptive. For instance, Figure 5.2 shows an excerpt from *Treatise*, Cornelius Cardew's Treatise, which uses shapes and other graphical marks to suggest types of musical
gestures, dynamics, and textures.[12] While still providing the basic ingredients
for a performance, such graphic notation establishes a relatively more indeterminate relation between sound and symbol. Such notation relies on the
bodily based sensory wholism, which allows us to transfer the significance of
a graphic symbol to musical object.

Sometimes traditional European notation is used in ways that blur the
prescriptive/descriptive boundaries. In the popular music world, it is often not
the creator who notates a "song." It is not uncommon for someone to tran-
scribe a song from a recording for the purposes of selling the "sheet music"
to fans, students or other performers.[13] And in studies of jazz and popular
music, scholars often define their research projects around transcriptions of
famous performers or performer/creators. For instance, Peter Winkler has
written eloquently about the politics of transcription in the instance of an
Aretha Franklin song. His article, "Writing Ghost Notes," addresses the issues of using European notation to capture precisely a musical performance
for the purpose of understanding what the performer does.[14] But as Winkler
observes, the traditional notation he employs can't capture some of the musical features he hears. One of Winkler's figures, shown here in Figure 5.3,
demonstrates his attempts to specify as exactly as possible the rhythm of
Franklin's vocal line in "I Never Loved a Man." His goal of capturing precisely Franklin's performance in the recording yields notations of considerable complexity with regard to pitch and rhythm. As Winkler points out, the
transcription, while accurate, does not give a sense of an underlying musical

Figure 5.3   Winkler's "attempted" transcription of Franklin's vocal line

simplicity that characterizes the performance. The complexity results from the attempt to make the notation visualize the "music" and from the use of a prescriptive visual tool for a descriptive task.

In ethnomusicological studies, the issue of visualizing music is long-standing since scholars in that field often study music from other cultures that have no

notation of their own. Nowadays, ethnomusicologists work from recordings and
the types of transcriptions they produce are varied. Some employ symbols and
a format similar to that of European notation, such as the transcription of a
"Hukwe melody" by Robert Garfias shown in Figure 5.4.[15]

Other scholars dispense entirely with European symbols and employ a
mode of representation that is more simply descriptive. Sue Carol De Vale,
in her study of harp and voice sounds in Uganda, invents or borrows graphical marks to represent sound features—as shown in Figure 5.5.[16] Like Cardew's

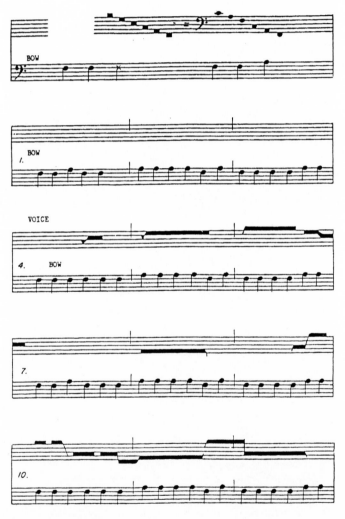

Figure 5.4   Robert Garfias, transcription of Hukwe melody

FIGURE 2: LEOPARD ON THE HUNT (TAPED EX. 1)
EXCERPT FROM NONESUCH H-72056 SIDE ONE BAND ONE
RECORDED AT ABERDARE NATIONAL PARK, KENYA, 1973
BIRD
LEOPARD
SECONDS
2 3 4 5 6 7 8 9
BIRD
LEOPARD
SECONDS
10 11 12 13 14 15 16 17

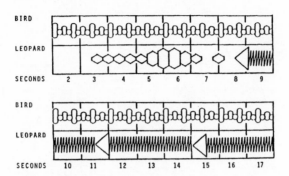

Figure 5.5 DeVale, Graphic Notation of Texture

in Figure 5.2, the symbols of De Vale's transcription depend on our ability to transfer the significance of a graphic symbol to musical object.

Such descriptive visualizations of sound play a role in the work of scholars addressing historical music in the European concert tradition. Music analysts and theorists in particular have relied on various types of descriptive visualizations that are used to represent some aspect of musical structure. Since "structure" is already itself a concept about musical sound, these visualizations are representations not so much of sound itself but of a concept about sounding relationships. For instance, some of the more famous visualizations of music structure include Johann Heinichen's musical circle. Figure 5.6

Muſicaliſcher Circul.
Pag. 261.

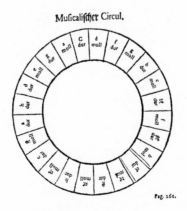

Figure 5.6 Heinichen's Musical Circle

J.S. Bach Prelude No. 1 in C Major

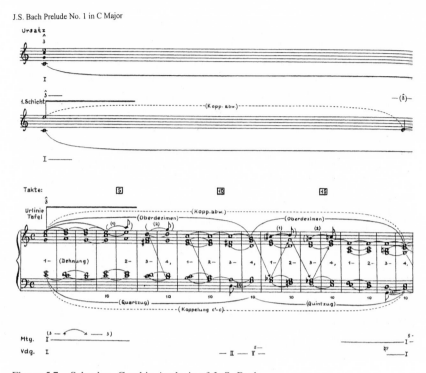

Figure 5.7   Schenker, Graphic Analysis of J. S. Bach

cites an instance of the circle, which occurred in his 1711 treatise, *Neu erfundene und grundliche Answeisung*.[17] The circle demonstrates that keys—both major and minor—listed in an order of increasing flats or sharps have a cyclical organization.[18]

A couple of centuries later, Heinrich Schenker visualizes the structure of a whole piece with his "graphic analyses."[19] Figure 5.7 cites his analysis a J.S. Bach Prelude. The uppermost system is the "Ursatz"—the deepest level of structure—and the bottom system is the "Urlinie Tafel"—the foreground or surface level.

Schenker uses traditional Western notation but has transformed it to serve purposes that are descriptive but rely on a good deal of instruction and practice in the reading of the notational symbols.

In the 1980s, Robert Cogan used new technologies in sound analysis to produce pictures of the overtone structure of music.[20] Figure 5.8 shows one of Cogan's "spectral photos"—this of the opening 54 seconds of Milton Babbitt's *Ensembles for Synthesizer*, an electronic work with no score. Cogan's

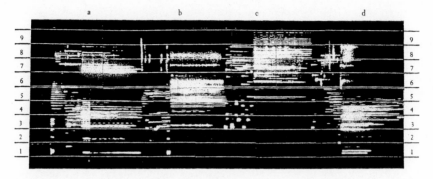

Figure 5.8   Cogan, spectral photo of Babbitt's *Ensembles for Synthesizer*

spectral photo here only depicts an excerpt of a longer work; and it is generated by a "machine-like" reading of sound, unlike the graphic depictions of De Vale and Schenker.[21]

Visualizing as Conceptualizing

The visualizations considered so far illustrate a range of possible ways that musical sound has been comprehended by graphic means. My focus next is on what is entailed by the act of putting onto paper a visual symbol that represents musical sound and its implications for the ways that we comprehend music.

For the composer, putting musical ideas onto paper is often part of the creative process itself. While there are stories of Mozart essentially transcribing whole movements that were already fully formed in his imagination, it is more typical that notating and creating go hand in hand. However, it is important to remember that the composer must be fully conversant with the conventions of notation and how its symbols refer to potential sounds. The notated symbols in this instance are primarily prescriptive—providing the ingredients necessary to "make" the music.

The issues surrounding the practice of descriptive visualization are more complex. Some of these issues have already been well articulated within the ethnomusicological community where transcriptions are often needed for purposes of study and discussion. Since the beginnings of ethnomusicological research, scholars were confronted with problems of notating music from non-Western cultures for the purposes of study. The promise of an automatic and hence "objective" transcription arose with the invention in the 1950s of such machines as the "melograph"—a machine that reads pitch variations and displays it graphically. In his article, "The 'objective and subjective' View in Music Transcription," Nazir Jairhaizboy points out some of the false assumptions about the possibility of an objective transcription process. Part of the debate on the virtues and drawbacks of "automatic" transcribers, Jairhaizboy's article argued that despite the promise of objectivity mechanical transcriptions always bear the trace of human intention. Since the move from acoustic signal to visual symbol is always mediated by some person, then the transcription records a subjective intention. Further, Jairhaizboy argues that the very idea of an "objective" transcription presumes the existence of an "objective" sound. Given that processes of human hearing are selective and depend on an explicit or implicit understanding of the distinctions between music and noise, the conventions of style and genre, and so on, the idea of an objective sound is largely illusory.[22]

Of the descriptive visualizations considered above, only Robert Cogan's spectral photo qualifies as automatic, or "objective," in Jairhazboy's sense. Graphic representations such as Heinichen's circle, De Vale's transcription, and Schenker's analyses are "subjective" accounts since they are made by a process in which a person makes decisions about how to depict musical sound graphically. Such a subjective process requires this person to ask questions about what is heard and to make decisions about how to put it down on paper. In other words, the act of "transcribing" musical sound into graphic symbols is very much like the kind of musical study named "analysis." If analysis entails "understanding how a piece works," to use a phrase from Ian Bent, then the process of subjective visualization is analytic in nature.[23]

Visualizing and Challenges

A visual representation of musical sound constitutes an understanding of that sound. From the vantage of this observation, I return to the three challenges considered above. These challenges arise because technological and cultural changes have diminished or eliminated the role that traditional European notation plays in our efforts to comprehend various genres of music. The preceding survey of the various ways that musical sound is and has been visualized provides a basis for addressing these challenges. In particular, I am interested in devising visual modes of access to music, which either has no notation or a notation that does not directly symbolize sound. My goal in devising such visual access is to make it possible to engage the music more fully and to comprehend it in more formal terms. The lack of notation hinders such an engagement for a number of reasons—some very practical, others having to do with issues of human cognition. For instance, without a visual representation musician-scholars must rely on their memory of occurrences and there is no simple way to refer to a particular occurrence in context. Such practical matters become conceptual problems since they have the effect of marginalizing the music, which does not offer some kind of visual access. In the absence of a prescriptive notation, a descriptive visualization can not only give us access to the musical object but further can already begin the process of conceptual understanding—that is, of analysis.

Maps

My project of visualizing music has been informed by ideas from "map theory"—that is from ideas about how maps represent the physical world.[24] A "map" is a visual object that represents parts of the world that we typically cannot apprehend as a visual whole. In *The Power of Maps*, the map theorist Denis Wood writes that maps give us a "reality that exceeds our vision...they make something visually present to us that would typically be perceptually unattainable as such."[25] Map-like visualizations of music work in similar ways—especially those that represent a piece or movement. Unlike the "recipe" offered by a score, a musical map is an attempt to capture "the music" as a lived phenomenon—to give us in visual terms a sonic reality. It shows us what happens over a span of time and frees us from the incessant flow of musical time. The visual representations of De Vale, Schenker, and Cogan (Figures 5.5, 5.7, 5.8) are instances of musical maps, giving us an all-at-once access to an excerpt or an entire musical work.

Wood draws attention to two aspects of maps that are instructive for thinking about music visualizations: they "serve interests" and "make present . . . the accumulated thought and labor of the past."[26] Wood argues that since the process of mapping is selective, it requires the mapmaker to make choices. The interests of the mapmaker are served through the various decisions that go into the mapmaking—what to include, what to exclude, and how to represent these. Maps then are not "objective" representations of the world; as Wood points out, "the point of the map [is] to present us not with the world we can see, but to point toward a world we might know."[27] Changing this to fit the situation with music I would say: maps, or visualizations, of music do not present us a direct analog of the sound we might hear, but rather they allow us access to a sound we may know. Since maps result from human decision-making, they must be understood as historically and culturally contingent records that bear the "accumulated thought and labor of the past." Similarly, a musical map represents the labor of the musician-scholar who both acts as an individual and as a member of a community of musicians. For this community, the map provides access to "sounds that we may know."

Another map scholar, Alan M. MacEachern, takes many of the same positions in his *How Maps Work*, but he goes into more detail about how the graphic symbols of maps both do the work of representing the world and generate meaning for the people who read them.[28] That is, he is also interested both in the decisions people make to represent things in a particular way and in how those symbols are utilized by the map-user. Both Wood and MacEachern approach the question of how maps generate meaning for map readers through semiotics, showing how meaning arises from various perceptual and cultural factors. Their approach is suggestive for thinking about the visual representations of sound and how they generate meaning.

One issue that clearly distinguishes "mapping of the world" from "mapping of music" is the question of performance. The distinction between prescriptive and descriptive visualizations engages this distinction directly. The prescriptive symbols of Western notation make possible performances of a piece. A descriptive visualization depends on the existence of a sound recording of the work. When the piece has no score, the recording represents it; when the piece does have a score, the recording represents one possible performance. This turn from prescriptive notation to recorded sound has some ramifications. In the instance of electronic works having no score, like Davidovsky's and Varèse's, there is only one performance—the one existing in the sound recording. In the instance of some other works, like Eleanor Hovda's *Lemniscates*, a score exists but its notation does not symbolize sound as such.[29] Rather it has graphic symbols that tell the performer what physical motions to make and verbal instructions to explain the kinds of sounds the composer desires. Figure 5.9 cites a page of the score,

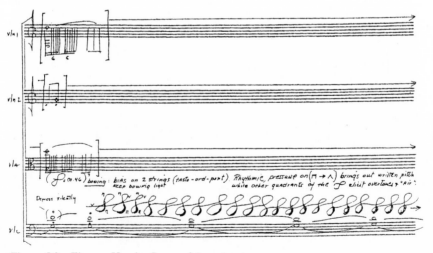

Figure 5.9   Eleanor Hovda, Score of *Lemniscates*

showing in particular the "figure 8" bow strokes for the string players. In cases such as this, a recording exemplifies only one possible performance—as would be the case of recorded performances of traditional notation. But also in this instance, the relation between graphic symbol and intended sound is much more indeterminate than traditional notation, and this indeterminacy undercuts the function of the notation for music study. A map of a recorded performance will describe only one possible performance, but it will provide access to the sounds of the piece in ways the score can not.

By way of concluding, some examples of musical maps will show the range of possibilities that visualizing may take. I am not interested at this point in codifying a system of representation; rather I want to explore the ways that such mapping can encourage a creative approach to musical understanding. Rather than specifying a fixed number of structural objects and a corresponding system of visual representation as does Schenker in his graphic analyses, I am interested in allowing more freedom to myself as mapmaker and others who might engage such a project of visualizing as understanding. The possibility of communicating visually with others when no restrictions are placed on the process of graphic representation rests on my belief in the function of metaphorical transference.

I offer below a "sound-picture" gallery, which shows parts of maps of three works. Two of the maps are mine and a third is by a graduate student.

The map, showing the first minute of the piece, depicts the temporal flow of events across the horizontal axis of the page and the relative pitch of events on the vertical axis—as they would occur in a traditionally notated score. The shapes of symbols and the "cotton" background are meant to suggest visually qualities of sound—indicating such things as the timbre, attack and endings of sounds, duration, connections between sounds. A

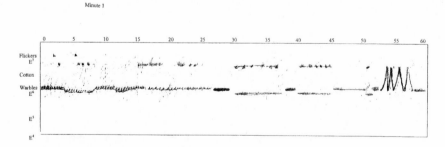

Figure 5.10   Map I—by Lochhead
Piece: Eleanor Hovda, *Lemniscates* (see discography for recording information)
For string quartet

Time	Close Sounds	Distant Sounds	Background
0:00	"Click"	Male Voice: Yelling	Tape Hiss
0:07		↓	↓
1:15	Female Voice: Today is 9/5....	↓	Change in Hiss
1:45	.	MV; banging	↓
2:06	FV: *I taped it...*	↓	↓
2:32	FV: *I'm taping this....so I remember it.*	↓	↓
3:00	FV: *I will start taping when I can...best journal that I have*	↓	Change in Hiss (higher)
3:14		↓	Change in Hiss (lower)
3:20	FV: *I went to look for...beating you up again*	↓	Change in Hiss (higher)
3:55	FV: *Can't even explain....*	↓	↓
4:10		Plus reverberation and echo	↓
4:40	FV: *He threw this music box off a table....*	↓	↓
4:45	←	←←←	↓
4:50	MV: *She's a fucking bitch and I will kill her*–into reverberation		↓

Key to annotations on "Map"

FV	First Female Voice
FV2	Second Female Voice
MV	Male Voice
← etc.	Change in "placement" of sound
↓	Continuation of sound type

Figure 5.11   Map II—by Lochhead
Piece: Rachel McInturff, *By Heart*[30]
This is an electro-acoustic piece with no score.

general timbral quality is suggested by verbal descriptors on the left (as if the layer were an instrument in a traditional score).

The map is organized like a train schedule, showing time on the vertical axis. It does not attempt an "analog" representation of events but is more "digital"—only indicating an event when it begins. The three columns distinguish sounds by their aural distance from the listener: close, distant, and background. The map shows events through 4 minutes and 50 seconds. The

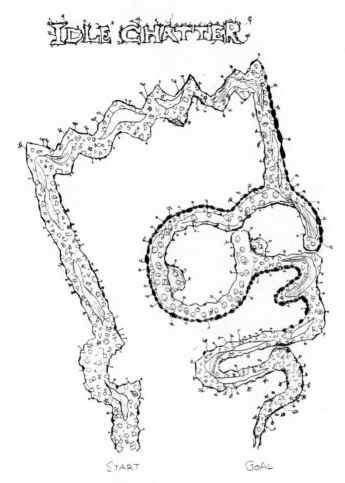

Figure 5.12   Map III—by Makiko Hirai
Piece: Paul Lansky, *Idle Chatter*[31]
This is an electro-acoustic piece with no score.

event at 4:50 is a significant one in the piece since it entails a change in which the Male Voice (MV) moves from the "Distant Sounds" to the "Close Sounds." The map uses verbal description to characterize the timbre of sounds and quotes phrases from the text of the piece.

This map was made by a student in a class I teach on contemporary music. Students were told simply to make a map of *Idle Chatter* without using traditional notation. This one by Hirai depicts the temporal flow of the piece along a kind of path that has some maze-like characteristics. The music begins at the Start and ends at Goal. The overall sound of the piece is depicted with closely packed symbols and letters. The letters suggest that bits of words are heard, never fully forming recognizable linguistic units. The spikes that jut away from the path indicate that there is a sense that sounds occasionally pop out of the busy surface. Myriad other details project the sense of constant change that characterizes the musical flow.

Conclusion

The examples from this "sound-map" gallery approach the project of visualizing quite differently, but in each instance the creator of the map must have already formed a concept of how the piece works in order to depict it visually. For instance, Hirai's map of *Idle Chatter* conceptualizes a busy, constrained texture from which sounds protrude, and a rather meandering process that leads the listener in often circuitous routes. For *Lemniscates*, I have categorized sounds into three types—Flickers, Cotton, and Warbles— and have shown their relation to one another texturally—the Cotton sound envelopes the other two. And for *By Heart*, I use a concept of aural distance as the primary organizational categories.

The project of mapping musical sound requires that the musician-scholar query and examine his/her experience of listening to a work. The process is not unlike a phenomenological investigation since the goal is not to valorize any single listening experience and to take it as unassailable evidence about the world or a musical piece. Rather the goal is to investigate the things as they arise in experience in order to understand them. The things of musical experience are not evidence of how a piece "is," but rather the things that arise in experience are the subject of our investigation. The project of visualizing music helps to give shape to the process of understanding musical sound. Rather than denying the possibility of sonic meaning, the project of visualizing the musical object requires that we listen intently in order to make sound visible.

Notes

1. I refer here to Bolcom's Rags, which were composed during the years 1967 through 1993. William Bolcom, *Complete Rags for Piano* (Milwaukee: Hal Leonard Corp., 1999).

2. I do not use the term in the way that Patricia Carpenter does in "The Musical Object," *Current Musicology* V (1967): 56–87. She suggests an opposition between "musical objects" as a static formal unit and "musical process" as acts of listening.

My focus here is on the fundamental things of musical understanding, which have an intentional shape in musical experience.

3. Ian Bent and David W. Hughes, "Notation," *Grove Music Online*, ed. L. Macy (Accessed July 8, 2004): http://www.grovemusic.com.

4. William Bolcom, *Incineratorag*, from *Complete Rags for Piano*. Milwaukee: Hal Leonard Corp., 1999.

5. The composer must also understand the "music" implicit in the notation when composing. Compositional ideas must be abstracted into notation.

6. Charles Seeger, "Prescriptive and Descriptive Music-Writing," *The Musical Quarterly*, 44, 2 (1958): 184–95.

7. This is typically referred to as "musique concrète" in the concert tradition and "sampling" in the popular domain. See Mario Davidovsky, *Electronic Study #1* (Composers Recordings Incorporated, 1976 [1962]) and Edgard Varèse, *Poème Èlectronique* (Electro-Acoustic Music: Classics. Acton, MA: Neuma, 1990 [1957–1958]).

8. Marco Stroppa suggests, in a contentious article, that analysis of electronic works is not possible. See Marco Stroppa, "The Analysis of Electronic Music," *Contemporary Music Review* IX (1984): 175–180.

9. Terry Teachout, "What Killed Classical Recording?," *Commentary* 111, 5 (2001).

10. Jose Bowen, "Finding the Music in Musicology: Performance History and Musical Works," in *Rethinking Music*, ed. Nicholas Cook and Mark Everist (Oxford: Oxford University 1999), 424–451.

11. Robert Philip, *Early Recordings and Musical Style: Changing Tastes in Instrumental Performance, 1900-1950* (Cambridge and New York: Cambridge University Press), 1992.

12. Cornelius Cardew, *Treatise* (Buffalo: Gallery Upstairs Press, 1967).

13. "Transcription" is the term used when a person takes a sound recording of a piece and notates it, usually in traditional European notation.

14. Peter Winkler, "Writing Ghost Notes: The Poetics and Politics of Transcription," in *Keeping Score: Music, Disciplinary, Culture* (Charlottesville: University of Virginia, 1997), 169–203.

15. Robert Garfias, "Transcription 1—Symposium on Transcription and Analysis: A Hukwe Song with Musical Bow," *Ethnomusicology* 8, 3 (1990): 233–240. Symposium organized by Nicholas M. England, with contributions by Garfias, Mieczyslaw Kolinski, George List, and Willard Rhodes, and moderated by Charles Seeger. Reprinted in *Ethnomusicology: Musical Transcription*, ed. Kay Kaufman Shelemay (New York: Garland Publishing, 1990 [1964]).

16. Sue Carol DeVale, "Prolegomena to a Study of Harp and Voice Sounds in Uganda: A Graphic System for the Notation of Textures," in *Selected Reports in Ethnomusicology*, ed. J.C. DjeDje (Los Angeles: University of California, 1985), 284–315.

17. Johann Heinichen, *Neu erfundene und gründliche Anweisung zu vollkommener Erlernung des General-Basses.* (Hamburg, 1711).

18. The cyclical structure depends on the enharmonic identity of keys, such as Gb and F#.

19. Heinrich Schenker, *Five Graphic Music Analyses* (New York: Dover, 1969 [1933]).

20. Robert Cogan, *New Images of Musical Sound* (Cambridge, MA: Harvard University Press, 1984).

21. Milton Babbitt, *Ensembles for Synthesizer*, (New Electronic Music: Columbia Masterworks, 1967). This piece is an electro-acoustic work with no score. I will shortly discuss some of the issues surrounding such music. Further, while this spectral photo depicts only the opening of Babbitt's work, other spectral photos in Cogan's book depict entire pieces.

22. While maintaining that an "objective" visualization is largely illusory, Jairazbhoy does not condemn such machine-based readings of sound but argues that they must be understood as conditioned by human processes of perceptual understanding. Nazir Jairbaizboy, "The 'Objective and Subjective' View in Music Transcription," *Ethnomusicology* 21, 2 (1977): 263–273.

23. Ian Bent and David W. Hughes, "Notation," *Grove Music Online* ed. L. Macy (Accessed 8 July 2004), http://www.grovemusic.com.

24. Ihde discusses issues of embodiment and map-reading in various places (*CP* and *PT*).

25. Denis Wood, *The Power of Map.* (New York: Guilford Press, 1992).

26. Ibid., 1.

27. Ibid., 12.

28. Alan M. MacEachren, *How Maps Work* (New York: Guilford Press, 1995).

29. Eleanor Hovda, *Lemniscates* (Cassatt String Quartet: Composers Recordings Incorporated, 1994 [1993]).

30. Rachel McInturff, *By Heart*, Music from SEAMUS #6, (Los Angeles: Society for Electro-Acoustic Music in the United States, 1997 [1996]).

31. Paul Lansky, *Idle Chatter More than Idle Chatter* (New York: Bridge, 1994 [1985]).

Part III

Normative Commitments:
Ihde at the Crossroads
of Ethics and Politics

6

Normative Phenomenology: Reflections on Ihde's Significant Nudging

Evan Selinger

Introduction

Don Ihde's phenomenological-hermeneutic framework overcomes long-standing epistemic deficiencies. He contests untenable premises embedded in determinist outlooks and establishes a unique view of the lifeworld that avoids the excesses of utopian prognostics and dystopian diagnoses. Before the philosophy of technology established itself institutionally, he identified several unjustified presuppositions that had permitted theorists and policy makers: (1) to overestimate the causal power of technological activity or human agency, and (2) to overlook (or repress) the nuanced, diverse, and existentially significant interactions through which humans and technologies can coconstitute one another's "identities."

Some critics maintain that Ihde's *oeuvre* is hindered by a considerable flaw: his philosophy of technoscience putatively lacks normative sensitivity.[1] This accusation is noteworthy, and it amounts to more than an indictment of Ihde's division of academic labor. Because Ihde is viewed as privileging epistemic over normative inquiry, he is vulnerable to being characterized as neglecting the most important relations among science, technology, and philosophy. Whereas the more empirically oriented disciplines—anthropology, history, and sociology—can, in principle, explain how technologies function and how technical cultures are organized, philosophical resources appear to be best used when put to another purpose. Despite the diminished public role of the "intellectual," philosophers present themselves regularly as "values experts," that is, as qualified to judge the proper place of technoscience in both the public and private spheres. This principally is the case with respect to identifying the dangers stemming from technoscientific progress, particularly threats which citizens and corporations dismiss as lamentable but tolerable tradeoffs. While applied ethics—medical ethics, environmental ethics, and computer ethics—dominate this arena, phenomenology, in both its secular and theological forms, has made important contributions as well.

In light of these considerations, it is illuminating to compare Ihde with normative phenomenologists such as Hubert Dreyfus and Albert Borgmann. In order to create a shared context through which this comparison can be made, it will be helpful to consider first the topics of situated analysis and phenomenological parity.

Phenomenological Parity

Ihde's metaphilosophical views on normativity center around two themes: situated analysis and phenomenological parity. Influenced by Edmund Husserl's injunction to "remember" the lifeworld origins of human activity—including the generation of conceptual thought—Ihde's epistemological inquiries are always reflexively positioned: through analysis of intentional structures, he correlates *noesis* and *noema* and thereby establishes a necessary experiential link between criteria for knowing and an embodied subject who makes the acquisition of knowledge possible. According to Ihde, understanding the being of a phenomenon necessitates understanding the being of the interpreter who accounts for it. A brief précis of paradigmatic examples of situated analysis in Husserl and Ihde can crystallize this point further.

When Husserl engages in "genetic" phenomenology to reconstruct the lost origin of geometry—ostensibly the mathematical analysis of all possible shapes of the world—he contends that our intuitions concerning the boundaries of clearly defined shapes emerged from a process of abstraction that is rooted in concrete lifeworld praxis. The carpenter's practical need to produce particular kinds of items facilitated the microperceptual recognition of a set of features (e.g., points, angles, straight lines, and surfaces) that served as the historical basis for the macroperceptual identification of idealized shapes (e.g., rectangles, squares, triangles) outside of their initial pragmatic context of discovery. Similarly, when Ihde engages in "genetic" phenomenology to reconstruct the origin of the subject-object split that defined modern epistemology in both its empiricist and rationalist variants, he contends that lifeworld practices pertaining to the *camera obscura* facilitated the production of an "epistemology engine." These practices captivated the philosophical imagination to such an extent that a variety of thinkers used analogical reasoning to conceptually abstract a model of subjectivity—the subject who could never be certain of transcending subjective experience—from the camera's optical ability to invert images (*BT* 71–75).

While this comparison illustrates clearly how the phenomenologist links theoretical claims, abstract intuitions, and lifeworld praxis, it fails to inform us explicitly about the phenomenological connection between lifeworld praxis and normative judgment. Such explicitness requires a discussion of phenomenological parity. Ihde contends that viable normative assessment must ontologically correlate with epistemic inquiry: "I do think there are normative dimensions in phenomenology, but they have to be normative dimensions that arise out of phenomenology" (*CT* 129). Put in terms of phenomenological parity, criteria for deciding what ought to be done should be correlated with a concrete subject whose engagement with lifeworld praxis makes such a recommendation possible. Commenting briefly on the proximity of this position to the Marxist treatment of praxis can clarify matters further.

Ihde claims that despite Husserl's "rationalism," Husserl and Karl Marx exhibit, to some degree, compatible philosophies; they both emphasize the primacy of praxis (*TL* 28). Similarly, despite his negative assessment of Marx's determinist views on technology, the praxis dimension of the political philosophy expressed in *The German Ideology* can be viewed as compatible with Ihde's attention to a situated critical subject in normative contexts.[2] Long before Donna Haraway's meditations on "situated knowledge," Sandra Harding's proposal of "standpoint objectivity," and Bruno Latour's analysis of the limits of modern critique, Marx and Friedrich Engels correlated critical resistance with self-criticism. As David Couzens Hoy notes:

> In the *German Ideology* Marx and Engels insist that when someone speaks, one should always ask oneself "Who is speaking and from where?" The contrast they intend is to the left Hegelians who they criticize for trying to speak from above and outside the world. Resistance is thus thought to be more effective if it is not only critical but also self-critical.[3]

What Hoy does not mention is that the degree of reflexivity that Marx and Engels actually demonstrate varies throughout their texts. Textual interruptions that feature self-reflexive gestures often exist in an unresolved tension with rhetorically grand moves of theoretical overreach. But put charitably, what Marx and Engels propose is that the analyst who fails to be explicit about the position from which he or she is interrogating the world runs the politically dangerous risk of reproducing unintentionally "ideological" biases. The unreflective critic potentially extends aspects of a tradition that he or she does not endorse and is vulnerable to mistaking partial for complete evidence.

These brief comments on Ihde, Husserl, and Marx suggest that Ihde's views on normative philosophy center around two traits typically associated with praxis philosophy:

(1) Ihde often inserts into his analyses reflexive comments about which personal experiences facilitated his disposition to frame a particular issue in a particular way. In this respect, Ihde demonstrates that he appreciates the value of answering the question, "Who is speaking and from where?" Such explicitness extends to reflections upon which life events enabled him to perceive certain phenomena as problematic and other phenomena as unobjectionable. However, being sensitive to postmodern criticisms of the "metaphysics of presence," Ihde does not rely upon biographical commentary to achieve reflective self-understanding. Recognizing that subjectivity is shaped significantly through specific environmental interactions, Ihde attends to the constitution of his own subjectivity through the use of "variational method." Variational method is a rigorous style of analysis that permits the phenomenologist to experience *Gestalt* shifts: the investigator engages in acts of perceptual variation—sometimes with the different perceptual possibilities that a single phenomenon can exhibit when viewed from different vantage points, and at other times with the different perceptual possibilities that a phenomenon can exhibit when juxtaposed comparatively with other phenomena—in order to discern what experiential invariants a phenomenon is constituted by. Should the variational method reveal that something the phenomenologist initially took to be essential turns out to be inessential, then the investigator would revisit the relevant guiding presuppositions. Because the use of variational method allows the phenomenologist to achieve reflective equilibrium, he or she learns about personal perceptual prejudices while coming to understand better the phenomena under investigation.

(2) Even as Ihde strives to present a general theory of intentionality that links inextricably humans, technology, and the world, he frames his analysis of technoscientific practice in terms of specific cultural situations. In this respect, he pursues the traditional philosophical goal of trying to discern universal truths, but does so without compromising fidelity to context, including the material dimensions of history. Assessing cuisine is the most commonplace example that Ihde discusses to illustrate this point as it relates to normativity: while he does not believe that a single best cuisine exists, he contends that one can judge culinary quality within the context of a particular style, that is, better and worse Italian, Indian, or Chinese foods.

In order to elaborate on these points, it will be helpful to consider the role they play in Ihde's metaphilosophy of technology.

Metaphilosophy of Technology

In *Technology and the Lifeworld* Ihde provides a metaphilosophical analysis of the prejudices that have historically limited normative judgments of technological practices. He exposes two kinds of biases: (1) the biases that have allowed theorists to obscure the situated dimensions of their position, and (2) the biases that have allowed theorists to present overly abstract and general analyses—while nevertheless positioning their views rhetorically in concrete and specific terms. The salient points that he discusses can be summarized as follows:

- "Social determinists" contend that social factors, such as decisions made by the elite in the context of technocratic bureaucracy, determine in crucial ways how technology is implemented. Their critiques tend to focus upon how the decisions made by the elite are oriented toward maintaining an established hierarchy that the elite benefit directly from. The value of their critiques is limited: social determinists do not reflect carefully upon the significance of their failure to focus upon the material dimensions of a technology (or technological system). Were they to reflect accordingly, they might have to revise their views. They might have to recognize that their guiding presupposition—that technologies are fundamentally neutral instruments whose significance is established by the causal power of human decision-making—is untenable. Put in terms of phenomenological parity, the social determinist fails to correlate his or her inability to perceive the richness of materiality with his or her sense that modern bureaucracy represents the danger of technology in general.

- "Technological determinists" contend that technological development determines in crucial ways how society evolves. For example, Ihde characterizes the view that the invention of the stirrup as a historical event that leads directly to the development of later Medieval technologies—such as lances, saddles, and armor—as a position that is predicated upon the assumption that technological innovation follows an inevitable causal trajectory: "there is the suggestion that, once invented, technologies simply follow a line of development, almost contextless, as it were" (*TL* 6). The value of this type of analysis, as well as any normative critique that is based upon its structure, is limited. Technological determinists fail to reflect carefully upon the multiplicity of relevant social norms and cultural practices that are found in the specific historical contexts in which technological development actually occurs. Were they to reflect accordingly, they might then have to revise the premises in their arguments that treat technologies as autonomous, transsocial/cultural forces. Put in terms of phenomenological parity, the technological determinist fails to correlate his or her inability perceive the richness of social-cultural context as a significant dimension of his or her sense that technology is an autonomous force.

- Theorists who approach technology from "utopian" and "dystopian" perspectives fail to examine carefully how the examples that they focus upon can be conducive to hastily defining the essence of technology in hyperpositive or hypernegative terms. On the dystopian side, Martin Heidegger characterizes the essence of technology as "standing reserve." Jacques Ellul and Herbert Marcuse equate modern technology with "calculative" techniques that unduly limit human freedom. On the utopian side, zealous optimism in the artificial intelligence community sanctions the conviction that the distinction between human and nonhuman will soon be eradicated. In all of these instances, theoreticians fail to reflect carefully upon the complexity of technological practices: utopians ignore or underplay technological disasters and the historical failure of previous technologies to live up to the hype that once surrounded them; dystopians tend to ignore or underplay how their focus upon military technologies and corporate bureaucracy over-determines their excessively negative and one-sided views. Put in terms of phenomenological parity, utopian and dystopian theorists fail to correlate their confidence/despair with their unjustifiably narrow sense of what counts as relevant evidence.

This summary suggests that when Ihde engages in normative metaphilosophy, he tries to expose theoretical distortions of lifeworld praxis. In this context, a brief comparison with Maurice Merleau-Ponty is warranted. As Edward Said notes:

> Merleau-Ponty's thought is best understood not as a way of uncovering new truths about man but as a way of intensifying participation in human experience. One does not read his work to discover what one had not known before. Instead, one is readmitted from distraction to one's own experience . . .[4]

For both Ihde and Merleau-Ponty, a keen sense of phenomenological description is the key to challenging untenable claims about lifeworld activity.

Phenomenology and Normativity

Having discussed Ihde's evaluation of many of the traditional views espoused in the philosophy of technology, we can now assess critically his relation to contemporary phenomenological inquiry. Living phenomenologists tend to address technoscience from a perspective that is foreign to Ihde's discourse; they focus on emancipation and proceed by using its correlative rhetoric of liberation. Husserl's discussion of the "crisis" concerning Europe, science, and the nature and possibilities of philosophy sets the tone for later investigations. But the most relevant primary sources turn out to be Heidegger and Merleau-Ponty.

Heidegger remains possibly the most significant European philosopher of technology. The lasting power of Heidegger's philosophy correlates in part with admiration for how he examines the "essence of technology." But the perception that his work deserves continual engagement is, perhaps, more a result of interest in the normative implications associated with his injunction to recognize the "saving power" of a "free relation" with technology. And while the critique of the "ideology" of cybernetics in Merleau-Ponty's later writing is remarkably prescient with respect to recent literature on the computational conception of consciousness, his early accounts of perception and intersubjectivity are also situated within a normative horizon. Said—one of the most vigorous critics of "aestheticized powerlessness" in academia— argues that Merleau-Ponty "never" succumbs to a *laissez faire* attitude toward ethics and politics:

> [Merleau-Ponty] clearly rejects what Hebert Marcuse has called one-dimensional man on the same grounds that made him in 1950 sharply criticize the Marxists with whose thought he had hitherto sympathized. To allow things to go as they are, whether or not commanded from above by a rationalized and monolithic superstructure, is bad faith. It means the surrender of the distinctively human activity of conscious perception, and hence the resignation of our task "to complete and conceive" the world.[5]

More recently, when Dreyfus tries to rescue the authority of expertise, he references Merleau-Ponty's account of perception and action, as well as Heidegger's views on "authenticity."[6] Borgmann's attempts to rescue tradition and community are rooted in Heidegger's "reflections on simple and eminent things." Even though Ihde's philosophical investigations are influenced considerably by Heidegger and Merleau-Ponty, important differences distinguish his views from the content and orientation expressed by the other accounts. I will consider each in turn.

Ihde and Dreyfus

Dreyfus argues that the intuitive dimension of expertise is "endangered" because of the widespread assumption that the human mind solves problems algorithmically due to is computational structure. Like Dreyfus, Ihde writes about the process of analogical reasoning through which theoretical accounts of the mind are modeled upon the organizational principles that permit technological artifacts to function. But unlike Dreyfus, Ihde is not terribly concerned that contemporary society is endangered by this process; it does not appear to be at significantly greater risk than previous societies have been.[7] Through phenomenological variation of different lifeworld shapes, Ihde demonstrates that "all self-interpretation takes its shape in a certain way with respect to some basic form of existential praxis which is projected upon the world and reflected back in ways which have become dominant ways of understanding ourselves and our world" (*ET* 22). Today, when the lifeworld is thoroughly mediated by technologies, we "project and interpret ourselves in terms of technology" (*ET* 22). But during a different period, such as when nomadic Amerindian society participated routinely in rituals involving animals and plants, the content of projection differs: "the Indian thinks himself to be 'brother' to the cult animal or, generalized, to be 'brother' to the animal kingdom (*ET* 16). In light of the fact that culturally specific interpretative projections seem to pervade all of human history, Ihde uses moderate rhetoric to recommend that we should be wary of reifying those models "which foreclose us in a totality" (*ET* 23). After all, the lasting power of any model can be expected to be temporary. As lifeworld praxis changes, it is likely that a shift will arise in our willingness to accept those models that fail to reflect our altered ways of being-in-the-world.

It is not only the matter of recognizing historical continuity with respect to praxis and projection that allows Ihde to proceed temperately when compared with the more prophetically stylized Dreyfus. He recognizes further that Dreyfus's philosophy of technology is based upon a significant misunderstanding. Despite his overt attempt to be sensitive to human-technology interactions, Dreyfus ultimately obscures the domain of praxis. In order to establish a polemical and normative framework for addressing the presence of computers in the contemporary lifeworld, Dreyfus depicts technologies as autonomous entities. Ihde thus claims:

> In the context I am tracing here, I now position myself between my two contemporary peers: Dreyfus and Heelan. To caricature the situation, Dreyfus, I believe, leaves the technology *outside*. For him, not only do computers "think" differently than humans, but they do not "think" at all. The computer remains an alien presence which, only through philosophic illusion, becomes a semblance of the human . . . For me, technologies are neither *outside* nor *inside*. (*EH* 45–46)

What Dreyfus fails to appreciate is that the basic ontological status of a technology is tied inextricably to the structure of intentionality that serves as the organizing principle through which it can be put to use.[8] Attending to praxis carefully reveals that computers can do and can fail to do many significant things. In this context, the structure of a computer is an index of the performance that may be expected from it. Dreyfus therefore pursues a fruitful path by examining the limits of computational processing. However, he provides the reader with very little sense that philosophically interesting computational outcomes—of both the successful and unsuccessful kinds— tend to arise because of how computers are used by specific users in specific contexts; the outcomes are often not attributable primarily to inherent limitations posed by a computer's ontological properties—although such properties limit the kinds of practices that computers can enter into. Likewise, humans might succeed or fail at some endeavor in part as a result of limitations posed by their being. However, when it comes to philosophically interesting cases of practice, human success or failure tends to depend on the outcome of its interactions with technologies; it is often not attributable primarily to intrinsic ontological limitations.[9]

Dreyfus might be insensitive to these points concerning the primacy of interaction because he did not reflect phenomenologically on his situated position as a normative critic. Had he been more sensitive to phenomenological parity, he might have recognized that in trying to prove that artificial intelligence (AI)—at least of the "GOFI" variety—is a "degenerating research program," he appropriates the AI enthusiast's manner of framing the debate. Such appropriation saddles him with all of the conceptual problems for examining technology critically that this ontologically reduced framework entails. By contrast, when Ihde analyzes computational power in his later writings, he focuses upon interactive uses of technology, such as practices of instrumentally mediated vision. In these instances, computer imaging makes it possible for the trained interpreter to see dimensions of the world that were not visually accessible to the human eye previously.

While the difference between Ihde and Dreyfus on this point might appear to be principally about topics of investigation—expert programs vs. imaging technologies—the contrast reveals something fundamental about their orientation toward theorizing technology. When he addresses the artificial intelligence debate, Ihde comments on the significance of IBM's Deep Blue beating Garry Kasparov at chess. Ihde argues that Dreyfus's position on chess playing and intuition might not be weakened by Kasparov's loss—but that in order appreciate this point, we should not fixate on the question: How can a computer beat a grand chess master? Instead, the chess match needs to be interpreted within Ihde's framework of "human-technology-world" relations:

> The crucial thing to realize is that Dreyfus would be defeated with respect to the mind vs. machine motif, if and only if a machine beat

a human beat a human at a task that is considered paradigmatic of intelligent behavior. We, however, would argue that this version of the Deep Blue-Kasparov narrative is badly framed. There never has been simply a chess-programmed, autonomous computer. Instead, there are humans plus computers in relations. It is, of course, possible for humans to program computers and then set the computers to running the programs; in this case, the human-technology relation remains in place, albeit located in the background. The "deistic" computer designer and programmer has set off the toy to spin by itself—until it runs down, crashes, or completes the run. The computer does not do anything on its own: it is not self-invented; it does not program itself; and it runs only within the input given. Those who play chess with computers at home are in this situation. But in the context of the Deep Blue-Kasparov match, there was a much more intimate human-technology situation at work.[10]

The relevance of Ihde's commentary on Kasparov extends beyond the topic of chess. The earlier phenomenologists reified diverse technological practices under the monolithic category of the "essence of technology." When viewed from Ihde's interactive framework, it can be appreciated how Dreyfus's monolithic description of the essence of the contemporary lifeworld as "endangered" is also an untenable gesture of theoretical over-reach. While Ihde commends Dreyfus for adopting a "research and development" position toward philosophy, his analysis suggests that when Dreyfus tries to liberate human expertise by contrasting its intuitive dimension with brute computational power, he frames the issue of emancipation poorly. "Society" is not endangered because computers are capable of doing certain things and incapable of doing others. Neither is "society" endangered because of general attitudes toward what computers can and cannot do. General attitudes and specific ontological limitations are important dimensions of praxis, but since the former and the latter tend to transform through interaction, it is not helpful to investigate praxis through either lens. It is not surprising, therefore, that when Dreyfus investigates "distance learning" in his later writing, he treats the topic reductively. He proceeds under the assumption that distance learning necessarily equates with the attempt to reproduce face-to-face classroom experiences through virtual means. By evading the relevant empirical literature, Dreyfus fails to address how different techniques have promoted or failed to promote specific pedagogical ends in specific pedagogical contexts.[11] Dreyfus thus never taps into the epistemic or normative possibilities that a situated and phenomenologically reflexive "research and development position" might make possible.

Ihde and Borgmann

While Ihde has not criticized Borgmann extensively in print, conversations that occurred during Borgmann's "roast" in Ihde's technoscience seminar suggest that while Ihde admires Borgmann's philosophy deeply, he nevertheless finds the contrast between "focal practices" and the "device paradigm" nostalgic. From Ihde's perspective, Borgmann's account achieves its persuasive force by: (1) romanticizing a past that never existed and (2) demeaning the actual present by interpreting its practices selectively and almost always disparagingly.

According to Borgmann, the premodern technological world is best depicted as a world of *poesis* and craft in which people actively engaged in practices that fostered the development of skill. This was a time in which the means were not separated typically from the ends of practice. By contrast, he depicts the modern technological world as one in which craft and skill is threatened: the inner workings of technological devices are, for most consumers, separated from the ends toward which they can be applied. For Borgmann, the predominantly welcoming attitude extended toward these readily available, easy-to-use, low-maintenance devices correlates with a particular configuration of subjectivity: an unengaged populace that spends much of its time pursuing distractingly trivial activities. The "focal practices" that Borgmann advocates as an antidote to the alienation of consumerism are supposed to provide central and illuminating orientation to our lives. "Focal practices" are ostensibly memorable, context-dependent experiences in which a sense of accomplishment can be experienced.

The culture of the table, as exemplified by the family meal, is, for Borgmann, a paradigm case of a focal practice: "The great meal of the day, be it at noon or in the evening, is a focal event par excellence. It gathers the scattered family around the table."[12] Unlike fast food, a home-cooked meal takes time to prepare. It is not meant to be eaten with disposable utensils on disposable plates. According to Borgmann, the primary purpose of the meal is to create a gathering space for the family—not to facilitate "grabbing a quick bite":

> In a Big Mac the sequence of courses has been compacted into one object and the discipline of table manners has been reduced to grabbing and eating. The social context reaches no further than the pleasant faces and the quick hands of the people who run the fast-food outlet. In a festive meal, however, the food is served, one of the most generous gestures a human being is capable of.[13]

Like Borgmann, Ihde notes that the practices associated with fast food can be problematic:

From every city and town in the most maximalist technological culture (the USA) the "double arches" now appear only a block from
Rome's Spanish Steps and, with the related varieties of fast foods,
throughout most of the developed world. Such fast food chains are
the epitome of the now-computerized assembly line processes pioneered in the days of Ford and Taylor. There is no skilled chef—the
workers are all de-skilled, and one can learn the steps of the process
quickly and easily. The marginal persons for employment—adoles-
cents and, more recently, the elderly—become the primary labor
sources for the fast food factory. The market, too, is interesting in
that, in Europe particularly, the fast food operation has become the
"hangout" for respectable youth. (*TL* 159)

In light of these damning observations, it may appear strange that Ihde
disagrees with Borgmann's sense that the prevalence of fast food indicates the
decline of cultural values.[14] Ihde and Borgmann part company, however, on the
issue of praxis. Ihde contextualizes the value that Americans place on fast food
within a broader framework of culinary practices. He notes that at the same
time that American-style fast food is exported all over the globe, Americans are
given opportunity to expand their culinary horizons, and in turn, to recognize
the aesthetic limits of traditional American culinary practices:

First, what was once "Prince Spaghetti Day" has now proliferated
into regional Italian cuisines . . . In Chinese food, once merely the
"chop suey" staple of non-Western food for Americans, the choice
must now be made between Hunan, Sichuan, Mandarin, etc. To these
finer differentiations must be added the whole spectrum of newer and
smaller culinary traditions such as Vietnamese, Thai, Afghanistani,
Indian in all its varieties . . . There is innovation springing from the
pluriculinary development. . . . (*TL* 158)

For Ihde, the critical point is that when Borgmann focuses on the loss
of American table manners, he (1) avoids looking at broader lifeworld patterns and (2) fails to justify his insular focus. All of the features associated with
focal practices can be found during a "take-out meal" that occurs in a pluriculture
context. A family gathering (or a gathering of friends, co-workers, etc.) in
which people eat the readily available cuisine that reflects non-American
culinary practices can be quite memorable, and for a variety of aesthetic,
political, and ethical reasons.

The issue of whether pluriculture provides unique opportunities for
reflection also functions as the decisive point of demarcation between Ihde
and Borgmann in their respective assessments of television—a technology

that Borgmann treats as paradigmatic of the corrosive effects of the "device paradigm."[15] Upon consideration of sociological data that reports how highly people esteem their television, Borgmann insists that: "Telephone and television are the technological devices that have weakened literacy and impoverished the culture of the world."[16] Writing letters, telling stories, engaging in conversations, attending plays, reading to one another, and silently reading books and periodicals to oneself have all taken a backseat to watching television. Television routinely provides an alienating experience that disengages subjects from one another and inhibits genuine intersubjective connection by promoting self-oriented comportment. Whereas the scattered family once gathered around the "culture of the table," today TV dinners dominate. Not only is food reduced to a meal to be grabbed, but the festive and conversational context of dining—a focal practice—is lost. Seduced by the soothing presence of the television, we have putatively come to experience engagement with others and with nature as exertion, as a cruel and unjust demand. When our favorite show is on, we presumably do not want anyone to interrupt and pull us away from our passive contentment.

Borgmann grounds his negative assessment of television in an ontological distinction between two kinds of reality: "commanding things" and "disposable devices." Disposable devices are readily available commodities that make technologically mediated experiences instantly available without the use of much skill. Indeed, learning to watch television requires little effort; young children ascertain how to do it, often without any formal instruction. Disposable devices thus belong to a world of pliable material; their emotional and moral significance is subjective and flexible. Their use, as Borgmann takes the example of television to illustrate, encourages a shallow life of distraction and isolation.

By contrast, commanding things are focal objects that express meaning on the basis of their own intrinsic qualities; the emotional and moral significance that people invest in them is largely based on the sense-bestowing capacity of the objects themselves. Commanding things direct our attention because they require skill to use and we treat people who can adroitly operate them with respect. Whereas we do not value someone because they know how to operate a television, we admire a musician whose disciplined training allows her to create beautiful, memorable music. Furthermore, in contrast to the withdrawn and individualist behavior that disposable devices such as television encourage, commanding things further the end of communal engagement. One of the reasons why a person learns to use an instrument is to be able to extend his or her range of communication, to be musically expressive.

Ihde takes issue with Borgmann's analysis on the grounds that Borgmann has to avoid dealing fully with praxis in order to equate television watching with the individual's withdrawal into solitude. Borgmann deals with television on such a general level that it never addresses the specific practices of watching specific kinds of programs. Ihde politicizes the philosophical problem of television by focusing on its extensive reach in highly developed countries. This is an unusual aspect of television for Ihde to highlight: his analysis combines the presentation of multiple variations with a cosmopolitan sense of multiculturalism. In order to best convey Ihde's point, it will be helpful to juxtapose it to some critics of globalism.

Some critics of globalism warn that the ever-growing reach of television, particularly the exportation of American ideals as embedded in the popular culture of American programming, presents a threat to local values. For example, during the Bhutto era in Pakistan, concern was raised over how to censor Western portrayals of women on publicly available programs. With the revival of Islamic fundamentalism in a number of countries, additional national examples that make the same point can easily be given: far from being neutral, the images that television presents are often acidic to a traditional community's sense of collective identity.

Although Ihde is highly sensitive to the non-neutrality of all technologies, including television, he has a different take on globalism. From Ihde's perspective, it is a mistake to view the global presence of television so reductively as to see it as mostly promoting Americanism. By focusing on the television habits of highly developed countries, Ihde highlights the prevalence of pluriculture as the presentation of "multiple otherness." For example, while international news programs depict a variety of countries, cultures, and perspectives in a single broadcast, pop-culture programs, such as shows that run on MTV, present us with fragmented images that draw from a multicultural mix of music, fashion, and ethnic traditions. In other words, the success of numerous "high" and "low" cultural programs can be attributed to their ability to deconstruct monolithic images and ideologies. As Ihde notes, such deconstruction implies relativism: "Implicit in pluriculture is a kind of *bricolage* relativism. One may pick and choose culture fragments, multiply choices, and in the process reflectively find one's own standards provincial or arbitrary— certainly no longer simply *a priori* obvious."[17] Whereas the prospect of relativism calls for criticism in many philosophical circles, Ihde does not oppose it in this case because it is a prospect that applies to all cultural forms. While traditional cultures will find themselves able to confront critically modern secular images, so too will provincial American (as well as Eurocentric) audiences have the opportunity to call aspects of their own identities into question as they are confronted with traditional religious images.

In sum, while Ihde acknowledges that the media exhibits bias routinely, he also insists that there are instances of regularly occurring programs that present an opportunity for individuals to engage with the international community. These programs allow viewers to become more reflective about the arbitrary nature of their own cultural identity; they can recognize that their cultural position is but one of many such perspectives within the wider cultural arena. For example, the multiperspectival international coverage of the recent "War on Terrorism" suggests that the conflict between East and West might not be adequately explained by the partial metanarratives that both sides present.

These remarks on where Ihde and Borgmann differ on the philosophical significance of culinary practices and practices of television watching reveal the main philosophical point that distinguishes them from one another. Since Borgmann's "deictic" philosophy is based upon abstracting two categories from the domain of practice for the purpose of appealing to one as a foundational standard from which the other can be judged deficient, it is likely that Ihde, a self-professed "post-foundational" thinker with pragmatic sensibilities, would object to such a move on the grounds of it being unjustifiably transcendental and totalizing. It is not the case that Ihde would doubt that focal practices exist, that focal practices can be socially valuable, or that focal practices can be threatened by the values embodied in the "device paradigm." However, for all of the reasons mentioned, he would agree with Andrew Feenberg who insists: "Borgmann's conclusions are too hastily drawn and simply ignore the role of social contextualizations in the appropriation of technology."[18] Put in terms of reflexivity, Ihde might contend that Borgmann downplays the role of social context when he chooses his paradigmatic examples because he is not sufficiently sensitive to phenomenological parity, that is, his "European" biases with respect to American culture, his biases with respect to living in Montana as opposed to a more urban city such as Manhattan.

Conclusion

I've attempted to prove that Ihde does indeed present a normative critique of the type of theorizing that obscures the subtler dimensions of engaging with technoscience. He shows how the troubling dimensions of the lifeworld that a variety of critics identify do not correspond adequately with empirical reality. To a great extent, these maladies are idealized constructions; they exist primarily as theoretical distortions that correlate with selective perceptual attention. In this context, Ihde's primary contribution to normative philosophy can be said to occur in a deflationary register that is comparable to Ludwig Wittgenstein's project of "philosophical therapy." By showing how many critics of technology and science obscure the situated dimensions that underlie their perspectives, Ihde reminds us of the normative relevance of a *Gestalt* shift: when a shift in perspective makes a problem disappear, then one is better placed to interrogate contextually situated technological dilemmas and propose

contextually situated solutions. This approach to normativity clearly corresponds with a deflated vision—at least with respect to its traditional ambitions—of the philosophical enterprise:

> It should be understood from the outset that the task of a philosophy,
> not matter how far-reaching or profound, is also limited. The philoso-
> pher cannot provide formulaic answers to the questions posed, nor are
> there in any likelihood such simple answers. There are two things that
> a philosophy can do: It can provide us with a perspective from which
> to view the terrain . . . Secondly, a philosophy can provide a frame-
> work or "paradigm" for understanding. (*TL* 9)

Viewing philosophical potential in these narrowly circumscribed terms does
not suggest that philosophical reflection is irrelevant to normative ends. Philosophers can make significant contributions by way of "significant nudging":

> I reject the notion made popular by Heidegger that "only a god can
> save us." Nor do I have any faith that this could or would happen. In
> what I shall claim is rather a heightened sense of contingency; we
> must more than ever see to our own fate, by deeply and even caringly
> looking after our technologically textured world...there are some
> directions that can be taken in crucial interstices that can do some
> significant nudging. (*TL* 163)

But what is "significant nudging" for Ihde? Ihde demonstrates that any
discussion that links intentional beings with their tools has an *intrinsically
normative dimension*: human-technology-world relations can be transformative at both the microperceptual and macroperceptual levels. Ihde also displays a *substantive normative commitment*: by examining critically (and
ultimately metaphilosophically) the theoretical positions that over-determine
and totalize our technologically mediated relations, Ihde actively deflates the
persuasive power of those views, which undermine our potential to interact
with technologies successfully. But these two dimensions of normativity do
not inform us as to which specific practices Ihde endorses. The clearest passage that speaks to this issue is one that also suggests that a tension might run
throughout Ihde's philosophy:

> And in the face of this situation, I find myself equally empathetic to
> those who defend a neo-enlightenment set of social and political
> values...In this analogy, the pluripalate dilettante is at least a harbin-
> ger if a new enlightenment, in so far as he or she can see that there
> is not single "core" or "foundational" cuisine and that many can be

equally tolerated, or better, deeply appreciated. There is a kind of cosmopolitanism implicit in this phenomenon which will always offend the countryman. But if, through the mediation of now omnipresent information, communication, and image technologies *there is no more "country,"* for the "global village" is not a village, but an urban complex of global diversity, including all the ethnic neighborhoods contained within the city, then neo-enlightenment cosmopolitanism may be the order of the day. (*PP* 66)

This passage indicates that Ihde's commitment to phenomenology and his commitment to pragmatism might not accord completely with one another. If a tension exists, it appears in the gap between the existence of multiperspectival phenomena and the contingent reasons that people have for interpreting them in particular ways. As an individual, Ihde admits to being empathetic to a neo-enlightenment set of values. But he never formally articulates why these values are useful for him to maintain or why others should want to endorse them as well. In this sense, Ihde suggests that an intimate connection exists between what someone "can see" in a multiperspectival phenomenon and a cosmopolitan ethos; apart from personal endorsement, however, Ihde never provides causal or logical arguments that substantiates why others should want to capitalize on this potential link. As Ihde suggests, viewing bricolage television and consuming multicultural cuisine can be practices that are acidic to traditional "identity politics." What Ihde does not highlight, however, is the fact that these practices can also result in the reaffirmation of traditional "identity politics." One can look at bricolage entertainment and find it lacking in substance when compared with more native productions. One can sample multiple cuisines for the purpose of experimentally proving to oneself that one's naïve cuisine is the best. The question at issue is thus: What, if any, norm suggests that multiperspectival phenomena ought to be experienced in cosmopolitan terms that promote critical reflexivity? Correlatively, we might wonder: Is there a single over-arching cosmopolitan norm that applies to all multiperspectival phenomena? Or should we be pragmatic and address the issue of cosmopolitanism on a case-by-case basis?

Notes

1. In an interview, Ihde notes: "And Latour wants to claim not being critical at all, wanting to eliminate the notion of the critical. The first thing I want to say is that in the early days I constantly experienced the critique of being a descriptive phenomenologist. I was continually asked why I was not normative and failed to develop axiological notions" (*CT* 129).

2. This brief comparison of Ihde and Marx is not meant to suggest that Ihde would endorse any of the key concepts in Marx's political analysis—"ideology," "consciousness," or "alienation"—as being useful for normative assessment.

3. David Couzens Hoy, *Critical Resistance: From Poststructuralism to Post-Critique* (Cambridge: MIT Press, 2004), 191.

4. Edward Said, *Reflections on Exile and Other Essays* (Cambridge, MA: Harvard University Press, 2000), 6.

5. Ibid., 9.

6. For a critique of the limits of Dreyfus's account, see Evan Selinger and Robert Crease "Dreyfus on expertise: The limits of phenomenological analysis," *Continental Philosophy Review* 35 (2002): 245–279.

7. Hubert and Stuart Dreyfus write: "The chips are down, the choice is being made right now. And at all levels of society computer-type rationality is winning out. Experts are becoming an endangered species. If we fail to put logic machines in their proper place, as aids to human beings with expert intuition, then we shall end up servants supplying data to our competent machines. Should calculative rationality triumph, no one will notice that something is missing, but now, while we still know what expert judgment is, let us use that expert judgment to preserve it." Hubert and Stuart Dreyfus, *Mind Over Machine: The Power of Human Intuition and Expertise In The Era of the Computer* (New York: Free Press, 1986), 195.

8. Specifically, what Ihde calls "human-technology-world" relations.

9. For more on Ihde's critique of Dreyfus, see Don Ihde and Evan Selinger, "Merleau-Ponty and Epistemology Engines," *Human Studies* 27, 4 (2004): 361–376.

10. Ibid., 371.

11. A brief comparison with Dreyfus and Andrew Feenberg on the topic of distance learning can be useful here. Feenberg was a member of the design team that created the first online educational program at the School of Management and Strategic Studies at the Western Behavioral Sciences Institute in 1981. During this time, online education was conducted through technologies that by today's standards appear primitive (Apple IIE's with 48k of memory and 300-baud modems). On the one hand, technological limitations translated into pedagogical limitations because the lack of graphical content prevented even the simplest of blackboard scribbling from being transmitted. On the other hand, technological limitations, which led to text-based communication, were also experienced as enabling; through experimentation Feenberg realized that "a Socratic pedagogy based on virtual classroom discussions" could lead to successful results. He goes so far as to claim: "Literally hundreds of highly intelligent comments were contributed to our computer conferences each month by students and teachers. The quality of these online discussions surpasses anything I have been able to stimulate in my face-to-face classroom." Andrew Feenberg, "Distance Learning: Promise or Threat," *Crosstalk* (2004): 12.

12. Albert Borgmann, *Technology and the Character of Contemporary Life: A Philosophical Analysis* (Chicago: Chicago University Press, 1984), 204.

13. Ibid., 205.

14. "I admit," Ihde writes, "that the previously mentioned dystopians could take these observations—and particularly given what I suspect is a hidden elitism combined with nostalgia for some folk past—and run rampant with this trend" (*TL* 160).

15. The contrast between Ihde and Borgmann on television was developed initially for my entry on "television" for the *Encyclopedia of Science, Technology, and Ethics*.

16. Albert Borgmann, "The Moral Significance of Material Culture," in *Technology and the Politics of Knowledge*, eds. Andrew Feenberg and Alastair Hannay (Bloomington: Indiana University Press, 1995), 90.

17. Don Ihde, "Image Technologies and Traditional Culture," in Ibid., 155.

18. Andrew Feenberg, "Critical Evaluation of Heidegger and Borgmann," in *Philosophy of Technology: The Technological Condition*, eds. Robert Scharff and Val Dusek (Malden: Blackwell Publishers, 2003), 331.

7

Ihde and Technological Ethics

Paul B. Thompson

Between Philosophy of Technology and Technological Ethics

Practitioners of technological ethics, if the term may even be used, have labored to carve out a modicum of philosophical turf. Against them on the one side are those who argue that there is just ethics, the philosophical study of norms for human action. For them, human actions are amenable to ethical reflection and judgment, and this is not changed by whether they make use of tools and techniques or not. On the other side are a few who have seen technology as inimical to ethical purposes, possibly as something like original sin or alternatively as an inexorable natural force that defies any ethical steering at all. The turf between these views is occupied on the one hand by people who think that it is possible to make fairly broad generalizations about the ethical significance of modern technology, and on the other by those, such as myself, who tend to focus on specific ways in which specific technology has modified particular forms of human agency, while making no broad generalizations about technology and moral problems.

Though simplistic, this analysis suggests four possible stances within (or against) technological ethics. First is the view that there is no such thing: technology is not in itself ethically significant. On this view, the use or development of technology is a form of human action that takes on whatever ethical significance it might have solely in virtue of being the kind of action that it is. Second, there are the dark views of technology. Here technology attains philosophical significance as a metaphysical force unto itself, possibly as a distortion of human purpose and meaning, and often autonomous. Even when the failing is ultimately a human one, as in the case of Martin Heidegger's influential essay "Die frage nach technologie," technology is associated with a world gone wrong, and the philosophical task is to reveal the source of evil or error.

The third and fourth stances are poles of a gradient. At one end are very general theories of technological ethics, theories that posit ways in which technology or technical practice as a whole can and should be made more ethical. But technology as whole can be readily broken down into general types of technology, though the typology might be done in different ways. Here biotechnology, energy technology and information technology might be thought of as distinct fields, each with distinct ethical problems. Alternatively, the breakdown might emphasize a distinction between large technological systems, on the one hand, and isolated tools and techniques, on the other. But one can be even more specific in one's approach, and as one reaches the opposite pole of the gradient, one is examining ethical issues associated with open source code or adult cell mammalian cloning with no expectation that these issues generalize to other areas of technical practice at all.

Though he has rarely addressed normative themes in his writing, Ihde's philosophy of technology bears on all four of these broadly characterized stances in technological ethics. First, Ihde's challenge to the conventional view of technology as applied science is also an implicit challenge to the philosophical attitudes that give rise to the view that technology raises no new or unique ethical questions. Second, Ihde's adaptation of postmodern themes can be read as an implicit endorsement of dark views, and especially of those that call for a check on technology's alleged tendency to lead us away from those aspects of being and praxis that are most crucial for understanding moral purpose. However, Ihde has often distanced himself from such strongly negative views of technology, suggesting that a more plausible reading of his postmodern critique might be more in line with someone like Langdon Winner, who challenges us to think more philosophically about technology in general. The fourth stance, the ethical analysis of specific tools and techniques, returns to work undertaken early in Ihde's philosophical career.

Stance I: The Denial of Technological Ethics

As used here, "technological ethics" is inclusive of any view that finds technology and technical innovation to pose philosophical questions that bear on normative topics. Such views are relatively uncommon among twentieth-century academic philosophers. One obstacle to technological ethics has been the view, hardly ever argued explicitly, that technology is just applied science. Science was thought to be largely a process of explanation, and the model of explanation that emerged from the logical positivist tradition held that explanations have the logical form of a deductive argument in which theory and empirical observations deductively entail a description of the phenomena to be explained. For Karl Popper and Carl Hempel, this tied scientific explanation closely to an ability to predict how material entities would behave under specified conditions. Technology was, on this view, simply a matter of setting up an apparatus that conforms to the conditions specified in the scientific theory, which in turn will produce the conditions entailed or predicted through a robust theory. One could theoretically predict how steel and concrete would perform under certain conditions, and one could measure or manipulate the conditions at a particular site so that steel and concrete would be predicted to bear specified loads. Voila; a bridge! Technology was, in other words, simply a replication the experimental procedures described in positivist philosophy of science for practical purposes.

Thus twentieth-century philosophy had a tidy view of technology. Epistemology and philosophy of science yielded an analysis of prediction under experimental conditions as a byproduct of the philosophy of explanation. Experiments could simply be repeated over and over and on larger scales "for practical purposes," which had nothing whatsoever to with science. Here, ethics would pick up the ball, specifying whether the purposes were consistent with either the conceptual specification of ethical action (as indicated by neo-Kantians) or the maximization of social utility (as indicated by consequentialists). This did not preclude the possibility that technology could have unintended consequences. Nothing in postpositivist philosophy of science entails that one can predict every possible consequence of a particular experimental apparatus, especially when it is being operated in uncontrolled and complex circumstances. But while twentieth-century academic philosophers were certainly capable of admitting that technology might have unexpected impacts, they were not inclined to see this as a philosophically provocative problem.

Ihde's philosophy is a direct challenge to the view that technology can be understood simply as applied science. These elements of Ihde's thought are discussed in other chapters and will not be rehearsed again here. What is relevant in the present context is simply the way in which this challenge was also a challenge to the assumptions implicit in twentieth-century analytic ethics' neglect of technological themes. If technology is constitutive of perception and practice (especially scientific practice), it cannot be understood simply as a logical extension of Popperian or Hempelian theories of scientific explanation. If technology is made interesting in the sociology, history, and philosophy of science, it should also be interesting in ethics. Although this is a fairly straightforward implication of Ihde's thought, it has emerged as an explicit claim only in recent work, as when he calls for philosophers to work with scientists and engineers in *Bodies in Technology*.

Stance II: Anti-Technology Ethics

I am using the phrase "anti-technology ethics" to indicate philosophical views that see modern technology as corrupting, as something that must resisted by those who wish to live well or rightly. While there are any number of intellectual traditions that contribute to such views (including 1960's hippie idealism), the forms of anti-technology ethics most relevant to Ihde's work are those that draw on phenomenology and especially on Heidegger's analysis of the way that technologies transform (some would say distort) key qualities in the experience of the world. Albert Borgmann, David Strong, and Michael Zimmerman have each combined phenomenology and environmental philosophies to produce sophisticated (if also somewhat moderated) articulations of the era's dissatisfaction with technology. Their analyses run parallel to those of Idhe with respect to technology's capacity to transform human consciousness.

In *Technics and Practice,* technology's effect on embodied experience is characterized as relative to the sensory capability of the technologically unaided human body. Phenomena as revealed or made evident through unenhanced senses become an implicit reference point susceptible to various types of modification through technical means. Here Ihde is consistent with Husserl's characterization of the *lifeworld*, the world as experienced or "lived." Husserl's phenomenology gives priority to the lifeworld in comparison to conceptions of the world (or nature). The world as constituted by such unenhanced forms of experience also becomes an implicit reference point, opening up the possibility for a normative conceptualization of authenticity relative to technological enhancement. At times, Ihde's characterization of amplification and reduction suggests that this implicit reference point is a point of origin, a neutral position, but there are many different ways in which philosophy can proceed from such an observation. Ihde *does* want to suggest that philosophies of the modern and analytic period have invested certain technically amplified features of phenomena with ontological significance simply in virtue of the fact that scientific equipment has made them readily available. He *does* argue that availability is not itself an adequate warrant for such an investment.

Ihde *does not*, however, argue that the neutral position of unaided, unamplified perceptual encounter constitutes a more authentic or ontologically correct vantage point, nor does he even endorse the view that any such vantage point or orientation to phenomena can ever be found. It is in this respect that Ihde differs from others who rely on Heidegger more than Husserl. Nevertheless, Heidegger's remarks on hammers in *Being and Time* clearly inspired some of the ideas in *Technics and Praxis*. Heidegger philosophizes with a hammer as his primary example in characterizing beings or things as "ready-to-hand" and compares with the way in which a thing, the hammer, is seen as a thing in the Kantian sense, as an entity present to the perceiving subject and phenomenally available as an spatially extended object having mass, density, etc. It is the latter sense of "thingness" that gives rise to the modern metaphysics of transcendent objects, available for characterization by modern science. As ready for deployment in hammering, however, the hammer is absorbed into the equipment with which an embodied individual encounters the lifeworld. As ready-to-hand, the hammer is experienced much as one might experience one's own body in various forms of physical activity.

Ihde use of this Heideggerian argument is intended to assert the ontological priority of the lifeworld (and of tools as ready-to-hand) over the metaphysics of things or beings that emerges out of the modern scientific world view. Borgmann uses it to call attention to the coherence and infinite richness of the lifeworld, and to contrast this with the attenuated and potentially brittle character of experiences and relations founded on specialized (e.g., reductive) modern technologies that have been developed to do one thing exceedingly well. Strong and Zimmermann both rely on Heidegger's claim in *The Question Concerning Technology* that the modern worldview results in seeing everything (and especially the natural world) simply as a resource to be consumed in human projects that grow thoughtlessly out of the modern project. For them, ethical imperatives emerge primarily in the realm of understanding, appreciating, and preserving the natural environment. Borgmann cautions more broadly against succumbing to the reductive tendencies of modern technology, urging us of the need to "hold on to reality." Thus though Ihde shares many ontological views with these anti-technology philosophers, he does not draw anti-technology conclusions from them.

Ihde praises Heidegger for his attentiveness to the way in which tools (such as the hammer) are "embodied," meaning that they become absorbed into the noetic dimensions of intentionality normally associated with the human body itself. Yet he believes that Heidegger (and by extension others who follow him) romanticizes the embodiment relations associated handcraft tools (such as the hammer), seeing only modern industrial technologies as indicative of a world gone wrong. However, it is not enough to dismiss these views as forms of romanticism, for while they may share many dissatisfactions with the romantics, the dark views of the twentieth-century have far more detailed and ontologically sophisticated discussions of *how* technology comes to be problematic than did anyone in the nineteenth-century. In distancing himself from this tradition, Ihde must either find these accounts to be flawed (though they share a great deal with his own work), or he must disagree with the negative valence that these philosophers associate with the "loss" of authentic, natural, or sufficiently rich and well-grounded orientations within the lifeworld. There are clues throughout Ihde's writings that it is the latter, but an argument for his more optimistic view of our circumstances has not been forthcoming.

Stance III: Technological Ethics in Broad Form

Although there are several philosophers who might be taken as exemplifying the attempt to provide a positive ethic for technology, two that have drawn Ihde's attention are Langdon Winner and Richard Sclove. Both were influenced by Jacques Ellul's analysis of technological systems. Ellul popularized the view that the development and use of certain types of technology requires very broad and systematic social, practical, and material coordination throughout society. Once the infrastructure and institutions for a particular configuration of the technological system is in place, it is very difficult (meaning mostly very costly in economic and political terms) to alter it. The choice of which technology to deploy in meeting a society's material needs is thus actually made very early in the process of developing the specific technical means for doing so. American political theorists such as Winner and Sclove have emphasized the fact that choices are made in developing and promoting technological systems. Despite the profound way that these choices affect the lives of everyone, they are typically made in rather autocratic fashion, and often by individuals who have little sense of public duty. As such, there is a general imperative to make technology "more democratic," and this means both that these early technical decisions must be made responsive to democratic political influence, and also that it is better to deploy technological systems that preserve many opportunities for further choice and adaptation by individuals, rather than centralized bureaucratic management.

While Winner and Sclove seem to derive an impetus from the anti-technology ethos of the late twentieth century, they derive alternative technology, rather than anti-technology, views from this impetus. In this respect they may share elements of mood and temperament with Ihde, and indeed, Ihde has cited all these figures approvingly in his writings. When pressed to make normative statements, Ihde is likely to echo Winner's call for democracy or Sclove's call for participation. Yet philosophically Ihde seems to share much more with figures such as Borgmann, Strong, or Zimmerman. First, there is the phenomenological tradition; second, the ontological analysis of technology; and third, there is the strong postmodern critique of modern science. Beyond this, Ihde's work actually does a great deal to undermine the modernist presumptions still at work in broad-form technological ethics. In emphasizing choices among technology and a reform of the scientific research process, broad-form technological ethics not only leaves much of apparatus from modern ethical theory and philosophy of science in place, it actually seems to rely on it. All of this suggests an enigma in Ihde's thought. Why, given his philosophical orientation and his substantive philosophical achievements, does he distance himself from those who would appear to share so much with him, and associate himself with those whose position he has done so much to weaken?

Stance IV: The Ethics of Technological Artifacts

It is commonplace that many problems with technology involve unwanted and unanticipated consequences. Part of the problem lies in the fact that the world is a very complex place. This is a real and largely insurmountable aspect of technology's unexpected impact, but the idea that technology is "just" applied science (and that "real" scientists were working on core theoretical problems arising within the framework of explanation) contributes to a particular interpretation of complexity. Because explanation yields prediction, well-developed scientific explanations can be adapted to specific ends: building bridges, making machines that fly, or harnessing energy. Although science may be reasonably good at prediction when most variables are controlled, it is not reasonable to think that science can actually predict outcomes in realistic applications where variables are uncontrolled. Furthermore, those who adapt explanations to technological ends are not the scientists who develop the theory, and scientists cannot be expected to anticipate all the purposes to which their theories will be put. Science and technology involve different agents, and the agents who discover and develop theory cannot anticipate the actions of the agents who apply this theory. If unwanted and unanticipated outcomes are simply inevitable, they must simply be accepted as a fixed cost of technological innovation.

However, many problems seem in hindsight to involve consequences that should have been foreseen. In these cases, complexity is no defense. Some of these cases are simply situations in which someone should have done something that they did not do, but others are cases in which something that is obvious in hindsight was not obvious beforehand because the attention of those developing and deploying the technology was focused in the wrong place. In such cases, an account of how attention is framed and directed would be extremely useful. While there may be any number of ways in which attention and interpretation can be framed and directed, Ihde's work on amplification and reduction has indicated key ways in which the tools being deployed can have this effect.

In *Technics and Praxis* Ihde turned his descriptive efforts to a characterization of the tool-wielding body. Discussing a dentist's examination of a patient's tooth, Ihde notes that the use of a probe allows the dentist to encounter the tooth quite differently than she might were she simply to look at the tooth or to touch it with her finger. The dental probe makes features in the surface of the tooth more evident to the dentist, including the tooth's resistance to various amounts of pressure. Throughout the examination, the dentist is never focused on the probe itself. Ihde describes the influence of the probe in terms of reductions and amplifications. Surface features such as small ridges or the relative smoothness, as well as the tooth's resistance to pressure,

Paul B. Thompson

are amplified, or made more perceptible. Other features such as the temperature or the wetness of the tooth are reduced: they are less available to the
dentist than they would have been without the aid of the technical device.

One of Ihde's important claims in *Technics and Praxis* is that it is possible for human beings to develop an interpretation or understanding of the
things in their experience that is profoundly shaped by the systematic
amplifications and reductions of their tools. On the face of it, there is no
reason to think that the surface features amplified by the dentist's probe are
"more real," more characteristic of the tooth, than those features (such as
wetness or temperature) that are reduced. Yet to the extent that people become
habituated to or enthralled with those phenomena made available through
technical means, there is always the possibility that it is those aspects that
"stand out," that are made more evident through amplification, which will
become associated with "the thing itself," while aspects that are reduced may
become forgotten or concealed. Amplification and reduction indicate the way
that using *a particular* technology creates an implicit focus, a form of selective attention. Although the applicability of these ideas to problems in technological ethics should be obvious, few have utilized Ihde's theoretical
apparatus for the purpose of ethical analysis.

Conclusion

Despite broad applicability to a number of problems and approaches in technological ethics, neither Ihde nor his students have articulated or developed
some of the most obvious and important extensions of his thought in the normative realm. Ihde has disassociated himself from those who take dark views
of technology and aligned himself with those who hope to democratize technology. Yet here, too, there is an enigma, for Ihde's work on philosophy of
technology shares much with the former, and little with the latter. Thus while
Ihde's work in philosophy of technology holds out great promise for technological ethics, it is a promise that one must regard as still largely unfulfilled.

8

The Morality of Things:
A Postphenomenological Inquiry

Peter-Paul Verbeek

Ethics appears to be at the eve of a new Copernican revolution. A few centuries ago, the Enlightenment, with Kant as its major representative, brought about a turnover hitherto unequaled by moving the source of morality from God to humans. But currently there seem to be good reasons to move the source of morality one place further. It increasingly becomes clear that we should not consider morality as a solely human affair, but also as a matter of *things*. Just like human beings, material objects appear to be able to provide answers to moral questions. The artifacts we deal with in our daily lives help to determine our actions and decisions in myriad ways. And answering the question how to act is the ethical activity *par excellence*.

This "material turn" in ethics raises many questions, though. Is the conclusion that things influence human actions reason enough to actually attribute morality to materiality? Can things be considered moral agents, and if so, to what extent? And is it morally right to go even one step farther and try to explicitly shape this morality of things, by consciously steering human behavior with the help of the material environment?

What Things Do

One of the first to propound the morality of things was the French philosopher of technology Bruno Latour. In 1988 he delivered a lecture in The Netherlands entitled "Safety Belt—The Missing Masses of Morality." He stated that it is about time to stop complaining about the alleged moral decay of our society. Such lamentations show a lack of understanding of our daily world. Morality should not be looked for only among humans, but also among things, Latour told his audience. Whoever is able to discern the moral charge of matter sees a society that is swarming with morality.

Latour illustrated his thesis by discussing the safety belt. Many cars refuse to start or produce an irritating sound until the driver is wearing his or her seatbelt. According to Latour, such cars embody morality. Designers delegated to it the responsibility to see to it that car drivers wear their safety belts. Apparently, the moral decision whether or not to wear a seatbelt is not made exclusively by the driver, but also by the car in which he finds himself.[1]

Latour's thesis that things can possess morality is based on the counterintuitive thought that things, just like human beings, are able to *act*. In his "a-modern" approach of reality, Latour gives up the rigid distinction between humans and things that has been playing such an important role in Western thinking ever since the Enlightenment.[2] Rather than making an *a priori* distinction between "humans" and "nonhumans," Latour prefers to approach them symmetrically. In order to be able to do that, he analyzes reality in terms of "actors" that are associated with each other and interact via "networks." These actors can be human or nonhuman in nature, and therefore he prefers to call them "actants."

The agency of things consists in their ability to help shape human actions. Latour indicates this ability in terms of "scripts."[3] Just like the script of a movie or a theater play tells the actors what to do at what time, material artifacts can embody implicit prescriptions for the actions of their users. Latour illustrates this not only with the safety belt that was discussed above, but also, for instance with a speed bump. Such a bump has a prescription "built in": slow down when you approach me.

Latour analyzes the script of artifacts in terms of "translations" of "programs of action." [4] From the perspective of his symmetrical approach, both humans and things possess programs of action. A speed bump translates the action program of a driver ("drive fast because I'm in a hurry," or perhaps "drive slowly because otherwise I might cause an accident") by merging it with the action program of a speed bump ("damage the suspension of cars that drive fast") into a new program: "drive slowly because otherwise I might damage my suspension." In this translation, the speed bump helps to shape the actions of human beings.

According to Latour, the scripts of things can be understood as the result of "inscriptions" or "delegations." The activities of designers can be understood as "inscribing" programs of action into artifacts. In doing so, designers delegate responsibilities to these artifacts. By inscribing a program of action into a speed bump, designers delegate the task to see to it that people do not drive too fast, which is usually associated with a police officer or a traffic sign, to a piece of concrete.

Latour is not the only philosopher who has explored the agency of things. In the philosophy of technology, the work of Albert Borgmann, Langdon

Winner, and, of course, Don Ihde takes this direction as well. As opposed to classical philosophy of technology, which was mainly interested in understanding the transcendental conditions of technology, contemporary positions increasingly approach technology in terms of specific material objects that play a role in human actions and experiences. As I elaborated earlier, the positions that have developed can be augmented and integrated into a philosophy of "technological mediation."[5] The central idea in this approach is that technologies play an actively mediating role in the relations between human beings and reality.

Virtually all positions in this new direction in the philosophy of technology, however, take a *descriptive* point of view. Their main ambition is to analyze the role of technology in the lifeworld. Against this descriptivist orientation, which is characteristic of many contemporary approaches within the philosophy of technology, in this contribution I would like to investigate to what extent the concept of technological mediation can be deployed in a *normative* setting.[6] Ihde's work will play a central role in this investigation, extending it to a domain the he himself has left untouched of most of his work: the domain of ethics.

Things as Moral Agents

To what extent can the mediating role of things be described in ethical terms? Should we recognize things as moral agents? When we limit ourselves to the main directions in ethical theory—deontology, consequentialism, and virtue ethics—there are good reasons to answer this question affirmatively. Deontological and consequentialist ethics are concerned with the question "how to act?" and Latour's work shows that not only human considerations but also material artifacts provide answers to this question. In virtue ethics, things can play a moral role as well. As Gerard de Vries showed, this classical form of ethics tried to answer the question "how to live?," rather than "how should I act?" In our technological culture, not only ethicists or theologians answer this question of the good life, but also all kinds of technological devices that tell us "how to live."[7]

Yet, the thesis that morality is not a solely human affair, because things provide answers to moral questions as well, is likely to receive a lot of criticism. Things, after all, do not have intentions. They are not able to make decisions about their influence on human actions, and therefore they cannot be held responsible for their "actions." On the basis of this argument, it would be a mistake to describe the influence of things on human actions in terms of morality. Steering behavior, as well as showing steered behavior, is something entirely different than making moral decisions.

A good representative of this criticism is Tsjalling Swierstra. He discusses how the "moral community" has been expanded many times since classical antiquity. "Women, slaves, and strangers were largely or entirely devoid of moral rights," but "over time all these groups were admitted."[8] But the current inclination to grant also things access to the moral community lets it go too far, as he argues from both a deontological as from a consequentialist position.

Consequentialist ethics assesses actions exclusively in terms of their outcomes. When the positive consequences even out the negative ones, an action can be called morally correct. From this perspective, things can indeed be part of a moral practice, since they can incite human beings to morally right behavior, and from a consequentialist perspective it is only the result that counts. But things can only do this because human beings use them for this. Things themselves are not able to balance the positive and negative aspects of their influence on human actions against each other. They can only serve as instruments here, not as fully fledged moral agents that are able to render account for their actions.

Deontological ethics is not directed at the consequences of actions, but at the moral rightness of the actions themselves. From a Kantian perspective, for instance, one should decide to act in a specific way by considering whether the action meets a number of rationally insightful criteria. Artifacts are not capable of such considerations. Moreover, if they incite human beings to actions that are morally right from a deontological point of view, these actions are not the result of a rationally insightful moral obligation, but simply as a form of steered behavior.

This means that both from a deontological and a consequentialist perspective, artifacts can only be *causally* responsible for a specific action, and not *morally*, for the simple reason that artifacts do not possess intentions and therefore cannot be held responsible for what they "do." "Compelling artifacts, therefore, are no moral actors themselves, nor can they make humans act truly morally. Therefore . . . there is not any reason to grant artifacts access to the moral community."[9]

I share Swierstra's hesitations regarding a too radical symmetry in approaches of humans and things.[10] Yet, the argument that things do not possess intentionality and cannot be held responsible for their "actions" does not justify the conclusion that things cannot be part of the moral community. For even though it does not happen intentionally, things do play a mediating role in the actions of human beings, and as such they provide "material answers" to the question how to act. Precisely this ability to answer moral questions, however different the medium and origins of their answers may be from those provided by human beings, justifies the thesis that things should be considered moral agents. We cannot call them to account for the answers they give—for that, we should address their designers or users—but this does not alter the fact that things do provide answers to moral questions. They may not belong to the moral community in the sense that they could claim moral rights, but they do belong to it in the sense that they help to *shape* morality.

Moreover, these "actions" of things can and should be assessed in moral terms—whether their mediating roles have been explicitly delegated to them or not. After all, not only was the architect Robert Moses racist, but so are the bridges he designed over the roads to Long Island Beach to keep away Afro-Americans. The fact that these bridges cannot be held responsible for the racist practice they install, does not imply that their role in this practice cannot be judged in moral terms.

Beyond the Autonomous Subject

There is, however, another important reason to grant things a fully fledged role in ethics. The observation that things play a mediating role in the actions of human beings also has implications for the ways in which ethics itself should be approached. For at the basis of the predominant ethical positions that were discussed above is an image of the moral subject that is seriously challenged by the concept of technological mediation.

The predominant approaches in ethics rest on the assumption that human beings should be understood as autonomous subjects: beings who are able to make moral decisions on the basis of entirely transparent and fully rational considerations. The opinions of ethicists may differ about the nature of the considerations that should be taken into account in moral reasoning; whether these considerations should be deontological or consequentialist, for instance. But the idea that human beings are able to make autonomous decisions is usually beyond dispute. If this autonomy is lacking, human beings are considered to be of unsound mind. Without autonomy, human beings could not be held responsible for their actions.

This view is at odds with the analysis of the mediating role of things, which was discussed above. When the actions of human beings are not only determined by their own intentions but also by the material environment in which they live, the central place of the autonomous subject in ethical theory needs to be put into perspective. And once we do that, it becomes clear that it might indeed be necessary to move the source of ethics, which had already been moved from God to humans, one place further.

Postphenomenology

The necessity to mitigate the importance of the autonomous subject in ethical theory does not only follow from the fact that things can play a mediating role in the *actions* of human beings. As can be explained on the basis of

Ihde's work, things are also able to mediate the experiences and interpretations of reality on the basis of which human beings make (moral) decisions. From a phenomenological point of view, the material mediation of action that is analyzed by Latour and that played a central role in this contribution up till now, can be seen as a specific aspect of the mediation of human-world relationships.

Phenomenology can be interpreted as a philosophical movement that aims to analyze the relations between human beings and reality. In order to make phenomenology relevant for analyzing the morality of things, it needs to be elaborated to what Ihde calls "postphenomenology."[11] Classical phenomenology aimed to produce "authentic" descriptions of "the things themselves" to counterbalance the alleged alienation caused by the scientific and technological approach of reality. Against this romantic essentialism, postphenomenology holds that humans and reality constitute each other in their mutual relationships. To the classical-phenomenological view that humans and reality are always related to each other by the irresolvable directness of humans toward reality, postphenomenology adds the idea that in these relations both the subjectivity of human beings and the objectivity of reality are shaped. Humans are what they are on the basis of the ways in which they can manifest themselves in reality, and reality is what it is on the basis of the way in which it can be experienced by human beings. Humans-in-themselves do not exist: they are always directed at and present in their world. The "things themselves" might exist, but not for human beings: for human beings, reality is always reality as it disclosed by them. A tree in which one climbs is another entity than a tree that is chopped down, and the one who climbs it is another subject that the one chopping it down.

The interrelation of humans and reality can be viewed from two perspectives. The first, "pragmatic-existential" perspective, starts from the human side and concerns the ways in which human beings can be present in their world. Central categories here are the *actions* of human beings and the ways in which their *existence* gets shape on the basis of this. The second, hermeneutic perspective, starts from the side of reality and concerns the ways in which reality can be present to human beings, both perceptually and interpretatively. Central categories here are human *experience* and *interpretations* of reality.

This postphenomenological perspective offers a suitable framework for analyzing the mediating role of things—and especially of technological artifacts—since the process of mediation should be localized precisely in this relation between humans and reality. Both perspectives sketched above offer a possibility to analyze processes of mediation. Latour's analysis of the mediation of action finds itself at the pragmatic side of the postphenomenological framework, but at the hermeneutic side a completely different form of mediation is at work. Here things help to shape human perceptions, and in doing so they coconstitute how reality can be present to human beings. A landscape is present in an entirely different way when viewed from a train than from a bicycle or when walking. As Ihde has elaborated, such mediations of perception always involve a structure of amplification and reduction; specific aspects of reality are highlighted, while others are weakened.

The transformation of perception, which thus occurs, has implications for the ways in which human beings can interpret their world. Scientific and medical instruments, for instance, allow scientists and medical doctors to perceive things that would be imperceptible without these instruments.[12] There is no equivalent in the perceptible world for many things that can be perceived with the help of radio telescopes or ultrasound scanners. These instruments "translate" imperceptible forms of radiation or sound to perceptible images. In doing so, they open an entirely new way of access to reality: they help to shape what rank as "objectivity."

Mediation and Morality

This mediating role of things in the perceptions and interpretations of human beings has important ethical consequences. It implies that material objects can make an active contribution to the moral decisions human beings make. Medical technologies like ultrasound imaging are a good example of this. The image of a living fetus in the womb cannot be made visible without ultrasound scan. But the machine that produces an ultrasound image of an unborn child is not simply a functional device that makes it possible to look into the womb. It also helps to shape how the fetus is perceived and interpreted, and what decisions are made about him or her.

Ultrasound scan, for instance, can be used for testing nuchal translucency, the thickness of the skin at the nape of a fetus's neck.[13] This gives an indication of the risk that the child will suffer from Down's syndrome. Because of this, the scan is no neutral way of depicting what is inside the womb, but it brings the fetus under very specific conditions; it lets the fetus be present only in terms of health and disease, and ultimately even in terms of desirability and undesirability. For the people who will have to make a decision about abortion on the basis of the outcomes of the test, the unborn child is translated into an organism with a chance to suffer from a disease. And the very act of having this test done already suggests what an appropriate response to its outcome would be.[14]

Moreover, the very possibility of having this test done even helps to shape the frame of interpretation of those who refuse it, in order to avoid having to make a decision about the life of their unborn child. When ultrasound is only used to determine the expected date of birth, there is a serious possibility that the practitioner who performs the scan sees the nape of the fetus's neck, and many more things that can give information about the condition of the fetus. Many people will find it difficult to repress the impulse to try to interpret the expression of the face of the practitioner. In this way, ultrasound scan fundamentally shapes one's experience of an unborn child, and even of being pregnant. It lets the fetus be present in terms of its possibility to suffer from a serious disease and in terms of our ability to prevent children with this disease from being born.

This ability to co-shape human interpretations of reality puts the autonomy of the moral subject into perspective, just like the mediating role of artifacts in the actions of human being does. Moral decisions and the actions that result from these decisions come about in a relation between the moral subject and its reality. And this relation is mediated in many ways by material artifacts.

This conclusion does not imply that human beings are merely languid playthings of their material environment. From the fact that human beings are not autonomous, it does not follow that they are entirely irrelevant in ethical respect. But the conclusion that the relations between human beings and reality are technologically mediated in many ways does imply that in our technological culture, ethics cannot pass over the moral charge of things. In order to analyze situations from an ethical perspective, and in order to make moral decisions, it is not sufficient to make an inventory of all relevant norms and the consequences of all possibilities of action. Ethics will also have to account for the ways in which technologies themselves help to shape moral questions, and suggest answers to them.

The Moralization of Technology

How difficult it is to say good-bye to the autonomous subject in ethical theory can be illustrated with the short discussion that arose in The Netherlands after the Dutch philosopher Hans Achterhuis pleaded for a "moralization of technology." Achterhuis proposed to apply Latour's analysis of "technological scripts" to the context of technology design. Designers should build morality into the technology they are designing, by deliberately shaping its influence on the behavior of its users. According to Achterhuis, we should stop moralizing each other, and start moralizing our material environment. To prevent that human beings will reach a state of permanent reflection on their actions, because of all new possibilities opened up by technologies that raise ethical questions, we should delegate specific moral decisions to the technical devices themselves.[15]

A good example of this is the automatic speed influencing. In order to make traffic safer we could pursue a change of attitude of car drivers, but we should not expect too much of this, given the availability of a large network of wide roads with faint curves that make it possible to drive very fast, and cars that are able to exceed the speed limit by far. Where should we start if we want to lower the number of traffic fatalities? "In 1991, on the A16 highway in The Netherlands, 300 automobiles collided in dense fog, with ten fatalities. They were driving much too fast. If the automobiles were forced automatically to slow down to a safe speed in dense fog, these lives could have been saved." And Achterhuis ironically adds: "But in this case, the freedom and responsibility of the drivers remained intact."[16]

Many objections have been raised to the call for a "material ethics." In the discussion, two arguments played an important role.[17] First, Achterhuis's proposal to let devices make decisions for human beings was seen as an unacceptable threat to human freedom. Human action can only be called moral when it is chosen consciously and in freedom. Second, Achterhuis was accused to make a plea for totalitarianism. Our democracy would be replaced with technocracy when human beings are deliberately steered with the help of the material environment in which they live. Yet, these arguments against the moralization of technology can be refuted.

Freedom in Restraint

The argument that human freedom is denied when technologies are moralized can easily be countered. First, there exist many agreements between human beings in that they explicitly and consciously limit their own freedom. Hardly anybody will find it immoral or beyond human dignity, for instance, to obey the law. And if only few people will protest against the legal prohibition to murder, why be indignant about installing speed bumps that prevent people from driving too fast at places where many children are playing outside?

A second reason why the moralization of technology does not need to be a threat to human freedom, is the fact that technological mediation does not need to have the form of compulsion. Artifacts can also "seduce" people to act in specific ways, as the work of the Dutch Industrial Designers Association "Eternally Yours" shows. Eternally Yours is working in the field of ecodesign. It focuses its attention to the throw-away behavior of human beings. Many products are discarded far before they are actually worn out, simply because people do not like them anymore. Therefore, Eternally Yours tries to design products in such a way that humans develop more attachment to them. This can happen, for instance, by making it easier to repair or upgrade products, or by making them age in an attractive way. The Dutch designer Sigrid Smits, for instance, designed soft furnishings for a couch, which prevents it from aging unattractively. In the velour, she stitched a pattern that is initially invisible, but which gradually becomes visible over time because of wear. A couch that is covered with this upholstery does not decay over time, but rather renews itself by getting older. Products like these do not compel their users to act in an environmentally friendly way, but seduce them to interact in a more durable way with their everyday things.[18]

Third, the analysis of technological mediation above shows that the actions of human beings who are dealing with technologies are *always* mediated. This implies that the explicit moralization of technology only comes down to accepting the responsibility given with the insight that technologies inevitably mediate human interpretations and actions. If technologies are always mediating human-world relationships, it seems wise to anticipate this mediation and give it a desirable form, rather than rejecting the whole idea of a "moralization of technology."

The fact that this technological mediation is always there does not imply that human freedom is permanently under attack. Freedom simply does not exist in an absolute sense. Human actions always take place in a stubborn reality, and therefore the ambition to reach a state of absolute freedom would require that we ignore reality, giving up the possibility to act at all. Freedom should not be understood as a lack of force and constraints, but as the existential space human beings have to realize their existence. Humans have a relation to their own existence and to the restraints it meets in the material culture in which it happens. This specific situatedness of human existence *creates* specific forms of freedom, rather than *impeding* them. Freedom can only arise where possibilities are opened up for human beings to have a relation to the environment in which they live and to which they are bound.

Democratizing Things

The second argument against Achterhuis's proposal of a moralization of technology regards its alleged technocratic character. When human actions are steered with the help of technology, this would threaten the democratic quality of society, the critics hold. After all, not human beings but material things would be in charge then.

This argument is highly important for ethical theory—albeit not as an argument against the moralization of technology, but as an incentive to deal with the morality of technology in a responsible way. Technocracy is not the inevitable result of accepting the influence of technologies on human actions. After all, this influence is *always* there, as became clear above. The danger of technocracy only arises when this influence is not shaped consciously but remains an unintended byproduct of technology design.

Designers materialize morality: they are doing "ethics by other means." Usually this happens in an implicit way. Precisely to prevent that technocracy comes about, democratic forms of moralizing technology need to be developed. If the built-in morality of technologies is not anticipated in the process of technology design, the devices and the engineers have free play. Not the moralization of technology, but the refusal to deliberately shape the moral charge of technology leads to a totalitarian threat to our free and democratic society.

Conclusion

Things, and especially the technological devices that increasingly form the world in which we live, deserve a place in the heart of ethics. Doing ethics in a technological culture implies that we recognize that things, just like humans, belong of the moral community. Things carry morality, since they help to shape how human beings act and interpret reality. Moral decisions are not made by autonomous subjects, but are coshaped by the material environment in which humans live.

Ethicists may count it among their tasks to make explicit this implicit morality of things, and to be involved in the ways in which this material morality gets shape. In Protagoras's time, "Man" was "the measure of all things." But in our technological culture, ethics cannot avoid the conclusion that things are at least as often the measure of all human beings too.

Notes

1. Bruno Latour, "Veiligheidsgordel – de verloren massa van de moraliteit," in *De technologische cultuur*, ed. Michiel Schwartz and Rein Jansma (Amsterdam: De Balie, 1998).

2. Bruno Latour, *We Have Never Been Modern*, trans. Catherine Porter (Cambridge: Harvard University Press, 1993).

3. Bruno Latour, "Where are the Missing Masses? The Sociology of a Few Mundane Artifacts," in *Shaping Technology/Building Society*, ed. Wiebe Bijker and John Law (Cambridge: MIT Press, 1992).

4. Bruno Latour, "On Technical Mediation—Philosophy, Sociology, Geneaology," *Common Knowledge* 3 (1994): 29–64.

5. Peter-Paul Verbeek, *What Things Do: Philosophical Reflections on Technology, Agency, and Design* (Pennsylvania: Penn State University Press, 2005).

6. Andrew Light and David Roberts, "Toward New Foundations in Philosophy of Technology: Mitcham and Wittgenstein on Descriptions," *Research in Philosophy and Technology* 19 (2000): 125–147.

7. Gerard de Vries, *Zeppelins—over filosofie, technologie en cultuur* (Amsterdam: Van Gennep, 1999).

8. Tsjalling Swierstra, "Moeten artefacten moreel gerehabiliteerd?" *K&M— tijdschrift voor empirische filosofie* 4 (1999): 317. (Unless indicated otherwise, all translations from Dutch to English in this chapter are mine—PPV.)

9. Ibid.

10. See Verbeek, *What Things Do: Philosophical Reflections on Technology, Agency, and Design.*

11. See Ibid. and *PP.*

12. *EH.*

13. Peter Paul Verbeek, "Pragmatism and Pragmata—Bioethics and the Techno-logical Mediation of Experience," in *Pragmatist Ethics for a Technological Culture,* ed. Jozef Keulartz (Dordrecht: Kluwer, 2002).

14. The test does not provide certainty but an indication of a risk. Because of this, it is often reason to have another test done, which does give certainty but which is also more risky: amniocentesis, which can result in a spontaneous abortion. Only when the woman who has the amniocentesis done at the age of 36 years or older, the chance that a child suffering from Down's syndrome is "intercepted" is equal to or larger than the chance that a healthy child dies because of the test. When this break-even point is reached, there is one death of a healthy fetus for every discovery of a child suffering from Down's syndrome. Leonoor Kuijk, "Prenataal Onderzoek: Abor-tus als logisch vervolg," in *Trouw,* January 3, 2004, Amsterdam: PCM Publishers (newspaper article).

15. Hans Achterhuis, "De moralisering van de apparaten," *Socialisme en Democratie* 52,1 (1995): 3–11.

16. Hans Achterhuis, *De erfenis van de utopie* (Amsterdam: Ambo, 1998), 379.

17. Ibid., 28–31.

18. Ed van Hinte, *Eternally Yours: Visions on Product Endurance* (Rotterdam: 010 Publishers, 1997).

Part IV

Heidegger and Ihde

9

Ihde's Albatross: Sticking to a "Phenomenology" of Technoscientific Experience

Robert C. Scharff

Ihde's work occupies a unique position in technoscience studies, no doubt due in part to his development of a creative but still recognizably Husserlian phenomenology. Ihde himself, however, has recently called phenomenology his albatross (*CT* 131–144, 128–130): he cannot get rid of it. He adds, however, that when phenomenology is properly defended against old misperceptions and expanded to concern itself with human-technology relations, does he need to get rid of it. Labels, he concludes, might just as well be embraced; they stick anyway.

Ihde's self-conception successfully highlights what is interesting and important about his work. It also, I think, hides a weakness. Without any doubt, give him three cheers for his systematic descriptions of our technoscientifically structured lifeworld and for his epistemic defense of the phenomenological approach he employs in developing these descriptions. Together, they offer a welcome alternative to the much less experientially astute and often epistemologically naïve accounts typically offered by analytic philosophers and social scientists. Do you want to consider concretely how it is to "be" with technology—and how a phenomenologically informed account of this is neither "objective" (i.e., causal and third-person) or "subjective" (i.e., as objectivity freaks assume phenomenology *must* be)? Read Ihde.

On the other hand, Ihde's phenomenological descriptions can often seem strangely apolitical and "neutral." Granted, he knows that technology is not an unmixed blessing, and he insists there should be "technoscience critics." Like science critics, he explains, those engaged in technoscience studies must not only be more expert than amateur about what they describe, but also less than "total insiders" in how they react to it (*EH* 127–136).[1] Only in this way can they achieve the proper evaluative distance from the technoscientific practices that concern them. Yet in the end, this seems to me to be too much a case of "do as I say, not as I do." In Ihde's own writings, new technologies are embraced, the expansion of technological mediation is everywhere noted, and some instances of technoscientific excess and inefficiency are mentioned. Yet for anyone who displays less enthusiasm than he does for human-technology relations, or whose criticisms of technoscientific culture are systematic or overtly political, Ihde has mostly dismissive names (e.g., romantic, nostalgic, utopian, absolutist, pessimistic totalizer). For thirty years, he has continued to believe that "a rigorous phenomenological analysis of [human-technology] relations poses . . . the best way into an understanding of both the promises and the threats of technology" (*TP* 15).[2] Here is Husserl having the last word, for it is above all Heidegger who is being rejected here. Heideggerians love their laptops, Ihde likes to say.

My interest in this paper, however, is not to see better justice done to Heidegger—though I think he deserves it. And Ihde is certainly right that some of Heidegger's followers are too quick to embrace "globally" the master's critique of technoscientific hegemony and too slow to ask locally where that leaves us now. So, Ihde's complaint does have a target. Nevertheless, I believe that his dismissiveness of Heidegger's allegedly "pessimistic totalizing" is off the mark. It has, moreover, the potential to diminish the power of Ihde's own findings, not just to help perpetuate the familiar Heidegger-bashing myths about how out of touch this poor Swabian peasant was with the real world. To the extent that it can be done in a short paper, I suggest below and argue a little for the view that Ihde's weakness here may well be a consequence of precisely his loyalty to that same phenomenology, which Ihde already, for other less worrisome reasons, calls his albatross.

Ihde's Pioneering Phenomenology of Technoscience

I start with Ihde's contributions. After all, without them, there would be nothing to critique. Consider this comparison. In a famous essay, Gadamer claims that the "central question" of our age is "how our natural view of the world—the experience of the world that we have as we simply live out our lives—is related to the unassailable and anonymous authority that confronts us in the pronouncements of science." Moreover, Gadamer thinks that precisely because this is the central question, as philosophers, "our task is to reconnect the objective world of technology, which the sciences place at our disposal and discretion, with those fundamental orders of our being that are neither arbitrary nor manipulable by us, but rather simply demand our respect."[3]

There are two main reasons why Ihde could never have written this passage. First, Gadamer's outlook here is too Heideggerian—implying as it does that technology is something alien that is imposed on our "naturalness." Second, Gadamer displays no feel for the reciprocal idea of "technoscience," but repeats instead the old-fashioned picture of science presenting us with an objectified world and technology, and then using science to do something with it.[4]

To take the second issue first, Ihde himself has been an active participant in the widespread, interdisciplinary effort to discredit the idea that technology is simply applied science. As he points out, it is historically false to claim that technology waited upon the rise of modern science—unless, of course, one makes a skyhook ontological claim, to the effect that whatever all that tool-using, artifact-creating, and gadget-loving activity we did until the sixteenth century was, it was not "really" technology. Moreover, there is overwhelming evidence that the rise of modern science itself depended crucially upon the prior existence of devices whose invention owed nothing to science, but owed much to systems of belief quite unconcerned with either modern science or its purposes. Today, these facts are acknowledged by almost everyone not still suffering from the old reconstructionist orthodoxies. It now seems obvious that the culture of science has always been as much technological as theoretical.[5]

It is Ihde's way of using this information, however, that singles him out. The point is philosophically more radical than it is sometimes represented by historians and social scientists. It is not that, at one time, there were two independent things—technological practices and theorizing about nature— and then later, scientists availed themselves of the external, artifact-using culture for needed experimental devices. As a picture of actual scientific practice, this has always been mere mythology. As a description of scientific self-understanding, it is recent and at best tendentious.[6] In fact, for as long as there has been a desire to know nature, there has only been "technoscience." For Ihde and a growing collection of other thinkers, moreover, the point is no longer even controversial; they simply begin with it. On this basis, some have gone on to reform the philosophy of science, enrich the history of science, or critically deconstruct the cultural and political damage that has resulted from acting in ignorance of the point. Ihde argues, however, that progress in all of these other directions may well depend on first understanding phenomenologically *how* technoscience and technoscientifically saturated life *are*—as lived, embodied relations. Here I return to his first point of disagreement with Gadamer. For Ihde, since most of our lives are actually lived technoscientifically, to obsess "globally" about how terrible such lives can be leads inevitably, and wrongly, to a "pessimistic" outlook on contemporary culture.

In earlier writings (e.g., *TP* and *TL*), Ihde develops this thesis by way of a "phenomenology of technology." More recently (e.g., *EH*), he has come to think of himself as working out a "phenomenologically expanded hermeneutics." The introduction to EH explains some of the reasons for this change. He has come to think of the "philosophy of technology" and the "hermeneutics of science" as complimentary parts of a larger project of "technoscientific studies"; and he has also (too generously, in my estimation) concluded that the time has come to specifically recognize the contributions made to this project by analytic philosophers (*EH* 1–6). Throughout his career, however, Ihde has continued to use a slogan that captures nicely the spirit of his work. "Husserl's Galileo," he says, "is not a telescope user but a mathematizer." In this slogan, one can detect references to all the major critical themes he is well-known for stressing—his critique of theory-bias in the traditional accounts of science that Husserl still shares, his complaint that Husserl's focus on a phenomenology of consciousness must in principle fall short of appreciating perceptual embodiment, and his refusal to follow Husserl's early trajectory *from* lifeworld experience out *to* (the more "metaphysically" interesting?) "scientific" articulations of it. On these themes, the influence of Merleau-Ponty and Heidegger is candidly acknowledged. Other commentators have spelled out the positive and original character of Ihde's contributions here.[7] Let me add just a few more words about this, in order to set up my argument that, at least in two related respects, Ihde still seems to have listened too hard to Husserl and insufficiently to Merleau-Ponty and Heidegger.

Ihde deserves all the praise he gets for his extensive and perceptive descriptions of the way human embodiment infects and is affected by our encounters with, use of, feelings for, and thinking about technology. Here Husserlians and Heideggerians can be equally pleased with his findings. Ihde is surely right that who we are and how the world is disclosed are everywhere subject to technological mediation. Moreover, such mediation is not merely a matter of our deploying neutral objects in ways that we find useful. This familiar double image of mere things and meaning-constructing people fits neither everyday affairs nor the scientific reconceptualization of those affairs. Technologies "belong" with us, says Ihde. On the one hand, "the human with the steel axe is different from the human without one" (*PP* 34). On the other hand, technologies themselves presuppose and manifest our embodiment. In everyday praxis as well as in knowledge production, the development of scientific instrumentation, communication technologies, virtual realities, and simulation and modeling devices—all the hardware of the twenty-first century makes it increasingly obvious that, to use Ihde's early "human-device-world" paradigm, reference to any one of these phenomena requires reference to the others.[8]

Yet earlier or later, whether as phenomenologist of technological relations or expansive hermeneut of science, Ihde continues to depict of human life as a "two-tiered" relation. In *Technology and the Lifeworld*, there are both bodily-proper/microperceptual and cultural/macroperceptual "levels" of experience. In *Expanding Hermeneutics: Visualism in Science* (26–38), there is both a bodily/visual/perceptual dimension (modeled on Merleau-Ponty's "existential phenomenology") and a linguistic/social/historical dimension (à la Heidegger's "hermeneutical phenomenology"). In *Bodies in Technology*, life involves both "body one" and "body two" experiences or "senses of being" (xi, 67–71). In this distinction, however, I see two related problems. The first concerns the viability of distinction itself; the second, the fact that assuming this distinction has made it much too easy for Ihde to oppose the so-called "global" theorists of technology.

Regarding the first problem, one should note carefully how "embodiment"—and with it, the correlative term, "perception"—moves between wider and narrower applications in Ihde's work, often without acknowledgement. Sometimes, as in *Technology and the Lifeworld*, "embodiment *relations*" are one of three forms of specifically body-based mediation of individuals with the world—that is, they constitute one form of microperceptual relation (72–80). Sometimes, as in *Bodies in Technology*, Ihde distinguishes between perceptual and cultural "embodiments" (xi–xii). In both cases, of course, it is assumed that virtually all of our relations with our surroundings are technologically mediated ones; and so they are—at least in, as "we" chauvinistically phrase it, the "developed" world. It is not clear, however, whether this means that the social and the cultural are to be understood (supposedly à la Husserl and the Merleau-Ponty of the *Phenomenology of Perception*) as "another" layer or level, capable of being descriptively added to or ignored by analyses of the perceptual, or whether the perceptual, social, and cultural are all merely dimensions of one seamless condition of being-in-the-world (à la Heidegger's "factical-historical existence" in *Being and Time* and the later Merleau-Ponty's notion of multi-dimensional "presence").

Matters are at least ambiguous enough here to have prompted one writer to state flatly that, in contrast to Haraway, "Ihde's method of investigation is a fixed, phenomenological approach, taking the human (body)/technology relation as its primary phenomenon of investigation,"[9] and another, to worry that Ihde's analysis of embodiment relations in the narrower sense raises a "problem," in that it may not properly acknowledge the "interrelation" that precedes and constitutes subject-object/human-world relations.[10] Eason, the first writer, ultimately comes down on Ihde's side, arguing that Haraway fails to sufficiently appreciate Ihde's point that "human embodiment is *not* merely just another aspect of . . . situatedness akin to all its other aspects . . . Our embodied condition is *the* central situation we find ourselves in as knowers of the world. We are situated first and foremost always as bodies."[11] Against someone like Haraway—who often does seem to have an ontological tendency to depict every worldly entity as swimming freely in a kind of semiological soup—this conclusion may well be justified. But is a self-described nonfoundationalist like Ihde really in a position to defend the idea of human embodiment as *grounding* the social, political, and economic aspects of technoscientific life (*PP* 3)?

Verbeek's worry is slightly different from Eason's, but related. He asks whether Ihde's descriptions of technological mediation—precisely because so many of them involve *individual* human beings, artifacts, and worldly phenomena—may have failed to overcome the subject-object schema. Verbeek's solution is certainly generous. He simply assumes that Ihde's viewpoint "does not necessarily clash" with "the central thought of phenomenology," which he formulates in this way: "Humans and the world they experience are the *products* of technological meditation and not just the poles between which the mediation plays itself out." This concept of "production," however, is ambiguous. Does it mean embodiment relations are *entirely* mutually determinative, so that a phenomenology of microperceptual life requires only that we keep our focus on the process of mediation instead of its "poles"? Or does it mean that technological mediation is always informed by *something more* than these "bodily" interactions—something like a social, political, cultural, and historical inheritance that permeates these interactions? How are we to understand the bodily and cultural parts of Ihde's technoscientific studies, such that his aversion to "transcendental" phenomenology remains in tact?

Bodies "in" Culture or Cultured Embodiment

To put the issue another way, it is hard to imagine a feminist or race-theoretical phenomenologist writing the chapter on microperception in *Technology and the Lifeworld*. In what philosophical mood does one write about embodiment, hermeneutic, and alterity relations—and never once mention issues of gender, race, political and economic power, or spiritual understanding, since these are cultural/macroperceptual matters covered in the next chapter? Conversely, is it ever quite right to say that a culture provides "the macroperceptual field *within which* our bodily involvements take place" (*TL* 124–25, my emphasis)? At times, Ihde's "shift of perspective" toward cultural hermeneutics does seem to be merely additive in this way—as when he traces the "failure" of neocolonialist technology transfers to the introduction of the "materials" of high technology without the requisite "cultural" structure needed to support it (*TL* 131–39). He never asks whether this might be precisely the kind of transfer that best serves the interests of transferring democratic capitalist countries—and hence, whether "their" very bodily relations with the transferred high-tech materials were never intended to be as rich and multifaceted as "ours."

It seems to be Ihde's own most frequent tendency is to depict language and cognition not so much as dimensions of *embodiment in the wider sense* but as cultural phenomena that "build upon" *perceptual* embodiment proper. Ihde and I agree that there is no God-like perspective on life, "only variations on embodied perspectives" (*BT* 70). But then I want to ask, "From what sort of perspective does he make the distinction between perceptual "embodiment" and cultural "context," put their discussions in separate chapters, and often discuss one without reference to the other?" Ihde's body-perceptual/ cultural-linguistic cut would seem to reflect his inheritance of a Husserlian dualism that was in its day even less successful in "adding" history and culture to perception. And this, it seems to me, would indeed be an albatross-like feature in any "phenomenology."

Or can Ihde's work be pushed in the direction of Verbeek's "central thought of phenomenology"—that is, move toward a wider and more integrated understanding of embodiment, perception, and cultural interpretation that would cover both micro- and macroperceptual life from the beginning and ultimately make it difficult to sustain the distinction? Ihde tells us that, in his view:

> there is no bare or isolated microperception *except in its field* of a hermeneutic or macroperceptual surrounding; nor may macroperception have any focus *without its fulfillment* in micro-perceptual (bodily-sensory) experience. Yet in the interrelation of micro- and macrodimensions of perception, there may lie hidden precisely the polymorphic ambiguities which most particularly emerge in the later work of Merleau-Ponty and Foucault.[12]

Everything depends here on whether we are provided with the means to read the italicized phrases, not serially—as so many of Ihde's accounts of the bodily *and* the cultural suggest—but together, as he sometimes says they should be read. For this, however, we need from Ihde something more than his general descriptions of human situatedness as a phenomenological topic and of the transformed Husserlian strategies he plans to use on it. We need an account of the character of *his* situatedness, *his* embodiment—a reflective account that can assure us that from his perspective, one does not see merely microperceptual "and" macroperceptual "levels." And, I think, we also need an explanation of how Ihde can be so sure that given all the "polymorphic ambiguities" that "lie hidden" in our admittedly problematic world, everything can be handled perfectly well by those with some phenomenological training and pragmatic good sense, who feel safe in abandoning all general pessimism or global concern about technoscience and simply get into the trenches, "where problems are complex, ambiguous, and interwoven" (*BT*

128), solutions always piecemeal, and all general diagnoses merely lead to the false promise of quick fixes.

Achterhuis praises "American philosophers of technology" like Ihde because they are less dystopian than their European forebearers, do not transcendentalize technologies, are more "empirical" in the sense that they spend a lot of time analyzing particular technologies, and are in general more pluralistic and pragmatic about the role of technoscience in life and for its problems.[13] This set of tendencies, declares Achterhuis, defines an outlook on technoscience that is thankfully replacing the outlook of the previous generation of philosophers of technology like Ellul, Marcuse and the later Mumford—philosophers that Achterhuis, like Ihde, characterizes as being more or less like traditional speculative philosophers of history who look for The Meaning of Technology, who think everything in large abstractions, and who complain about History's essential drift in one inevitable—and mostly bad—direction. As Achterhuis reports, Ihde lumps Heidegger together with these "alarmist" totalizers of Technology—that is, sees him as ultimately abandoning his promising but flawed account of everyday life in *Being and Time* (*TP* 103–29), turning away from any further phenomenology of the "multiple possibilities of [our] admittedly non-neutral technologies" (*BT* 113), and embracing instead a romantically disappointed, congenitally dystopian macroperception—what *Technology and the Lifeworld* characterizes as the bad "dream" of a single massive trajectory of taking nature into culture (*BT* 123).

I certainly agree that we should have nothing but praise for Ihde's sort of "empirical turn," especially if it is indeed a turn away from speculative (metaphysical?) macroperceptions. I do not think, however, that this settles accounts with Heidegger. Ihde seems eager to construe all "general" statements about technology as cultural and macroperceptual, and as always threatening *not* to be articulations of embodiments. But this is Ihde's dichotomy, not Heidegger's. Of course, one can define the issue away by simply assuming that Heidegger's whole *Denkweg* is linguistically and culturally structured, *rather than* bodily and perceptually so (*EH* 36–37). But again, it is Ihde who defines culture and language as "body two" phenomena, and as always threatening to take us on a kind of disembodied head trip.

Yet whether Ihde can be persuaded of my reading of Heidegger or not, there is an issue that, with or without Heidegger's help, I think Ihde does not take seriously enough. It is this: The widespread, "materially pervasive" presence of technology in our lives—so deserving of Ihde's kind of concrete phenomenological analyses—*is also, at the same time, existentially intrusive.* Strangely, Ihde seems to assume that this claim is transcendental, pessimistic, and alarmist when it is said critically and out loud, but that it is perfectly all right if it is said quickly, merely descriptively, and then followed up by phenomenological accounts of all the ways in which this is very interesting.

In fact, however, my (and I believe Heidegger's) complaint about technoscientific hegemony goes precisely into the same space as Ihde's technoscientific studies. The complaint is neither a representation of something in the heads of pessimistic human beings—a macroperceptual part of their "culture"—nor out there in the world, as the manifestation of some inevitable causal process. It articulates, I think, an experiential sense of the dominant mood "between," and as clearing the space "where," we encounter things, and it differs from Ihde's own understanding of the age only in being more explicit and less joyful.

In his eagerness to define his position *against* Heidegger, Ihde seems not to realize that he himself *is displaying in his writings* a sense of technoscientific existence that is just as "global" and "general" as Heidegger's. And indeed, once one understands what Heidegger is really trying to do, this fact about Ihde's writings will be understood as something inevitable, not something one might choose to avoid. In other words, Ihde and Heidegger both understand themselves to be thinking and acting "in the midst of" the pervasive technoscientific character of life in the democratic capitalist West. They differ mainly in the fact that Heidegger thinks a "free relation" to technoscience has to be reflectively won, and Ihde thinks we already have it. Either way, we are speaking of Technology, but without reifying it. What follows is my explanation.

Technoscience with a Capital "T"

Ihde is right; there is more to our technoscientifically mediated experiences than what "a specific, and reduced, interpretation of the world . . . as standing reserve" makes of it. Indeed, a totalizing account of the world is as impossible as would be a totally technologized world; it could never be recognized as such. But it is recognized; hence totalizing accounts "cheat." They tell us only what they want us to see and keep to themselves their own means for seeing it. Yet for Ihde to show how he is no mere enthusiast for technoscience, albeit one with some willingness to identify problems that need fixing, he will have to engage in something like Heidegger's reflection on technoscience as "the" currently dominant ontological *Ereignis*. Or if he thinks Heidegger is an incurable totalizer, then he still owes us something very much like the reflection I am defending under the illusion that I am modeling it on Heidegger's.

To summarize what I have argued elsewhere, one might explain this point about reflectiveness by contrasting the general philosophical orientations of Comte and Heidegger, not regarding this or that instance of technology and technoscientific embodiment, but regarding a life in which technoscience is definitive of the dominant atmosphere.[14] Against this sort of consideration, it seems to me, Ihde cannot really raise objections. After all, from *TP* and *TL* on, he himself insists that technological mediation has all but eclipsed "bare perceptions" (i.e., experiences in which there is no technological mediation). This, it seems to me, obliges Ihde just as much as it does Comte or Heidegger to reflect upon how this "generally technological" state of affairs—this current "site" where everything "real" happens—strikes him. *Is* it now, easily and subject only to phenomenological clarification, an atmosphere of expansive understanding, openness to ontological variety and difference, free on all the appropriate occasions from "mere" repetitious or methodologically standardized thinking, from just saying and doing what "one" says and does?

Comte, we might well imagine, would respond "yes" to these questions (or at least assure us that the answer will soon be "yes"). He still speaks from an understanding and at a time when empirical ("positive") science is more a matter of promise than of actualization, when naturalistic models for human-historical study are still in their infancy (i.e., eagerly projected more than reductively deployed), and when prescientific thinking is mostly seen as ill-fated rather than meaningless.[15] In this milieu, he has no experiential basis for asking whether his "positivist age"—the time of an endless flourishing of a dominant technoscientific way of being-in-the-world—might, in its eventual unfolding, mark out an essentially oppressive and occlusive ontological site. Comte simply has, in Heidegger's phrase, no factical-experiential incentive to move beyond his internalist vision of an allegedly final, culminating "third stage" of human development. Thus, he is able to think technoscience *as* a culmination, but he cannot think *at* its culmination. As a result, he cannot ask whether "the world civilization just now beginning might one day overcome its technological-scientific-industrial character as the sole criterion of our world sojourn."[16] Comte lived at a time when one could easily see science and its modernizing effect on our technologies as a happy, progressive, even utopian event. For him, given that the positive stage promises to establish the orderly and predictable relationship to our surroundings that we human beings have always sought, the very idea of a fourth, or post-technoscientific stage makes no sense.

For many today including Heidegger, however, there is no avoiding the depressing, retrograde, and dystopian threat that now appears at least *equally* constitutive of the very same event. Indeed, for him at least, we now increasingly experience the danger in our condition first; and we must learn how, in his technical sense of the terms, to "destroy" and "rethink" everything we inherit in order to find in this condition a "saving grace." Using Heidegger's terminology, we might say that Comte does not yet experience any "distress" regarding the suitability of our currently dominant understanding of the relation between Being and human being.[17] My argument, however, is not that we must all identify with Heidegger rather than Comte. It is that failing to con-

sider this Technoscientific question does not make the issue it asks about—
or the somewhat naïve default position "one" is already likely to "have"
regarding it—go away. Here, I think, Ihde remains too Husserlian and not
sufficiently Heideggerian.

Heidegger considers his technoscientific "distress" at the same reflective
level and in the same determinately historical manner as does Comte in
registering his satisfaction. The treatment for this distress cannot lie either
above, beyond, or anterior to technoscience *in general*. Hence, Ihde is right.
There is no vantage point from which one might envisage the possibility of
an idyllic pretechnological or entirely post-technological world.[18] He is also
right that we are all, to some extent, happy Comtean pragmatists. Many of
our technological practices enhance our lives in just the ways that Comte
expected. Hence, in a black mood we might imagine giving all of this up, but
we cannot really, as Heidegger says, "think" it.

At the same time, however, there is the whole disturbing array of experiences to be had at the margins of these dominant practices. To express the
ambiguity of this situation, some today have in effect recast Comte's vision
by reflectively separating everything good that happens *within* the practices
guided by technoscientific understanding from everything else that lies essentially *outside* these practices. Then, one hopes, the latter might be addressed
without much disturbance to the former. Recall, for example, Gadamer's idea
of "reconnecting" our "natural view of the world" with "the unassailable and
anonymous authority . . . of science." What would be the character of the
reconnection? Would this reconnection itself be either "natural" or "anonymous"? By whom would such matters be determined? *Who*, in short, *is* the
"reconnector"?[19] Most importantly, especially in the present context, when
does the reconnector's situation—its (her? his? our?) factical-historical
Stimmung—get questioned?

I conclude, then, with a modest proposal: let Ihde ask, Who am I, and
for whom do I speak, as philosopher of technology? As hermeneut of technology? of science? of technoscience? What sort of "phenomenologist" is
able to declare, and do it with knowing irony, "Heideggerians love their
laptops?" Does this phenomenologist understand "our" ambivalent situation
better than they do? Are they being reflectively less astute about an embodied
situation which Ihde, as *another* thinker in the democratic-capitalist West,
very largely shares with them but about which he assumes he is
more . . . "perceptive"? In other words, what does Ihde already regard himself
as understanding about our times that makes it seem so right to him to
dismiss Heidegger's "general" assessment of our technoscientifically saturated situation? At the same time, what does he understand that makes it seem
equally right for him to stick to "rigorous phenomenological analyses" and
beyond that, simply proclaim the dominance of technoscientifically mediated

experience and the scarcity of experiences not so mediated, and then urge us
into the trenches? What makes him so sure that our current state of affairs is
not the display of an excessive, or threatening, or dangerous technoscientific
hegemony, and that "working out a free relation" to it is *not* an urgent task?

In short, what sort of thinker, with what sense of being-in-the-world,
says all the things Don Ihde does, but when asked about the degree to which
he is being "normative," replies only that he does not "have a program that
I am trying to follow in which I want this, that, or the other thing," and then
wonders whether having such a program is even possible (*CT* 130)? I think
avoiding the cluster of questions I ask above is already answering them—and
I am not sure that the "optimism" in this silent answer is . . . untimely enough.

Notes

1. The citation here is to a chapter called "Why Not Science Critics?" which,
perhaps a little misleadingly, never really distinguishes between science critics and
technoscience critics. It seems clear, however, that for both sorts of critics, possession
of the "distance" I describe here is crucial. Cf. Ihde's "Humanities in the Twenty-first
Century" (*PP* 137–155).

2. The 1975 essay reprinted here has "human-*machine*" relations, but I have
changed this to avoid a misleading narrowness this phrase might be taken to have
which Ihde does not intend.

3. "Die Universalität des hermeneutischen Problems" [1966], in *Gesammelte
Werke*, vol. 2 (Tübingen: J.C.B. Mohr, 1986), 219 ["The Universality of the Herme-
neutical Problem," in *Philosophical Hermeneutics*, trans. David Linge (Berkeley:
University of California Press, 1976), 3].

4. I suspect that Ihde might also detect a whiff of Heideggerian "nostalgia" for
the supposedly pre-scientific life here, but I'll ignore this third possibility in what
follows.

5. See, of course, Steven Shapin and Simon Schaffer, *Leviathan and the Air-
Pump: Hobbes, Boyle, and the Experimental Life* (Princeton: Princeton University
Press, 1985) and Bruno Latour, *Science In Action: How to Follow Scientists and
Engineers through Society* (Cambridge: Harvard University Press, 1987); and from
other angles, Patrick Heelan, *Space Perception and the Philosophy of Science* (Ber-
keley: University of California Press, 1983), Jan Golinski, *Making Natural Knowl-
edge: Constructivism and the History of Science* (Cambridge: Cambridge University
Press, 1998), and Joseph C. Pitt, *Thinking about Technology: Foundations of the
Philosophy of Technology* (New York: Seven Bridges Press, 2000).

6. It is useful to recall, for example, that "confirmation" in the logical positiv-
ist/empiricist sense of checking consistency and testing consequences of allegedly

predictive theories is a child of the mid-19th century, not part of (as these allegedly anti-metaphysical folk routinely express it) the "essence" of science as conceived from its very beginning. See, e.g., Larry Laudan, "Why Was the Logic of Discovery Abandoned?" in *Science and Hypothesis: Historical Essays on Scientific Methodology* (Dordrecht: D. Reidel, 1981), 181–91.

7. See, e.g., Hans Achterhuis, *American Philosophy of Technology: The Empirical Turn* (Bloomington: Indiana University Press, 2001), 119–46; and the sections on Ihde in *CT.*

8. See especially Ihde's *Bodies in Technology*. As Ihde points out, in one respect the development of simulation and virtual reality technologies has loosened up the inherited modern tendency to think of devices as one-purpose, mechanical devices that have a single main function in helping us subjects handle and represent the world's objects, so that it is now easier for us to think "magically" again, both in and outside of science—so that we can regard ourselves and the world we encounter as being and having multiple "realities" simultaneously or serially, forever capable of transforming and morphing into multiple shapes and interactions. The point to remember, however, is that "both RL and VR are part of the lifeworld, and VR is thus both 'real' as a positive presence and a part of RL" (*BT* 13). Another way to make the point is to explain why the National Rifle Association's "guns don't kill people, people kill people" is phenomenologically block-headed (*TL* 26–27; *CT* 137–38). See also, Aaron Smith, "Do You Believe in Ethics? Ihde and Latour in the Trenches of the Science Wars (Or: Watch Out Latour, Ihde's Got a Gun)," *CT* 182–194.

9. Robb Eason, "Hypertext: Rortean Links between Ihde and Haraway," *CT* 114.

10. Hans Achterhuis, *American Philosophy of Technology: The Empirical Turn,* 130–131.

11. Eason, "Hypertext: Rortean Links between Ihde and Haraway," 179–180.

12. *PP*, 77, my emphasis. Ihde goes on to claim that his micro-/macroperceptual style of analysis is confirmed in Merleau-Ponty's note in *The Visible and the Invisible* that "there is an informing of perception by culture which enables us to say that culture is perceived" (trans. Alphonso Lingis [Evanston: Northwestern University Press, 1963], 212). Ihde's interpretation is not, I think, an obvious one. It is at least as plausible to read this note—which is after all a note—quite differently, by bringing it together with what Merleau-Ponty goes on to say, viz., that we must put perceptual and cultural openness to the world *in continuity*, rather than think of them as one thing built on top of another via "learning." Moreover, his point, as the end of the note stresses, is that sensible, bodily perceiving "masks itself to itself" by enacting and becoming aware of itself *as if it had to be Euclidian* (213, my emphasis); and the next note explains that a recognition of this fact permits us to understand how "the sensible is precisely that medium in which there can be being *without it having to be posited*" (214, my emphasis). For me, this passage reflects Merleau-Ponty's struggle to work out a more intimately and simultaneously perceptual/cultural understanding of existence

than his early start with a phenomenology of perception, followed by phenomenologies of language, culture, history, etc. could permit him. And this is not Ihde's own trajectory.

13. Hans Achterhuis, *American Philosophy of Technology: The Empirical Turn*, 6–8.

14. See "On Philosophy's 'Ending' in Technoscience: Heidegger vs. Comte," in *The Philosophy of Technology: The Technological Condition—An Anthology*, ed. Robert C. Scharff and Val Dusek (Oxford: Blackwell, 2003), 265–76.

15. It is often overlooked that according to Comte's 3-stage law of intellectual and social development, theology and metaphysics are not at all the mere superstition and nonsense they are to the later logical empiricists. For detailed discussion, see my *Comte After Positivism* (Cambridge: Cambridge University Press, 1995), 73–91.

16. "Das Ende der Philosophie und die Aufgabe des Denkens," *Zur Sache des Denkens* (Tübingen: Max Niemeyer, 1969), 67 ["The End of Philosophy and the Task of Thinking," trans. Joan Stambaugh, alterations by David Farrell Krell in *Basic Writings*, rev. ed. David Farrell Krell (New York: Harper Collins, 1993), 437.]

17. Heidegger uses these expressions to characterize his central topic on that part of his path of inquiry that runs from the pre-*Being and Time* "hermeneutics of facticity" to his "immanent criticism" of it in *EP* 67 [437]; and in the 1956 "Zusatz" to *Der Ursprung des Kunstwerkes* (Stuttgart: Reclam, 1960), 100 [trans. Albert Hofstadter in *Basic Writings*, 211].

18. For discussion of this impossibility, see *TL* 1–20, 42–71.

19. Ihde seems to me at least to come very close to having this problem when he assures us that although technologically mediated experiences can significantly "magnify, amplify, or reduce" our perceptions, this need never be regarded as a danger because we can always "locate the difference" between naked and mediated perception by referring back to the former's role within the "privileged position" of "ordinary" bodily praxis and action, and so have the means for marking out and evaluating this difference (*TL* 76, 79–80). Where is this situated, concretely embodied and encultured "locator" standing, and how can it (he? she? we?) be so sure that there is anything to "privilege" rather than just compare against the more recently magnified, amplified, and/ or reduced perception? Cf. *PP* on "variational" phenomenology (*PP* 7, 70).

10

Technology: The Good, the Bad, and the Ugly

Richard A. Cohen

Introduction

Based on a lifetime of careful investigation into the significance of human embodiment and technology, the work of Don Ihde has revolved around the central insight that technology represents an extension of human embodiment.

Intimately related to this central insight Ihde has elaborated on two important corollaries. The first, which has far-reaching ramifications both within and beyond the subdiscipline called "the philosophy of technology," is that there is no "bodily-sensory perception that is without its socio-cultural dimension" (*BT* 133). The human body is not first an object or a subject, but a way of being-in-the-world inseparable from sociocultural contextualization. Therefore the meaning of technology must also be grasped in terms of its sociocultural context.

Of course, introducing the dimension of the sociocultural introduces the imperative force of moral values and the human judgments that sustain values. Examining this dimension—the role of morality and justice in relation to embodiment and technology—is the central concern of the present paper.

Ihde's second corollary already takes up this topic: the specific modification of the body's essential sociocultural significance by its technological extension provides no basis for either *utopian* or *dystopian* glosses of its value. The extension of the human body through technology is both quantitative and qualitative, to be sure, but not such as to enable overarching blanket value judgments. These valuations of technology (or anything else for that matter) depend rather on metaphysical presuppositions that are necessarily external and untrue to a phenomenological-hermeneutic understanding of

the human embodiment of which technology is the extension. As a philosopher, Ihde wisely rejects all *a priori* totalizing interpretations.

Technology, whatever its contribution to human life, offers neither the
universal panacea optimistically claimed by utopians nor the universal bane
pessimistically declaimed by dystopians. True to the results of his earliest
phenomenological investigations of perception, Ihde writes: "The possible
uses [of technology] are always ambiguous and multi-stable" (*BT* 131). Another concern of this paper is to contextualize and in this way to criticize,
along with Ihde, the false dyad of utopianism and dystopianism in understanding the significance of technology.

I am in complete agreement with Ihde on the points above: technology
is an extension of human embodiment; human embodiment, and hence technology, must be understood within sociocultural contexts; and finally, these
contexts, and not the fantasy of a technology divorced from its proper fields
of significance (body and world), provide the only legitimate grounds for
the evaluations too broadly and hence illegitimately drawn by utopians and
dystopians. Technology is "good" or "evil" as the human hand or foot are
good or evil, or rather as human action, of which technology is an extension, is good or evil. Putting aside the *metaphysical* presuppositions of
utopians and dystopians, the human body and the technologies that extend
it are neither good nor evil a priori. Technology is, in a word, instrumental.
Instruments can be used for good or evil, and are historically usually used
for both.

Nevertheless, evaluation is as essential to the sociocultural context of
human being-in-the-world as is the latter's technological dimensions. Indeed,
to go one step farther, the thesis of this paper is that evaluation is a *more
profound* dimension of being-in-the-world than technological instrumentality.
Hence the latter must be grasped within an appreciation for the imperatives
of the former. Despite their own evaluative zeal, it is precisely this, the priority of ethics in sociocultural life, which the utopians and dystopians fail to
recognize. The human world attains its "humanity" insofar as it always already determines the meaning of "importance" as an ethical category. While
both utopians and dystopians seem to value ethics, loudly crying "good" and
"evil," in the end they overvalue it and misunderstand the ethical character of
sociocultural life. And by misunderstanding the place of ethics they inadvert-
ently do something terrible: they undermine the possibility of a genuine
appreciation for its role in human affairs.

The thesis of this chapter is not, however, that technology is "value-
free." In one sense, divorced from all else, in its pure instrumentality, technology is indeed value-free. But such is an analytical abstraction, essence
divorced from existence. Technology is value-free in the way, as I have said,
a hand is value-free. Technology, in other words, does not ultimately alter a

human condition founded on ethical values because those values at once permeate *and transcend* technology.[1] They are its condition and not its product.

The true philosophical issue with regard to technology is to probe and discern the specific manner in which technology, as an extension of the human body, contributes to and modifies the root ethical constitution of humanity. This question has become all the more pressing with recent advances in technology whereby technology now permeates our worldly being to an extent, and in a manner hitherto almost unimaginable.

Utopias and Dystopias

Something of the transcendence demanded by the above question seems to be preserved in Heidegger's teaching that "the essence of technology is not technological," namely, the idea that technology can only be understood in a nontechnological way.[2] Nevertheless, Heidegger undermines his own effort to understand technology by locating it within what remains, contrary to his own claims, a metaphysically totalizing context. Returning, as he believes, to a strand of thinking initiated in Western culture by the pre-Socratics, for Heidegger the root of significance, and hence the true ground of technology, is not the imperative of the ethical but rather a quite different imperative deriving from the *essential*. That the essential underlies the ethical is the earliest theme, it seems to me, which runs through and characterizes the entire work and career of Heidegger. This is less surprising when we consider that it is also a core theme that runs through most of Western philosophy.

By "essence" Heidegger does not intend to mean something abstract, intellectual, or ethereal. Rather, he means the concrete epochal dispensations ("worlds") of being, whereby being is understood dynamically. Being both withdraws and "gives" itself in such a way as to fundamentally determine the root meaning—the "spirit," as Hegel called it—of an entire historical period. So, for example, the "essence" of the medieval period of Europe was, for Heidegger, a being-in-the-world that was theological, determined throughout, permeated in all its particulars, by relationship to the God of Christianity. Being manifest itself, came into "essence," in the medieval period theologically. In the "ontological difference" between withdrawal and manifestation of meaning, which is a dynamic rather than a static absence and a presence, being as essence at once determines and transcends its particular epochal manifestations. To think or be in the medieval period was, wittingly or not, to think or be theologically. Though the later Heidegger will eschew the very term "being," because he thinks it overloaded with preconceptions, he will continue to maintain that underlying essential epochs there remains an inexhaustible and primordial fund of significance. The ultimate source, let us call it, is at once what has been, what is, and what will be, the "temporalizing" or "historicizing" ongoing creation of historically manifest worlds. Heidegger concern, as a thinker, is to preserve the openness, the fruitfulness, the "generosity" of this ultimate source of meaning, to be its mouthpiece.

Within this encompassing philosophical framework, for Heidegger the role of technology is twofold. First, in our present world, being's essential manifestation today is precisely the "epoch of technology." Technology represents the fundamental character, the essence, the spirit, of our epoch of being's ongoing revelation of meaning. Therefore technology permeates all the particulars of our world, determining in its own special way the meaning of meaning, what counts as meaningful and what counts as insignificant. Technology is the very temper of our times, what "goes without saying."

But what specifically is the distinctive characteristic that orders and permeates our epoch as technological in essence? Heidegger's answer is purely negative. The essence of technology is the conversion of all reality into means without ends. Worse yet, technology represents the *endless* conversion of all ends into means without ends. As such, because it makes our age one without proper ends and because it therefore also occludes the very possibility of hearkening to being as ultimate source, it is the "greatest danger." The philosopher—Heidegger—is the guardian of the ultimate source, while technology is the unsurpassable foreclosure of any future novel revelations or dispensations of epochal being. Technology is the opening of being that shuts down being as openness. Ours is the age of technology, but the essence of technology is to be the final age. This final age without finality blocks any future ages. Technology is the essence that ends the dynamism of its own emergence; hence it is also the anti-essence par excellence: a never-ending, ever-increasing efficiency for the sake of efficiency alone—the greatest danger.

Obviously Heidegger takes a strong dystopian view of technology. His dystopianism is a deep one because instead of complaining about this or that technological problem (e.g., pollution, global warming, identity theft), it contextualizes and demonizes technology within a vast philosophy of historical revelation. Technology is the greatest danger because Heidegger's interest, given his interpretation of philosophy as openness to "ontological difference," is to remain open and to keep the world open to the questioning-poetic-thinking that alone remains attentive to future revelations of essential being.

Technology is not only blind to its own true origin in the generosity of the ultimate source, but in its unbounded willfulness it is essentially blind to its own blindness. Its form of blindness is thus incurable. It is endless construction, insatiable development of human command and control. In an idiosyncratic and even perverse way, Heidegger will label this willfulness "humanism," and proceed, notoriously (i.e., oblivious to the monstrous and disastrous anti-humanism of the Nazis), to attack it. The technical discourse of technology, concerned exclusively with speed and efficiency, is endlessly superficial because, so Heidegger argues, it is endlessly *merely* human. Its discourse avoids any deep questioning because, caught up in an endlessly instrumental reasoning, it is what Heidegger in *Being and Time* called the chatter of *"das Man,"* the "they." From the noisy wasteland of mass production and mass consumption, from a ceaseless blitz of advertising, publicity, and passing fame, from unending demolition and construction, from ever more refined intrusions into privacy, only an oracle ("a god"), only a genuine thinker (Heidegger, surprise!), he who is somehow still attuned to the ultimate source, can save us. Woe, woe, bereft and abandoned are we, toys are us. Heidegger's is a deep, baleful, almost apocalyptic dystopianism.

Heidegger's thought has been criticized many times in many ways for a number of related problems: the *a priori* character of its underlying metaphysics of ontological difference and the latter's alleged "generosity" (which, as Levinas remarks, also "gave us the Holocaust"); the abstractness of its philosophical framing of the question of historical epochs, and, more particularly, its reductive flattening of significant differences in technological issues; its selective blindness and complicity, despite its own appeal to history, to important concrete events of its own time, most obviously Nazism and the Holocaust; its own unacknowledged and contradictory subjectivist and controlling interests, as manifest in its cult-doctrine of salvation through "great thinkers," of which the most recent is clearly Heidegger himself; the again unacknowledged and contradictory naturalism of its derivation of "ought" from "is"; its typical "Germanic " philosophical-idealist anthropology, that is, its projection of human spirit onto being; and much else. I believe that all these criticisms hit the mark. The main point, here, however, is simply to invoke Heidegger's ontology as a recent and widely disseminated dystopian framing of the issues raised by modern advances in science and technology. As Ihde has made us acutely aware, however, Heidegger's dissatisfaction with modern technology stems from his assumption of a decontextualized attitude of nostalgic romanticism (*PP* 103–115) based on the unacknowledged construction of a myth of lost pretechnological ages of harmony. As such, and paradoxically contrary to its own self-interpretation, Heidegger's account remains a willful subjectivist dialectical partner and reflection of the technological age it invents to criticize.

In fact, technology has always been part of the human landscape, from chipped stones, from plows and altars, to trains, super-highways, telephones and computer generated virtual realities. Each technology involves gains and losses. To build a temple is to create a quarry or deforest a wood. To gather here is to separate there. The issue in understanding technology is not to deride it as such, which is equivalent to deriding the human condition as such (which is a theological rather than a philosophical position), but to grasp and then evaluate what is peculiar about its contemporary manifestations in our time of modern science.

Utopians, in contrast to dystopians, envision in technology a marvelous solution to perennial human problems, ameliorating or eliminating the sufferings of illness, deformity, hunger, aging, natural disaster, crime, poverty, war, inequity, boredom, death, and all the woes that have plagued a hitherto primitive and unenlightened humanity. Such wide-eyed optimism regarding technology's potential contribution to human affairs arose with the general European enthusiasm that surrounded the rise of modern science. Far before such twentieth-century horrors as mass murder, the totalitarian state, and nuclear meltdown, the threats facing an earlier humanity originated primarily from the natural environment: floods, earthquakes, plagues, wild animals, starvation, and the like. Combining the new-found Renaissance respect for worldliness with an appreciation for the amazing new empirical discoveries of modern science (e.g., the astronomical reckonings of Copernicus, Galileo, Kepler, and above all Newton), utopians envisioned a world no longer misled and disordered by the superstitions of religion, but one reconstructed and controlled according to the enlightened logic of verifiable scientific knowledge. Only through an enlightened political and social application of the new-found knowledge of modern science, would a genuine rather than a merely fancied human redemption become actualized. Modern science, along with the technologies that both made it possible and that it made possible, would open a new era of human amelioration and perfection on earth.

Enthralled by modern science, "progressive" European thinkers—one thinks of Fourier, Comte, Saint-Simon, Marx, Bakunin, among others—have constructed more or less elaborate articulations of a desired future society organized according to purely scientific principles. Even the founder of contemporary phenomenology, Edmund Husserl, who is rarely thought of as a social thinker, concluded his philosophical career opposing the rising European fascism of the 1930s with his saving vision of a rigorously and completely scientific humanity. If a god can no longer save us from science, science can save us from God. In every case, however, the utopian vision of technology mistakes the contribution of an important part of the human project, its scientific-technical component, for the whole of that project. Just as the dystopian vision underestimates the role of technology in humanity's past, and therefore exaggerates its impact on the present and foreseeable future, the utopian vision overestimates the role of technology in humanity's future, and therefore diminishes the positive role of the nontechnological in humanity's past, present, and future.

Quantity and Quality: Scientism and Romanticism

Another illuminating way to understand the conflicts and distortions generated by the opposed interpretations and evaluations of modern science and
technology is to recognize what is gained and what is lost in the initial
motivation and driving force of philosophy conceived of as science. To put
the matter as succinctly and boldly as possible (and therefore also to put aside
a variety of legitimate qualifications), we can say that philosophy begins as
the overcoming of creative imagination in the name of objective knowledge.
As "mere" opinion (*doxa*) must give way to knowledge (*episteme*), so, too,
all "mere fanciful" myth must give way to reason. What is too often forgotten
in this project, forgotten precisely because of the intellectual gains and achievements of this very project, is that "opinion" and "knowledge," "myth" and
"reason," arise at the same time, each the dialectical partner of the other. The
opinions to be corrected by knowledge are precisely the opinions whose
insufficiency are first insisted upon and revealed by standards appropriate to
knowledge. So, too, the inadequacy of myth derives from the adequacy of
reason. The "failure" of particularity derives from the elevation of universality. What is deemed "inauthentic" depends on what counts as "authentic."

The Socratic project of philosophy, originating in a time of social and
political upheaval and uncertainty in ancient Greece, demands nothing less
than a radical regrounding of human discourse and life upon reason. The
sage, the oracle, the poet, the rhetorician, and the tyrant (whether demagogue
or aristocrat) as well, are to give way to the scientist. One would no longer
"merely" do the good (out of filial piety, religious obligation, adherence to
tradition, etc.), one would first have to *know* the good, and only the good
known would be truly good. Only the life of reason—the philosophical life—
would be the true life, authentic life. Knowing would now and henceforth be
the ground of being. All else would become superstition, ignorance, näiveté,
immaturity, if not malice and machination.

Here is not the place to elaborate a history of Western intellectual development. Suffice to say of the origins of philosophy, of a life guided by
knowledge, that it finds its principle in Parmenides' identification of being
with thinking, and of thinking with the strictures of a formal logic (principles
of noncontradiction and excluded middle), organized by Aristotle in a manner
authoritative for two thousand years. The culmination of this approach came
with Kant and/or Hegel (Marx), for whom the real—whether determined by
an ongoing representational project as with Kant or through an immanent
dialect as with Hegel (Marx)—was that which was rational, and only the
rational could qualify as real. What is too often overlooked, however, is that
between Parmenides and Kant/Hegel, the notion of reason itself underwent a

drastic revision, usually called "Cartesian." With the rise of modern science (and technology) a rationality modeled on mathematical analysis, deductive logic, and efficient causality substituted itself for a reason, which, though oriented by epistemology, was nevertheless always conceived far more broadly. The reduction of reason to conformity to the quantitative approach of modern science yielded great rewards in clarity and system-building, to be sure, but at the price of a great delegitimatization—one might even say banishment or repression—of everything having to do with quality and value.

However, the broad is never or never easily eviscerated by the narrow. Rationality as the hegemony of modern mathematical science produces as its unwanted and now desperate byproduct a Romantic reaction: the equal and opposite exaltation of quality and value at the expense of quantitative objectivity. Extremes produce and mirror one another in their narrowness. In place of the prior unity of quality and quantity envisioned by reason, rationality now monopolizes and exalts an abstract and dehumanized quantification while romanticism, its dialectical partner, monopolizes and exalts a no less abstract and dehumanized sentimental enthusiasm. When Heidegger bemoans that "only a god can save us now," he means that only creative poetic-thinking can save us from objective scientific-technological rationality. The truth, however, is that one is the warped mirror image of the other. Both arise in the same reduction of reason to rationality, whether in celebration of, or in rebellion from the powers unleashed by this reduction—Blake vs. Bacon.

Ethics and Politics

But how can one today express an alternative to this royal family quarrel between rationality and romanticism? It is certainly impossible insofar as one accepts the parameters of a mathematical logic or a sentimental enthusiasm, which each sees itself as exclusive and hegemonic worldview. Both have severely limited notions of transcendence that make each fall short of a full account of the real that perforce must include and take seriously human being. To point to the ongoing free development of science as an open horizon of sense is misleading insofar as science is only open to more science, open only to more precise and coherent science. To point to the "revelation" of creative being as the ongoing free fund of world dispensation is no less misleading because such openness, as Ernst Cassirer tirelessly pointed out throughout his career, lacks sufficient standards of individual and social criticism to evaluate or even to distinguish regressive from progressive "gifts." Neither the world as knowledge nor the world as art can serve as comprehensive accounts of the world in its fullness, though each poses as absolute.

To find an answer to this dilemma and to overcome the narrowness of its alternatives, we must return to the initial premises suggested to us by Ihde: technology is an extension of human embodiment, and human embodiment is inseparable from its sociocultural context. Taking this one step further we must grasp what is the depth structure of human sociocultural embodiment, recognizing that it is something, or some way, that cannot be fully explained without distortion in either epistemological or aesthetic terms. Ihde, invoking the phrase of Langdon Winner, suggests that the solution lies in the "politics of the artifact."

For my part, I think the answer lies one step further, because I believe that the term "politics," by itself, without greater specification, can be misleading. Both knowledge and aesthetics have their own politics, as we have been taught by Nietzsche, Thomas Kuhn, and Foucault, among many others. In other words, if politics means nothing more than the command and organization of force relations, then, given the interpretation of knowledge taken from an aesthetic point of view, or of aesthetics taken from an epistemological point of view, both science and art are already political. Spinoza makes this explicit in the title of the one work he published in his own name: *Theological-Political Treatise*. Theology could not be extricated from politics because, from the point of view of a strictly scientific worldview, and despite its own masquerade to the contrary, it is nothing other than irrationally enforced command and obedience. So, too, from Nietzsche's strictly aesthetic point of view, science, despite its claims to the contrary, is itself nothing other than slavish obedience, a "faith in truth," which remains nothing more than a "natural" and elitist rather than an "unnatural" and plebian form of traditional religious command and obedience.[3] In introducing the idea of politics as an essential element of the sociocultural context of meaning within which embodiment and technology must be understood, I am confident that Ihde means to affirm neither of these essentially relativist and ultimately nihilist positions.

I think that the proper term Ihde is seeking, or the term that lies beneath the term "politics" that he has chosen, the term that overcomes the narrowness and dilemma created by the opposition between scientism and romanticism, and indeed the term that directs us to the genuine root of politics, is the *ethical*. In contrast to a long tradition of political thought running from the Greek sophists to Machiavelli, Hobbes and Marx and beyond, one that makes ethics a subset of politics ("Might makes right"), but in line with a no less ancient tradition of political thought for which politics finds its proper ground in ethics, and whose beginnings go back to Plato and Aristotle and find a compelling modern advocate in the political liberalism of T.H. Green, this inquiry must now turn to the ethical thought of a leading twentieth-century phenomenologist, one who was, it seems to me, the most radical adversary and critic of both Spinoza's scientism and Heidegger's romanticism, namely, Emmanuel Levinas. What is missing from Heidegger's account, just as it is missing from Spinoza's, and what is missing, too, from both the utopian embrace of modern science and technology and the dystopian rejection of the same, is a proper appreciation for the imperatives of morality and justice that constitute the "humanity of the human," to invoke Levinas' phrase, that is to say, the specifically human character of the sociocultural dimension within which human embodiment always finds itself situated. Deeper or higher than its engagement in science or aesthetics, deeper or higher than its engagement in political negotiations, human embodiment—intersubjective embodiment— is "constituted," or rather *elevated* by ethical responsibility.

Here is not the place for a detailed elaboration of Levinas' phenomeno- logical analyses or of the "ethical metaphysics" that ultimately undergirds and ruptures the phenomenological method in its search to understand the meaning of the human. Given our concerns, what is important to note is that, for Levinas, ethics enters the domain of human signification not as a second- order cultural, social, or political metastructure, but rather as the core dimen- sion of human embodiment itself. The body is not merely a locus of a generalized "flesh of the world," a perceptual reflexivity that finds itself mirrored in social, cultural, and political engagements, as it is so brilliantly described by Merleau-Ponty, but also, and from the very heart of its consti- tution as embodied subjectivity, it is an ethical responsiveness to the moral imperative of the other. The irreplaceability ("election") that determines the individuation of an embodied subjectivity lies neither in the mobility of Merleau-Ponty's "I can" nor in the anxiety of Heidegger's "being-toward- death," but rather in the "being-for-the-other," the "suffering" for the suffer- ing of another" of responsibility. To clarify the proper ethical signification of technology and to highlight the value of Ihde's rejection of both utopian and dystopian contextualization of technology, I will conclude with a closer look at modern technology in relation to an embodied ethics of responsibility. It is an analysis that begins with an historical-conceptual contextualization, moves to an all-too-brief phenomenology of technology, and ends in what I have elsewhere[4] called "ethical exegesis."

Modern Technology and the Tower of Babel

Given the astonishing advances in science and technology of the past one hundred years, it is sometimes easy to forget that technology and the human condition arose simultaneously or at least quite close together in time. This is not, however, to define the human by its technology, to define the human as the "tool user," say, but rather to point to a fact confirmed by modern anthropological studies. Nevertheless, it is obvious that modern technology is of a different order than premodern technology. What happened in the modern period that made technology so much more prominent in human affairs than hitherto? How do modern technologies differ from premodern technologies?

A broad historical-conceptual answer to the first question is fairly clear: modern technology arises with the rise of modern science. Having said this, let us immediately point out that while science and technology are not synonymous, it is nevertheless a mistake to divorce one from the other as if they were two entirely different things, or, more precisely, as if one were, as if often said, the "application" of the other. Technology is not simply the application of science; it is an active ingredient of science itself. Modern astronomy, for instance, depends on the telescope just as modern chemistry and biology depend on the microscope. So, in pointing to a difference between modern and premodern science, we are at the same time pointing to a difference between modern and premodern technology.

One of the key differences between modern science and premodern science is that the former is nonteleological while the latter is teleological. Modern science asks "how" or "of what" is something constructed; premodern science also asks "why," "what purpose does it serve?" With this shift in the meaning of scientific explanation a new problem arises: modern science, unlike premodern science, cannot so easily be conjoined to the value imperatives that rule in the social, political, cultural, and religious dimensions of human life. When creation and nature were both understood in terms of goal-orientation, humanity and nature could be grasped within one coherent whole, where divine providence was interpreted in terms of scientific purpose, as was done by the greatest of the medieval theologians, whether Islamic, Jewish, or Christian. When nature is understood divorced from goal-orientation, however, then humanity, with its inherent value-driven actions, and nature, indifferent to value, diverge.

Like Humpty Dumpty after his fall, it has been difficult to put fact and value back together again. If nature is value-free, humanity is certainly value-laden. If values are no longer scientifically verifiable, are no longer found in nature, then their status, in relation to the awesome successes and status of modern science, come into question. Knowledge and wisdom are for the first time fundamentally at odds with one another. Hence the modern problem: What is the value of values in the face of value-free science?

But let us not go too far astray from our specific question concerning science-technology. How does modern technology differ from premodern technology? Both are instruments, to be sure, and hence premodern and modern technologies are not different in kind. But it is clear, nevertheless, that a drastic change has occurred with the rise of modern technology-science, a change that began to have great public impact as early as the time of the

Industrial Revolution, and a change whose impact continues to accelerate to our own day. It seems to me that the central characteristic of modern technology has to do with a *quantitative increase in and qualitative abstraction of* (1) temporal simultaneity; (2) spatial proximity; (3) standardization; (4) scale; and (5) specialization. Premodern books were each one handwritten and handcopied; modern books are each one precisely the same and machine manufactured to any specified quantity. A donkey carried one person and small quantities of goods; trains, planes, and trucks carry many persons and many more goods, and they do so far more swiftly. A handwritten letter delivered by post differs vastly—in quantity and quality—from an e-mail sent to various addressees almost instantaneously across the globe. For the first time, modern technology has created one universal time across the planet, indeed, for our purposes, across the universe. To put the matter succinctly: modern technology is increasingly turning the human world into one metropolis, with universal and interchangeable standards, with one language. It unifies and reduces differences to sameness. In a word, it globalizes.

What, if any, are the ethical consequences of this qualitative leap in quantification? Walter Lippmann, in his book of 1936, *The Good Society*,[5] argues that modern technology has created a division of human labor, a growth in specialization hitherto inconceivable, burgeoning to the point that it might lead to an unhealthy fragmentation of what had been relatively well-rounded and integral lives. One could also point to the operational opacity inherent in ever more complex and ever more miniaturized technologies. How many of us know how the Internet works? How many of us know how a television or even a telephone works? As the world becomes increasingly unified, as knowledge increasingly permeates and transforms practical life, organizing it ever more efficiently, producing an ever more convenient and comfortable everyday existence, it seems that fewer of us understand how all this is happening. Hence, as we become closer to one another in a world increasingly unified, at the same time the same world is becoming increasingly mysterious, increasingly beyond our understanding, increasingly alien.

But this same fragmentation and alienation are counter balanced, as it were, by an increased availability of expertise and a heightened transparency also produced by technology. If many of us do not understand the inner workings of televisions, telephones, or electricity, they nonetheless bring vast amounts of information into our living rooms, open up lines of global communication, light up our streets and homes through the night, and provide warmth in the winter. In other words, one cannot point to an overarching evil, or to an overarching good, that is inherent in technology. Such was the error of the utopians and dystopians, and the compellingly simplistic temptation of their perspective. What technology does do, however, because it does represent a vast leap in quantity (in time, space, scale, standardization, and abstraction), is that it makes the opportunities for good and evil *both* greater. Just as never before could so much good be done—for example, to feed the starving in faraway places, to provide cheap housing for so many, to open universities to the masses—so, too, never before could so much evil be done—for example, the Holocaust, Chernobyl, open-air nuclear testing, deforestation. And at the same time scientific knowledge has nothing to say about values!

Wisdom does not grow the way scientific theory grows, by throwing away the old for the new. Rather, wisdom grows upon itself by building, maturing, and refining, to produce an ongoing and living tradition. This is why the wisdom of the past is relevant to today in a way that the science of the past is not. For this reason I wish to turn to a biblical story that seems to me to have everything to do with technology, or, more precisely, with an understanding of what can go wrong with technology, instructing us, thereby, in how to better grasp and better create a more humane relationship between technology and humanity, one governed by ethical considerations. I am thinking of the story of the Tower of Babel (*Genesis* 11:5–9).

As with most biblical stories, its literal rendition is quite short. Owing to its brevity and, more importantly, to it compactness, as well as to the long fascination this story has exerted on human imagination, it demands commentary. In what follows, I will rely primarily on rabbinic commentaries taken from the *Talmud* and *Midrash*, without citing specific texts.

What has immediately struck all commentators is that no explicit reason, no fault is ever given to justify God's dispersion of humanity, the termination of the tower's construction, or for the confusion of tongues in place of one universally understood language. Technology is not in itself bad. Communication is not in itself good. Metropolitan life by itself is neither good nor bad. To find a reason for God's displeasure, the rabbis rather turn to the manner in which the tower was being constructed and the purposes it was meant to serve. A Midrash focuses on the relative value of bricks and humans. Kiln-fired bricks, the ones used in building the Tower of Babel, are perhaps the instance of technology par excellence, for the brick is an artifact that "served them as stone." It replaces a more natural building block, one that God insisted upon for altars that would thereby not be touched by iron, an instrument of war. Furthermore, baked in a kiln it does not even make use of the natural heat of the sun. It is completely artificial, as much as any artifact can be artificial. As the tower grew in height so too did the difficulty in transporting bricks to its top—a construction problem. The evil, however, begins when, due to the greater labor, time, and expense of transporting bricks, they come to be treated as more valuable than humans. According to the Midrash, when a brick fell from the top it was more lamented than when a worker fell from the top. Indeed, the loss of the brick was lamented; the loss of the worker was ignored. A technology serving humanity is quite different—morally—than a humanity serving technology.

The rabbis also find evil in the purpose for the tower. While the text literally only says that it was constructed to "make a name," such as we readily understand when we think of London and Big Ben, Paris and the Eiffel Tower, New York City and the Empire State Building, or Kuala Lumpur and its Petronas Towers, the rabbis read a moral hubris into the aims of these citizens of Shinar. They want the top of the tower to reach the heavens, the "place" of God. They want to exalt their name *above* God's. It is idolatry, an idolatry encouraged by a misinterpretation of technological prowess. The whole earth is ours, and so too, therefore, the heavens!

The rabbis distinguish three sorts of rebels according to their differing motivations: (1) those who wanted to ascend to heaven to dwell there; (2) those who wanted to ascend to heaven to erect idols there; and (3) those who wanted to ascend to heaven to wage war against God. The first God dispersed; the second God turned into apes and spirits; and the third God confused their languages. In all three cases, rebellion consists in making one's own name greater than that of God, in not recognizing the legitimacy of a hierarchy of values wherein humanity remains between the beastly and the divine but oriented toward the above. Technical accomplishments alone are not equivalent to moral and spiritual development, nor do they make the latter obsolete or less difficult. There were towers at Auschwitz too.

A related evil pertains to the totalitarian rule of Nimrod, great-grandson of Noah through Ham and Cush, ruler of Shinar and, as the rabbis interpret it, the whole world. We must not forget that the story of the Tower is related to the story of the depraved generation destroyed in the Flood. Nimrod had a most peculiar and secret technology, one no doubt desired by the CIA and KGB: a cloak made of the heavenly garments given to Adam and Eve by God. It enabled him to see and not be seen and to hunt and subdue all the animals. Hence his reputation as a great hunter, a power and a reputation that led to his political dominion. The Bible calls him the "first mighty man" (*Genesis* 10:8), which, according to the rabbis, means that he was the first to seek dominion over the whole earth. He ensnared humanity with his cunning and deceptive words and technology (the garments). Through the example of his great successes, which he attributed to his own abilities, he incited his subjects to rebel against God. Unlike David or Solomon, he attributed his hunting skills and political success entirely to his own efforts rather than acknowledge a higher hand or goal. Who needs God when we have such powers! The Fuhrer—Hitler, Stalin, Mao, Pinochet, et al.—always knows best, and he will protect us.

But the city of Shinar and the Tower of Babel are not unmitigated evils. Unlike the generation of the Flood, who hated one another as well as hating God, and are hence all drowned by God, except for Noah, who is called the "most righteous of his generation," and Noah's family, the generation of the city of Shinar and the Tower of Babel are not killed but dispersed, their language is confused, and the construction of the Tower of Babel is halted. Why? Again, according to the rabbis, this is because they lived in peace and harmony with one another, gathered in one place speaking one language. Just as technology is in itself neither good nor evil, humanity, in itself, is neither good nor evil. Or rather it is both. When humans hate one another, and thus hate God, they are unworthy of life. When they love one another, then regardless of their other faults, they remain worthy. To make the value of bricks greater than that of humans, to create a world where one is either tyrant or slave, this is the path of evil. To speak one language, to live in proximity in peace and harmony, to make a name for oneself without destroying the names of others—this is the path of good.

Conclusions

The central problem with both utopians and dystopians is the same: they both project their own totalizing visions onto technology and the world. The utopians see technology as a cure-all, a panacea. But there are no universal technical panaceas when it comes to healing the moral and juridical ills of human society. The dystopians see technology as the bogeyman, the devil, but there is no single devil when it comes to accounting for the source of the moral and juridical ills of human society. What they neither realize nor appreciate is the inherent multiplicity of human endeavors, the varied levels of signification within which humans live, the social, political, cultural, and religious diversity of human life. This is not to suggest that meaning is anarchic or chaotic, that anything goes, or that everything means anything. Nor is it to substitute an overwhelming and discouraging complexity when it comes to tackling humanity's moral and juridical problems. Perhaps the utopians and dystopians fear chaos too much, which explains their retreat into totality. What is certain is that they both see technology in a reductive way: either it is completely good or completely evil. In both cases it controls us rather than we it.

Technology is an instrument appearing within the same sociocultural worldliness within which human embodiment makes sense. Like all things it can be used wisely or unwisely, producing more good than evil or more evil than good. Today it can even be used to destroy all human civilization. But it remains an instrument nonetheless, an instrument that is and has always been part of embodied being-in-the-world with its inherent and diverse cultural, political, social, and religious values. It is when we see that the "humanity of the human" depends fundamentally on moral responsibility, on putting the other person first, on caring for the needs of the other, and built upon moral responsibility that it demands an unrelenting quest for justice, that one can properly assess the value of technology, as of all else human. Here, then, lies the solution to the fact/value dichotomy that has so plagued modern thought in the wake of the rise of modern science-technology. Science and technology are not themselves sources of value. Science is objective, and as such not determined by scales of relevance. But science and technology remain powerful elements in the human quest for justice—for equitable law; fair production and distribution of food, clothing, shelter, goods; universal health care; education; environmental protection; and the like— which is itself in the service of morality. To maximize a justice that maximizes morality—to contribute to a humanity so constituted, herein lays the great value of science and technology. Every fact is already an occurrence within an inevitable value situation. Will a tower serve humanity? Will it contribute to and promote humane relations and a just society? Will it do the opposite? These are the questions—always asked, whether implicitly or explicitly—within which all scientific inquiries and technological accomplishments find their human context and value.

Notes

1. In invoking the ethical as the "ground" of the sociocultural, I am in no way suggesting or proposing a new ethics. This strikes me as ridiculous. I have argued elsewhere that technology does not by itself create a new ethics. Rather that it must be assessed on the basis of the ethics with which we are already long familiar. In this paper I am attempting to carry through that program, to elaborate the precise modification, the specific difference, effected by the technological that ethics—the old ethics, the only ethics— must assess. Richard Cohen, "Ethics and Cybernetics: Levinasian Reflections," *Ethics and Information Technology* 2, 1(2000): 27–35.

2. Martin Heidegger, *The Question Concerning Technology and Other Essays*, trans. William Lovitt (New York: Harper & Row, 1977).

3. Friedrich Nietzsche, *On the Genealogy of Morals*, trans. and ed. Walter Kaufman (New York: Random House, 1989), Third Essay, 148–156.

4. Richard A. Cohen, *Ethics, Exegesis and Philosophy: Interpretation After Levinas* (Cambridge: Cambridge University Press, 2001), 216–265.

5. Walter Lippman, *The Good Society* (New York: Grosset and Dunlap, 1943).

11

Breakdown

Peter Galison

Preface

The themes traversed in this essay, particularly the matter of thematizing the existential relation between the formation of identity and the activity of instrumental praxis, overlap in interesting ways with Don Ihde's philosophy of technology, including his interpretation of Martin Heidegger.

Breakdowns: Reflections from Failure

Just before 9 AM EST on 1 February 2003, the space Shuttle Columbia disintegrated fifty miles above Dallas, Texas. In a few seconds, the hundreds of engineers, managers, and technicians who were running the complex space mission faced their equipment—and themselves—very differently. No longer acting with the world-spanning array of machinery and technicians to track and land a spaceflight, they were now contemplating a catastrophe, a ship raining from the skies from New Mexico and Texas to Louisiana, a failure that had killed the astronauts and was evidently going to shake the space program to its core.[1]

In a sense, the inquiry into the Columbia disaster was an accident investigation of an accident investigation. Sixteen days before, or more precisely 81.7 seconds after the 16 January 2003 launch, a piece of insulating foam, much like store-bought spray-on insulation, detached from the rocket assembly where the orbiter attaches to the External Tank (the enormous cryogenic fuel carrier). Two-tenths of a second later, the insulation struck the Orbiter at 500 miles per hour. For the next two weeks, while the Orbiter ran science experiments and maneuvered in space, NASA engineers, contractors, and managers confronted that foam strike. Was it a routine event? An acceptable

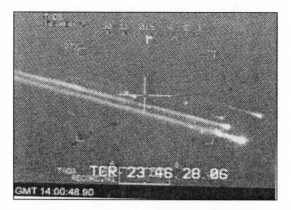

Figure 11.1 Disintegration of Space Shuttle Columbia, over Fort Hood, Texas, 1 February 2003. *Source: Columbia Accident Investigation Board Report,* Vol. 1, p. 40.

risk? A catastrophic accident? At stake in that evaluation was everything, across a nearly infinite scale of consequences. Would it require nothing more than tile replacement, rather like switching tires after touchdown? Or was it, at the other extreme, a crew—and ship—threatening puncture in the protective shields of the craft?

Once Columbia disintegrated, this first inquiry was, tragically, over. The "second" investigation began, their task enormous, a different order of magnitude. On the narrow side the Accident Board had to determine the proximate

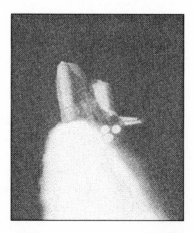

Figure 11.2 Foam Strike. Foam debris from the impact of the strike on Columbia's left wing. Source: *Columbia Accident Investigation Board Report,* Vol. 1, p. 34.

physical cause—as every accident investigation must. What were the actions that actually broke up the Shuttle as it entered the atmosphere? But once the Board began its explorations, it brought into view far more than detached foam and reinforced carbon-carbon: NASA engineering, NASA "culture," NASA management—even Congress and the International Space Station accords fell under the investigative spotlight. In the end, the Board came to address the very nature of handling dangerous technologies. How do we, how should we stand when we work with objects on the edge of destruction?

Objects are mirrors, to be sure, but their optics are vastly more complex than the silver-backed glass we peer into every day. Objects can serve as lensed mirrors of architecture that refract back to us who we are or who we aim to be; Rorschach Plates show us our selves rearranged, recast in new shapes. But the kind of self-object relation that concerns me here is rather different from any of these: In our desperate search to normalize the manipulation of dangerous, failing objects, we face the world in a highly unstable stance. This more existential mirror flickers, sometimes frighteningly, between two pictures of the Self with objects. One image shows us in confident self-possessed control of the world. There we are, the very picture of Cartesian (or perhaps more precisely Kantian) subjects who reason about what we want and make it so using the world of objects as tools and resources. We can build jumbo jets, nuclear reactors, hydrogen bombs; we can construct city-sized submarines and Space Shuttles to launch on demand. We are actors moving without undo self-consciousness, not just with the assurance of tapping with a hammer, but with the hubris of decapitating mountains or vaporizing cities.

And yet from time to time, the most powerful arms of technology break down and that bright image, the one starring us at the commanding center, flickers out of view. Another, more anxious picture arises. We stare, uncomprehending, at technologies when they no longer behave as we expect by all earlier experience. We engage: recalibrating, calculating, testing, investigating—desperately, trying to haul runaway objects back into grip. The self is thrown into unstable relief, theoretically contemplative and yet all at once outside the flow of easy absorption in the world, challenged by the confrontation with deeply threatening objects.

For centuries, philosophers have noticed that a working tool in use is often invisible. There is no need to pay attention to a tool that works—a hammer or a microscope that is functioning disappears, not unlike the way in which a blind man's cane becomes an extension of touch itself. All focus shifts from tool to the object that is being worked. But when the tool breaks, this relation alters. Suddenly, instead of a hammer being simply "available" (as Heidegger famously put it), its transparency in use suddenly becomes opaque. The easy, unconscious, carrying-on with things is broken. I can confront the hammer as a suddenly visible and *unavailable* object as I struggle to fix it—both "I" and hammer now very present. Alternatively, I can just gaze at the object without a plan at all, a blank, stare, "an isolated, self-contained subject confronting an isolated, self-contained object." This, Heidegger argues, is the impoverished but fiercely defended relation that undergirds the long and usual philosophical picture of an isolated, passive subject facing an entirely separate object. Opposing both the un-self-conscious stance of absorption and the mouth-agape contemplation of the spectator, is a third possibility. The subject in this third scene is neither absorbed nor spectating, but instead skilled, involved with the object; a scientist, for example, struggling to make use of theories to understand.[2]

Accidents, especially accidents involving our most complex technological systems, force us to confront what we mean by things and causes as nothing else. Mission Control was tracking Columbia's descent into the atmosphere when, on 16 January 2003 at 8:54:24 it became apparent that things were, as pilots laconically put it, no longer "nominal." MMACS [Maintenance, Mechanical, and Crew Systems officer]: "FYI, I've just lost four separate temperature transducers on the left side of the vehicle..." Then the tire pressure readings dropped to zero. CAPCOM: "And *Columbia*, Houston, we see your tire pressure messages and we did not copy your last call." FLIGHT [The Flight Director]: "Is it instrumentation, MMACS? Gotta be..." Here disbelief ("gotta be") hovered between absorption in the expected procedure and recognition that things were not right. All signals suddenly vanished, precipitating a frantic effort to re-establish contact with the craft until, at 9:12 AM, one of the Mission Control team members walked to the Flight Director's console to tell him that live television had, at 9:00:18, shown the Orbiter disintegrating. The Flight Director then made his final call: "GC [Ground Control],—Flight, GC—Flight?" Ground Control acknowledged. "Lock the doors."[3] Before the rain of debris ceased, the investigation started—into an accident that had begun, twelve minutes earlier. Or maybe the count-down had started two weeks earlier with that hurtling foam. Or had the disaster begun thirty years ago, its ramified causes deep in the infrastructure of spaceflight?

In disappearing, the Shuttle reappeared as the subject of a massive inquiry. That inquest drove contemplation inward—to the tiniest fault from which the accident sprang. But concern also surfaced in a vastly *larger* field, one in which the Shuttle was not an isolated object hurtling through the upper atmosphere, but instead was inseparably joined to the whole of NASA's human flight program. Indeed, the investigation spiraled beyond NASA's mission to Agency's funding by Congress, to the industrial contractors, to the Agency's management style, to NASA's half-century old way of life. Tracking this dual movement *in*—to the core of the technology—and *out* (to the wider culture) is the aim of "An Accident of History" where we dissect the assembly of several accident reports to make visible the strange and elusive grail of "probable cause."

In the formal investigation of the cause of the Columbia disaster, the weight of history pressed hard on the Accident Investigation Board—no one at NASA could avoid comparing the Columbia break-up with the Challenger explosion in 1986. In that earlier accident, investigators hunted the physical cause back to an O-ring that, on the cold morning of the launch, had failed to completely seal hot gases inside the combustion chamber. In the case of Columbia, following a massive search for debris and a huge inquiry, the investigators once again localized its cause:

> The physical cause of the loss of *Columbia* and its crew was a breach in the Thermal Protection System on the leading edge of the left wing, caused by a piece of insulating foam which separated from the left bipod ramp section of the External Tank at 81.7 seconds after launch, and struck the wing in the vicinity of the lower half of Reinforced Carbon-Carbon panel number 8. During re-entry this breach in the Thermal Protection System allowed superheated air to penetrate through the leading edge insulation and progressively melt the aluminum structure of the left wing, resulting in . . . failure of the wing, and breakup of the orbiter. . . . [T]here was no possibility for the crew to survive.[4]

The road to this conclusion was long. Some 25,000 searchers had pursued debris through swamps, fields, and lakes, recovering some 84,000 pieces over 2,000 square miles. Thirteen Principle Investigators, 120 staff members, and 400 NASA engineers combed through electronic, paper, and physical data. Interviews, fault charts, reconstructions followed, capped by a startling re-enactment of the accident in which a nitrogen gun shot a piece of frozen foam gun at a Shuttle wing. Against expectation, the foam projectile pounded a seventeen-inch hole through the wing.

What interests me most is that catastrophe both could and could *not* be kept within a tiny physical nexus, in the case of Columbia, to the foam fragment's breach of Reinforced Carbon-Carbon panel 8. Indeed, from early in the investigation, it became clear that the panel would not rest with a proximate, physical cause. No sooner is the physical cause displayed, then the panel opens the second volume of their report under the title, "Why the Accident Occurred" with the words, "Many accident investigations do not go far enough." It would not be sufficient to lay the blame on hurtling foam and a broken panel 8. Accident investigations, the Board continued, "identify the technical cause of the accident, and then connect it to a variant of 'operator error'—the line worker who forgot to insert the bolt, the engineer who miscalculated the stress, or the manager who made the wrong decision. But this is seldom the entire issue." Reducing a causal chain to this technical flaw or using human failings to punish a particular individual would not solve the problem. "The Board did not want to make these errors."[5] It insisted that dramatic budget cuts had hurt safety; so had the associated and premature "freezing" of the Shuttle design.

Back in 1995, former Johnson Space Center Director Christopher Kraft had embraced that freeze in a prominent report, arguing that upgrades could be deferred on this "mature" vehicle. The report concluded that funds could be husbanded for the planning of a dramatic new replacement ship: the Shuttle was *operational*, "about as safe as today's technology will provide," ready for transfer out from NASA's hands and into those of a single prime contractor. Eight years later, with a second shuttle lying in fragments and its crew dead, the Accident Board dissented, insisting that the Shuttle should *always* be considered as *developmental*, subject to constant intervention by NASA engineers who would pore over the anomalies and dangers that each flight presented. On this view, the Shuttle was *never* in routine flight, but on the contrary every time it flew it did so "in the realm of dangerous exploration."[6]

On the one side, an organization's tracking and production facilities— facilities big enough to sprawl over the whole of the United States—was pressing the Shuttle toward normalcy, toward routine. This was the spirit that, not too many years before, had expected NASA to be flying its Shuttles every week. And it was this same stance that took the Shuttle to be an available instrument, quasi-invisible as it served as the supply barge to Node 2 of the International Space Station. *Against* this routinization stood a blurry photograph of a foam strike, a few engineers, a couple of managers, and an old computer program. Together they tried, however unsuccessfully, to wrench the Shuttle and NASA into another mode of being. For this counter-assembly of people and techniques, the Shuttle was no longer effectively an everyday tool ready-for-use; instead, it became, to use Heideggerian language, quite the opposite: "conspicuous," "obtrusive," "obstinate."[7]

Heidegger wrote much about the *breakdown*, that sudden changeover, in which failure turned the invisibility of the hammer suddenly into an irreducible.[8] But there are differences in the kind of breakdown that intrigue me here: I am interested in exploring these "change overs" as a historical process, fiercely contested by an often fragmented collectivity. Consider, in this case, the position of Linda Ham, Mission Management Team Chair for Columbia's mission STS-107. She and many other STS-107 managers had just worked through an analysis of another mission where that had been a smaller foam loss from the bipod. Indeed there had been numerous foam strikes—at least twelve that NASA knew about, including one back in November 1997. This past experience with "harmless" foam strikes coupled to immense pressure to fly—to get the Space Station Node 2 lofted—left the mission managers of STS-107 within the ordinary. If the foam strike was classified as an "In-Flight

Anomaly," the next launch, of the Shuttle Atlantis, would become a major problem for the already tightly scheduled Space Station.[9] Ham and her colleagues saw the foam strike as a managerial-scheduling issue, not as an existential one.[10]

After reviewing the old flight rationale from STS-112, Linda Ham emailed the Space Shuttle Program Manager to say she found it "lousy": "Rationale states we haven't changed anything, we haven't experienced any 'safety of flight' damage in 112 flights, risk of loss of bi-pod ramp [Thermal Protection System] is same as previous flights . . . So [External Tank] is safe to fly with no added risk. Rationale was lousy then and still is . . . ." McCormack e-replied: "FYI—it kinda says that it will probably be all right." Expert opinion cascaded down, some reassuring ("[Thermal Protection System] took a hit—should not be a problem . . . .") and some worrisome as team members acknowledged the vulnerability of the Carbon-Carbon leading edge, the main landing gear door—knowing the damage depended crucially on the energy of the foam debris.[11]

The managers' relation to their object—the Orbiter—was not simple. Columbia was certainly *not* merely "available." It was not a tool so effortlessly in use that its very being could be forgotten, assimilated into the intentional actions of its pilots and ground controllers. Nor did the Orbiter suddenly appear torn out of the world, thrown, so to speak, onto the physical world outside understanding. Instead, the managers showed an ambivalent concern, a concern that oscillated between a desire to absorb the foam impact into routine, and an anxiety that registered it might be anything but normal. This unstable state left a myriad of traces. Even as Linda Ham dismissed the old flight justification as "lousy" (we've flown safely 112 times, why not again), the overall tendency of the managers, including her other statements elsewhere, was to fall back precisely on inductive arguments of this kind. To the Accident Investigation Board, the managers' stance as they pressed for the normalization of the flight reflected an institutional culture stamped by history—by the history of flying with partially singed O-rings, with dents, scratches and tears in the thermal tiles damaged by hurtling small blocks of foam. "History is not just a backdrop or a scene-setter," the Board commented. "History is cause. History set the *Columbia* and *Challenger* accidents in motion"[12] When foam hit the craft on launch, NASA adjusted the maintenance schedules, and adjusted budget for tile replacement.[13] Problems that might have been "safety-of-flight" issues, ones capable of stopping a countdown, launching emergency measures, or shutting down the program became "acceptable risks." This was deviance under control, deviance that the Shuttle team uncannily labeled "in-family."

Living in routine, managers were not looking to jar the Orbiter into a crisis state, into the genre of the headless hammer. Far from it. Even as requests came in to enlist national spy telescopes to snap pictures of the Orbiter, the managers dismissed them. In one attempt to mobilize the tele-spooks, Sydney Rocha (the NASA Co-Chair of the Debris Assessment Team) e-mailed—it should be said outside proper channels—to ask "Can we petition (beg) for outside agency assistance?" That plea was shot down with zinging rapidity—unauthorized request, not absolutely necessary and, as one personal note reported: "Linda Ham said it was no longer being pursued since even if we saw something, we couldn't do anything about it. The Program didn't want to spend the resources."[14]

On Wednesday 22 January 2003, Wednesday, Rocha banged out a forceful email:

In my humble technical opinion, this is the wrong (and bordering on irresponsible) answer from the [Space Shuttle Program] and Orbiter not to request additional imaging help from any outside source. I must emphasize (again) that [if critical tiles were damaged, it] could present potentially grave hazards. The engineering team will admit it might not achieve definitive high confidence answers without addi-tional images, but, without action to request help to clarify the dam-age visually, we will guarantee it will not . . . Remember the NASA safety posters everywhere around stating, "If it's not safe, say so"? Yes , it's that serious.[15]

And yet—and *yet*—Rocha never pushed the "send" button. Here too the simple opposition of manager and engineer is more complex than it looks. What was Rocha's stance? He was not reduced to a passive spectator. He typed, "It's that serious"; yet he held back from sending it; he showed the printout to some of his colleagues; yet he stopped short of putting it in the hands of upper management. His and the others' decisions were, in a sense, anything but individual. They reflect anticipation of responses from others, managers and engineers alike. Each person speaks separately, true, but when someone speaks it is also the team who is speaking.

No doubt the Columbia Investigators' category of "Institutional Culture" is an enormous improvement over simply nailing the poor soul who inserted the bad bolt or flipped the wrong switch. The Board knew very well that all too many accident investigations considered such indictments their terminus ad quem. "Engineers' failed attempts were not just a matter of psychological frames and interpretations. The obstacles these engineers faced were political and organizational. They were rooted in NASA history and the decisions of leaders that had altered NASA culture, structure, and the structure of the safety system and affected the social context of decision-making for both accidents."[16] All this seems exactly right—and all too reminiscent of that

Challenger Senior Vice President who had urged one of his cautious engineers during the launch deliberation: "Take off your engineering hat and put
on your management hat."[17] Culture talk, insofar as it emphasizes the need to
consider *shared* values among many individuals, may well be a useful part of
any analysis of things and self-hood. That said, as the VP and two-hatted
engineer showed, it is clear that the locution "*an* institutional culture" is
inadequate to capture the heterogeneous relations among these engineer-
managers and managing-engineers. Both the raw scale of NASA—and its
overlapping, crisscrossing *sub*-cultures—form crucial parts the story.

Faced with dangerous objects, we find ourselves traveling along strange
passages. Every individual's intervention is against and with the behavior of
others. Every *thing* is easily re-described as actions by people; every action
by staff easily can be embodied in an *object*. Dig into a chunk of frozen foam,
carbon-carbon, or telescope you find yourself among the clashing practices of
engineers and managers; dig deeper and you rediscover the broader world of
NASA hierarchies, industry contractors, and governmental organizations from
the bureaucratic to the super-classified. What seems like a simple question of
identifying the boundary of a thing isn't: Where is the perimeter of the Shuttle
accident? Surely it was not just that piece of insulating foam or carbon
section 8. Nor could we draw a bright line around the Orbiter, the launch
tower, the Kennedy Space Center, or the debris field. We would need to
extend the perimeter line around the Johnson and Marshall space centers, up
to the still-under-construction Node 2 of the Space Station, out to the contractors and over to 1600 Pennsylvania Avenue and the Capitol. Here is a debate
that cannot be confined to the eternal struggle over whether machines fail
because individual or groups of components went wrong. It is not even graspable as a classically conceived technological "system." The Columbia disaster
forces us to see double. We see that through the six-inch hole in the leading
edge of the Orbiter's left wing one finds ramified bits of the whole space
program, indeed of an institutionalized stance towards the domestication of
dangerous technology. We may try to view the problem in terms of available
and dysfunctional technology. But soon it becomes clear that what we have
is neither. Instead, we have a technology that reveals our own unstable oscil-
lations. We begin, with technology, as masters of a pliant world, but we soon
re-appear as fearful victims of a threatening apparatus out of control. We are
drawn into detailed flaws and thrown out to a world-covering technology.

* * *

Heidegger asks over and over: "In what way is the self given?"—and
answers not by relying on the philosophical turning back of the self (ego) on
itself, but in our engagement in the world. He puts it this way: "In everyday
terms, we understand ourselves and our existence by way of the activities we

pursue and the things we take care of. We understand ourselves by starting from them because [our being, the *Dasein*] finds itself primarily in things." That is, our understanding of our self does not require an "espionage" by the ego of the ego, there is no contorted observation for an eye-like ego to peer in on itself. Instead, we come to be this way and not that way because of our immediate involvement in the world, "as we have lost our self in things and humans while we exist in the everyday."[18] The self is reflected from its engagement with things, that is the self is constantly being formed and reformed by our *use* of things.

At the moment of technological breakdown we can see the contemporary self in a harsh and somewhat unforgiving light. True, we may confront the situation mouth agape or calculator at the ready. But as the Columbia disaster makes all too clear, these may be the first reactions we point to in an (exaggerated) psychology of the individual—and they do not exhaust the possibilities. We might, instead, look to the social, to the classically defined, homogeneous culture that constrains individuals, grouping them into fixed patterns of meaning, symbol, and value use. (Put on your "engineering hat" or take it off and don your "management hat.") More revealing, more human, more complex, more troubling, I believe, are the actual responses of a Linda Ham or a Sydney Rocha. Their responses were more ambivalent: a message and no hitting of the send key; a comment that old argument for flight readiness was "lousy" and a procedural advance of the schedule nonetheless. "Institutional Culture" in scientific-technological contexts may prove too rigid, too structural, and too simple to help us grasp the stance of a scientific worker faced with a system in collapse.

Immersed in overlapping professional roles and identities, facing a catastrophic failure, we may well find ourselves, not just individually but also corporatively, in a stance not unlike these NASA ground crew. We act and don't act, warn and comply. Global climate change, groundwater draining, species extinctions . . . we know these things and don't know them. We believe contradictory positions, sliding effortlessly between conflicting identities; we gasp at disaster and continue to work. Our world stars us in the midst of powerful effective, and failing technology—here we are, neither as tragic hero, broken hammer in hand, nor as Enlightenment scientist, laboratory at the ready.

Notes

1. This contribution is an excerpt from Galison, *Building Crashing Thinking* (in preparation) about the relation of technology to the historical self. On accident investigations and the nature of explanation see Galison, "An Accident of History," in Peter Galison and Alex Roland, *Atmospheric Flight in the Twentieth Century* (Dordrecht: Kluwer, 2000), 2–43.

2. Hubert Dreyfus, *Being-in-the-World* (Cambridge: MIT Press, 1990), 84.

3. Columbia Accident Investigation Board Report, Vol. I, 43–44.

4. CAIB, part I, 9.

5. CAIB, part II, 97.

6. CAIB, vol I, part I, 25; also vol II, 114–118, on 118.

7. Martin Heidegger, *Being and Time* (New York: Harper Row, Inc., 1962), 102–104.

8. Ibid., 412.

9. CAIB, Vol. I, part I, 138.

10. On Flight Day Six (21 January 2003), Don McCormack, Chief Mission Evaluation Room Manager, spoke with the Debris Assessment Team and reported to the Mission Management. Mission Management was interested in the strike, but their concern was rooted in flight scheduling, not in a foreboding about a catastrophic burn-through of the wing during re-entry. CAIB, Vol I. part II, 147.

11. CAIB, Vol. I part I, 148–49.

12. CAIB, Vol. I, part II, 195.

13. Ibid., 196.

14. Ibid., 153–54, 157.

15. Ibid., 157.

16. Ibid., 200.

17. Ibid., 202.

18. Martin Heidegger, *The Basic Problems of Phenomenology* (Bloomington: Indiana University Press, 1982), 159–160.

Part V

Perceiving Bodies

12

Crittercam: Compounding Eyes in NatureCultures

Donna J. Haraway

"[I]t is in the interactions, in the mutual questioning and interacting of the world and ourselves, in the changing patterns of the lifeworld that things become clear...In this interconnection of embodied being and environing world, what happens in the interface is what is important."

—Don Ihde (*BT* 86–87)

"I am concerned with how aquatic imaging and hydro-optics cause optics and haptics to slide into each other...Fingery eyes literally plunge the viewer into materialized perceptions."

—Eva Shawn Hayward

"Anything can happen when an animal is your cameraman."

—*Crittercam* advertisement

Infoldings and Judge's Chambers

Don Ihde and I share a basic commitment: as Ihde puts it, "Insofar as I use or employ a technology, I am used by and employed by that technology as well . . . We are bodies in technologies." Therefore, technologies are not mediations—that is, something in between us and another bit of the world—rather, technologies are organs, full partners, in what Merleau-Ponty called "infoldings of the flesh." I like the word "infolding" better than "interface" to suggest the dance of world-making encounters. What happens in the folds is what is important. Infoldings of the flesh *are* worldly embodiment. The

175

word makes me see the highly magnified surfaces of cells shown by scanning electron microscopes. In those pictures, we see the high mountains and valleys, entwined organelles and visiting bacteria, and multiform interdigitations of surfaces we can never again imagine as smooth interfaces. Interfaces are made out of interacting grappling devices.

Further, syntactically and materially, worldly embodiment is always a verb, or at least a gerund. Always in formation, embodiment is ongoing, dynamic, situated, and historical. No matter what the chemical score for the dance—carbon, silicon, or something else—the partners in infoldings of the flesh are heterogeneous. That is, the infolding of *others to each other* is what makes up the knots we call beings or, perhaps better, following Bruno Latour, things. Things are material, specific, non-self-identical, and semiotically active. In the realm of the living, critter is another name for thing. Critters are what this essay is about.

Never purely themselves, things are compound; they are made up of combinations of other things coordinated to magnify power, to make something happen, to engage the world, to risk fleshly acts of interpretation. Technologies are always compound. They are composed of diverse agents of interpretation, agents of recording, and agents for directing and multiplying relational action. These agents can be human beings or parts of human beings, other organisms in part or whole, machines of many kinds, or other sorts of entrained things made to work in the technological compound of conjoined forces. Remember also one of the meanings of compound is an enclosure, within which there is a residence or a factory—or, perhaps, a prison or temple. Finally, a compound animal in zoological terminology refers to a composite of individual organisms, an enclosure of zoons, a company of critters infolded into a one. Connected by cittercam's stolon—that is, the circulatory apparatus of its compounded visualizing practices—zoons are technologies, and technologies are zoons.

So, a compound is both a composite and an enclosure. In this chapter I am interested in querying both these aspects of the early twenty-first-century composition made up of marine nonhuman animals, human marine scientists, a series of cameras, a motley of associated equipment, the National Geographic Society, a popular television nature show, its associated Web site, and sober publications in ocean science journals.

At first glance, strapped to the body of critters like green turtles in Shark Bay in Western Australia, humpback whales in the waters off southeast Alaska, and emperor penguins in Antarctica, a nifty miniature video camera is the central protagonist. Since the first overwrought seventeenth-century European discussions about the *camera lucida* and *camera obscura*, within technoculture the camera—the technological eye—seems to be both the central object of philosophical pretension and self-certainty, on the one hand, and of cultural skepticism and the authenticity-destroying powers of the artificial, on the other hand. The camera—that vault or arched chamber, that judge's chamber—only moved from elite Latin to the vulgar, democratic idiom in the nineteenth century as a consequence of a new technology called photography. A camera became a black box with which to register pictures of the outside world in a representational, mentalist semiotic economy, on analogy to the seeing eye in brainy, knowing man, for whom body and mind are suspicious strangers, if also near neighbors in the head. Nonetheless, no matter how gussied up with digitalized optical powers, the camera has never lost its job to function as a judge's chamber, *in camera*, within which the facts of the world—indeed, the critters of the world—are assayed by the standard of the visually convincing and, at least as important, the visually new and exciting.

At second glance, however, crittercam, the up-to-the minute photographic judge's chamber packed by the likes of dugongs and nurse sharks, entrains us, compounds us, within heterogeneous infoldings of the flesh that require a much more interesting dramaturgy than that possible for any self-reporting, central protagonist, no matter how visually well endowed. This second glance will occupy most of this essay, but first we have to plough through some very predictable semiotic road blocks that try to keep us to a cartoonish epistemology about visual self-evidence and the lifeworlds of human-animal-technology compounds.

First Sight

In 2004 the National Geographic Channel launched a series of TV shows called *Crittercam*.[1] The announcements and framing narratives for the show present an easy target for chortling ideology critique with a superiority complex.[2] The animals who carry the attached cameras into their watery worlds are presented as makers of home movies that report on the actual state of things without human interference, or even human presence. As the AAAS online Science Update put it in 1998, we will learn "why one marine scientist started handing out camcorders directly to the sea creatures he wanted to study. The result: Some very unique home movies." Crittercam, we are told in the voice-over of the 2004 television shows, "can reveal hidden lives." The camera is a "National Geographic high-tech scientific video tool worn by species on the edge." The reports come from that sacred-secular place of endangerment, of threatened extinction, where beings are needy of both physical and epistemological rescue. Reports from such edges have special power. "Anything can happen when an animal is your cameraman," declaimed a brochure for the series that I picked up at the Hearst Castle gift shop in February 2004.

National Geographic Channel's Web site whetted the audience's appetite for dis- and re-embodiment through identification: "Meet our camera crews—they're all animals!…Sit back and imagine you are taking a ride on the back of the world's greatest mammal, or seeing life from the point of view of a penguin. The new Crittercam series takes you as close as you can get to the animal world." The camera is both physical "high technology" and immaterial channel to the interior reaches of another. Through the camera's eye glued—literally—to the body of the other, we are promised the full sensory experience of the critters themselves, without the curse of having to remain human: "Sense water rushing past, hear the thunderous roar of the wind and experience the thrill of the hunt…Dive, swim, hunt, and burrow in animal habitats where humans can never go." Addressing children, the February 6, 2004 online Crittercam Chronicles asked, "Have you ever wondered what it would be like to BE a wild animal?…You can experience their life the way they do." Speaking to adults, National Geographic tells us that crittercam is rapidly changing science fiction into reality by "eliminating human presence and allowing us entry into otherwise virtually inaccessible habitats."

Immediate experience of otherness, inhabitation of the other as a new self, sensation, and truth in one package without the pollution of interfering or interacting: these are the lure of *Crittercam*. Reading these promises, I felt like I was back in some versions of early 1970s Women's Liberation Movement consciousness raising groups and film projects, where self-reporting on unmediated experience seemed attainable, especially if women had cameras and turned them on themselves. Become self by seeing self through the eyes of self. The only change is that National Geographic's *Crittercam* promises that self becomes other's self. Now, that's point of view!

Second Sight

The National Geographic Web site tells a little parable about the origin of the crittercams themselves. In 1986, in the waters off Belize a big shark approached a diving biology graduate student and film maker, Greg Marshall, and swam away with three quick strokes of its powerful tail. Marshall looked longingly after the disappearing shark and spotted a small sucker fish, a remora, an unobtrusive witness to sharky reality, clinging to the big predator. "Envying the remora its intimate knowledge of shark life, Marshall conceived a mechanical equivalent: a video camera, sheltered by waterproof housing, attached to a marine animal." Now things are getting interesting; we are no longer inside a cartoon ideology of immediacy and stolen selves. Instead Marshall longed for—and built—*the remora*'s intimate view of shark life.[3] Endowed with second sight, we can now enter the compounded world of infoldings of the flesh because we have left the garden of self-identity and risked the embodied longings and points of view of surrogates and substitutes. At last, we get to grow up—or, in another idiom, get real. Neither cynical nor naïve, we get to become savvy about reality engines.[4] We are, in Ihde's words, bodies in technologies, in fold after fold, with no unwrinkled place to stop.

If we take the remora seriously as the analogue for crittercam, then we have to think about just what the relationships of human beings are to the animals swimming about with sucker cameras on their hides. Clearly, the swimming sharks and loggerhead turtles are not in a "companion animal" relationship to the people, on the model of herding dogs or other critters with whom people have worked out elaborate and more-or-less acknowledged cohabitations.[5] The camera—and the remora—are more about accompanying than companioning, more about "riding along with" rather than "cum panis," that is, "eating bread with." Remoras and crittercams are not messmates to either people or sharks; they are commensals, neither benefactors nor parasites, but devices with their own ends who/which hitch a ride. So, this paper turns out to be about a commensal technological lifeworld. Same housing, not the same dinner. Same compound; distinct ends. Together for a while, welded by vacuum-generating suckers or good glue. Thanks to their remora-like technological surrogates, in spite of narratives to the contrary crittercam's people are decidedly *not* absent from the doings of the animals they are interested in; technologically active humans get to ride along, holding on best they can.

At this point, the science and technology studies scholar starts asking about how the crittercams get designed and built; how that design changes for each of the 40-odd species who have gotten their techno-remoras fitted so far; what things look like from the attached cameras, some of which seem to be at very odd angles; what the devices' technical and social history is over time; how well they hold on; how the joint gets broken and data collected and read; how audiences (scientific and popular, child and adult) learn the needed semiotic skills to watch animal home videos and have any idea what they are seeing; what kinds of data besides the visual can the devices collect; how do those data integrate with data collected in other ways; how do the National Geographic crittercam projects attach themselves to established, ongoing research projects on the animals; are those collegial attachments parasitic, cooperative, or commensal; and whose (animal and human) labor, play, and resources make all this possible. Once one gets beyond the numbing narratives of diving with/as the gods and feeling the divine wind in the abducted face, it turns out that all of these questions can be addressed from the TV shows themselves and their associated Web sites.

It is impossible to watch *Crittercam* shows and not be exhausted and exhilarated by the scenes of athletic, skillful human beings lustily infolding their flesh and their cameras' flesh with the bodies of critter after critter. The sheer *physicality* of all that is crittercam dominates the television screen. How could a mentalistic "camera's eye" narrative ever take hold in the face of such immersion in boats, sea spray, waves, immense whales and slippery dugongs, speed and diving, piloting challenges, team interactions, and the materialities of engineering and using the plethora of cameras and other data-collecting devices that are crittercam? Indeed, the visual structuring of the TV episodes emphasizes bodies, things, parts, substances, sensory experience, timing, emotions—everything that is the thick stuff of crittercam's lifeworld. The cuts are fast; the visual fields littered; the size scales of things and critters in relation to the human body rapidly switched so that the viewer never gets comfortable with the illusion that anything much can be physically taken for granted in relation to oneself. But never is *Crittercam*'s audience allowed to imagine *visually* or *haptically* the absence of physicality and crowded presences, no matter what the voice-over says. The word may not be made flesh here, but everything else is.

Consider first the boats, the people in them, and the animals pursued by them. The TV-show audience learns quickly that each crittercam project requires fast boats; expert pilots; and agile, jocular, well-muscled scientist-divers ready to jump off a moving boat and embrace a large swimming critter who is presumably not especially longing to hug a human. In the episode about green turtles and loggerhead turtles off western Australia, the host Mike Heithaus tells the audience that "chasing after turtles is kind of like being a stunt driver." Of course, first the crews have to find the animals to whom they want to attach their sort of commensal remora. Looking for leatherback turtles off Costa Rica, crittercam people worked with former poachers turned tour guides to find these biggest—and acutely endangered—marine reptiles on earth, who make a living eating jellyfish. Crittercam scientists and entertainment producers also have to consider that some critters can't wear the current generation of videocams safely—too much drag could lead to the animal's early demise. Thus, we learn, imperial turtles will have to wait for more miniaturization for their remora-like accompaniments.

In the waters off Shark Bay where the National Geographic Remote Imaging Team and television crew were looking for dugongs, local Aboriginals worked on the boats as sea trackers. Implicit in that labor practice are the complex metamorphoses of these particular Aboriginal people from hunters of dugongs to their conservationists and comanagers of research permits and ecotourism. The only plant-eating mammals on earth that spend all of their lives in the sea, dugongs are marine relatives of elephants, who shared their last common ancestor about 25 million years ago. TV show host Heithaus, himself a Ph.D. scientist who studies predator-prey interactions among marine animals, with a special taste for sharks, never fails to remind the viewer of the conservation message in all crittercam projects. Such messages include the reassurance that special permits were obtained to harass endangered animals with research boats, such harassment was kept to a minimum and never pursued to the point of exhausting of the animals, and all of the operations are part of saving organisms and habitats of the edge of extinction. That has always been the argument of natural history extravaganzas, whether colonial or postcolonial. It might even be true. It takes believing that, under current conditions, knowledge saves; or at least if not a sufficient condition for enduring and flourishing, finite secular knowledge called science is definitely a necessary condition. Sign me on to that religion.

Not all cameras are attached with a hug. Besides considering whether a barnacle-crusted hide will accept suckers cups, be better off with epoxy glue, or need some other attachment technique, crittercam people have to solve— *physically* solve—how to get the videocam packages onto beings as different from each other as humpback whales, nurse sharks, and Emperor penguins. Take the humpback whales off southeast Alaska. Computer simulations helped Remote Imaging engineers design special suction cups for these critters. We hear on TV that "technology, teamwork, and a federal permit were required to get this close to the whales." Almost a whole research season of many weeks of unsuccessful attempts to attach a camera to a whale were reduced to a couple of minutes of TV time showing one failed attempt after another to plant a camera hanging off a long pole onto a giant moving whale from a boat. Sixteen crittercams (each worth about $10,000) were finally successfully deployed. Getting those cameras back after they came off the whales is an epic tale in itself; witness the 90 miles traveled and seven hours in a helicopter following elusive VHF signals, that lead engineer Mehdi Bakhtiari logged to get one camera back from the sea. Thankfully, the remoras on the whales got an eyeful, but more of that later.

Crittercam units get assembled on the TV screen. Attachment devices (sucker, fin clamp, or adhesive mount), integrated video camcorder and data-logging system, microphone, pressure and temperature gauges, headlights, the tracking system for both cameras that are still attached and cameras after their release from the animals, and the remote release button, all get screen time. However, the technology is put together so quickly in a burst of fast visual cuts from component to component that the viewer is dazed more than informed. Still, it would be impossible to get the visual impression that the camera is a mentalistic, dematerializing black box.

In a more relaxed mood, the interested viewer has easy Internet access to technical descriptions and timelines for the crittercam packages. We learn that the cameras record on Hi-8 or digital video tape; that housings are modified for different conditions, with titanium-encased units equipped with visual intensification capability that can record at 2,000 meters or more; that field reprogrammability of key elements is facilitated by on-site personal computers; that other sorts of data are logged by sensors for salinity, depth, speed, light level, audio, and more; and that data and imaging sampling can be segregated for different time-scheduling demands corresponding to the research questions being asked. We learn about time-sampling schedules and capacities of the data-collecting devices. Three hours of color recording by 2004 is pretty impressive, especially when those hours can be parsed to get, say, 20 seconds every three minutes.

On the Internet we learn about the progressive miniaturization and greater powers of crittercams from the first model in 1987, when outer diameters were 7 inches or more, to outer diameters of 2.5 inches with increased data-collecting capabilities in 2004. Snuck into the Web site narrative is the information that most of crittercam's complex body is proprietary, but was initially built off existing systems from Sony and JVC. Property matters; by definition, it is about access—and crittercam is about access. We are told about Gregg Marshall's early unsuccessful hunt for both funding and scientific credibility and his eventual success with the backing of the National Geographic Society. That took the savvy instincts of a National Geographic television producer, John Bredar. Development grants followed, with the first successful deployments on free-swimming sharks and sea turtles in 1992. Now Gregg Marshall heads up National Geographic's Remote Imaging Program, which is engaged in worldwide scientific collaborations. Finally, we aren't allowed to forget the dreams for the future— some day crittercam packages will tell us about physiological parameters like EKG and stomach temperature. Then, there is the 2-inch camera in the near-term imagination of the engineers. These are home movies with a future twist.

The TV screen itself in *Crttercam* episodes deserves close attention. Especially in scenes featuring crittercam footage, the viewer is invited to adopt the persona of a videogame player by the semiotic design of the screen. Blocking any naturalistic illusions, the screen is literally outlined like a game space; and the shots from the heads of the critters give forward-pointing motion like that of a videogame avatar. We get the point of view that searchers, eaters, and predators might have of their habitat.

But perhaps most striking of all is the small amount of actual crittercam footage amid all the other underwater photography of the animals and their environments that fills the episodes. Actual crittercam footage is, in fact, usually pretty boring and hard to interpret. Cameras might be askew on the head of the critter or pointed down, so that we get lots of muck and lots of water, along with bits of other organisms that make precious little sense without a lot of other visual and narrative work. Or the videocams might be positioned just fine, but nothing much happens during most of the sampling time. Viewer excitement over crittercam imagery is a highly produced effect. Home movies might be the right analogy after all.

The most visually interesting—and by far the largest amount of—underwater photography in the episodes gets no technical discussion at all. We learn nothing about who took this plentiful non-crittercam footage, what their cameras were like, or how the animals and camera people interacted. Reading the credits doesn't help much. On the other hand, the genre of footage is familiar to anyone who watches much marine natural history film and TV. That in no way diminishes its potency. Focused by Eva Shawn Hayward's lens in her analysis of the 1965 film, *The Love Life of the Octopus* (*Les amours de la pieuvre*), by Jean Painlevé and Genevieve Hamon, I experience in *Crittercam*'s "conventional" footage some of the same pleasures of intimacies at surfaces, fast changes in scale, ranges of magnification, and the immersive optics of refraction across varying media.[6] Painlevé and Hamon's films are aesthetically much more self-conscious and skilled than *Crittercam*'s assemblages, but once one learns how the dance of magnifications and scales shapes the join of touch and vision to produce the "fingery eyes" enabled by the biological art-film work, one seeks—and finds—that kind of vision much more widely. In addition, the haptic-visual symphony of *Crittercam* is helped immeasurably by the intense watery physicality of the whole package. For that, I will watch a lot of odd-angle shots of sea bottoms taken from the hides of critters equipped with techno-remoras.

Crittercam episodes promise something else too—scientific knowledge. What gets learned about the animals' lives matters a great deal. Without this dimension, the whole edifice would come tumbling down. Visual-haptic pleasures in part objects and voyeuristic revels in athletic maneuvers in surging waters by vigorous people and other critters would not hold me or, I suspect, much of anyone else. In this matter, I am no cynic, even if my eye is firmly on the culturally located technosocial apparatus of knowledge production. Folks in technoculture need their juicy epistemophilic endorphin surge as much as they need all sorts of sensory engagement. The brain is, after all, a sensory organ.

All the episodes of *Crittercam* emphasize that the Remote Imaging people from National Geographic hooked up with marine zoologists doing long-term research. In each case, the crittercam folks thought their apparatus could help resolve an interesting and ecologically consequential question that was not easily—if at all—addressable by other technological means. The long-term projects provided nearly all the information about habitats, animals, research questions, and grounds for worries about habitat degradation and depleted populations. For example, before crittercam came on the scene, more than 650 sea turtles caught and tagged over five years had yielded information crucial to understanding the shark-turtle, predator-prey ecologies of Shark Bay in western Australia. But the crittercam people offered a means to go with the animals into places humans otherwise could not get to see, things that changed what we know and how we must act as a consequence, if we have learned to care about the well being of the animals and the people in those ecologies.

Probably because I work and play with herding dogs in real life, the humpback whale collaboration is my favorite one to illustrate these points. Fifteen years of research about how humpbacks live and hunt in the waters off southeast Alaska preceded the arrival of crittercam. The scientists knew each whale individually by his or her calls and tail-fluke markings. The biologists had strong ideas about collaborative hunting by the whales as they collected giant mouthfuls of herring. But researchers could not prove that collaborative hunting was indeed what the whales were doing, with each whale taking its place in a choreographed division of labor like that of pairs of expert Border Collies gathering the sheep on the Lancashire countryside. Whale scientists suspected that individually known humpbacks had been knowledgably working together for decades to harvest their fishery, but the limits of humans diving with the giant cetaceans stopped them from getting crucial visual evidence. Getting crushed is no way to secure good data. Crittercam gave questing humans a way to accompany the whales as if the people were merely commensal sucker fishes along for the ride—and the photo op. In Bruno Latour's science and technology studies idiom, the scientists and the natural history entertainment jocks "delegated" parts of their work to the crittercam multitasking package and to the animals who bore the devices into their worlds.[7]

We have already seen how hard it was to get the cameras onto the whale hides and then recover them afterward. The sixteen successfully deployed crittercams from near the end of the season were precious. The scientists wanted to test their hypothesis that certain whales deliberately blew bubbles from below to surround and trap herrings that had been herded into tight congregations by other whales, forming a kind of net around the prey. In unison the whales surged upward with their mouths gaping to collect their teaming dinner. People could see the bubbles from the surface, but they could not see how or where or by whom they were produced. Humans could not really tell if there were a division of labor and social hunting by the whales.

Footage from the first fifteen crittercams did not show what the biologists needed. Suspense on television mounted; and, I like to think, suspense and worry were also rife in the non-TV labs where people were trying to make sense of the confusing, vertigo-inducing pictures the videocams usually brought back. Then, with the sixteenth videotape, shot by a crittercam-bearing member of the pod, came a few clear seconds' view of a whale going below the gathered herring that were surrounded by other whales and blowing a bubble net. Callers, bubble blowers, and herders were all accounted for. Bits of footage put together from several cameras gave a reconstructed, visually supported narrative of the Border Collie-like whales gathering their fish-sheep, penning them flawlessly, and eating them enthusiastically. Good Border Collies don't do that part; but their cousins and ancestors, the socially hunting wolves, do.

There was also a knowledge bonus from crittercam in the humpback whale social hunting story. Bits of whale skin adhered to the detached suction cups once the videocam packages were released, and so DNA analyses could be done of individually known (and named) whales who had taken attributable pictures of each other and their habitat. The result: whales in the social hunting groups were not close kin. The close teamwork over years would have to be explained, ecologically and evolutionarily, in some other way. I know I should suppress my pleasure in this result, but I raise my California wine glass to the extra-familial social worlds of working whale colleagues. My endorphins are at high tide.

Third Sight

So, the compound eyes of the colonial organism called crittercam are full of articulated lenses from many kinds of coordinated, agential zoons—that is, the machinic, human, and animal beings whose historically situated infoldings are the flesh of contemporary naturecultures. Fugal accompaniment is the theme, not humans abstemiously staying away to let the animals tell an unmediated truth by making pictures of themselves. That much seems clear. But there is something missing from my story so far, something we need to be at home in the hermeneutic web that is crittercam. The question I have been deferring is simple to ask and the devil to answer: What is the semiotic agency of the animals in the hermeneutic labor of crittercam?

Are they just objects for the data-gathering subjects called people and (by delegation) machines, just "resistance" or "raw material" to the potency and action of intentional others? Well, it shouldn't take recounting twenty-five years of feminist theory and science studies to get the answer there: no. OK, but are the animals then completely symmetrical actors whose agency and intentionality are just cosmetically morphed variants of the unmarked kind called human? The same twenty-five years of feminist theory and science studies shout the same reply: no.

It's easy to pile on the negatives. In the crittercam assemblage, the hermeneutic agency of the animals is not voluntary, not that of the first-person cameraman, not intentional, not like that of coworking or companion animals (my Border Collie analogy notwithstanding), not a weaker version of the always strong human hermeneutic game. It's harder to specify the positive content of the animals' hermeneutic labor in crittercam's particular naturalcultural encounter.

But it is not impossible to get started. First, there is no way even to think about the issue outside the relentlessly fleshy entanglements of this particular techno-organic world. There is no general answer to the question of animals' agential engagement in meanings, any more than there is a general account of human meaning making. Ihde insisted that in the human-technology herme-neutic relation, the technology adapts to the humans and vice versa. Human bodies and technologies cohabit each other in relation to particular projects or lifeworlds. "Insofar as I use a technology, I am also used by a technology" (*BT* 137).

Surely the same insight applies to the animal-human-technology hermeneutic relation. Hermeneutic potency is a relational matter; it's not about who "has" hermeneutic agency as if it were a nominal substance instead of a verbal infolding. Insofar as I (and my machines) use an animal, I am used by an animal (with its attached machine). I must adapt to the specific animals even as I work for years learning how to induce them to adapt to me and my artifacts in particular kinds of knowledge projects. Specific sorts of animals in specific ecologies and histories make me adapt to them even as their life doings become the meaning-making generator of my work. If those animals are wearing something of my making, our mutual but nonidentical co-adaptation will be different. The animals, humans, and machines are all enmeshed in hermeneutic labor (and play) by the material-semiotic requirements of getting on together in specific lifeworlds. They touch; therefore they are.

That's the kind of insight that makes us know that we have epistemo-logical-ethical obligations to the animals. Specifically, we have to learn who they are in all their nonunitary otherness in order to have a conversation on the basis of carefully constructed, multisensory, compounded languages. The animals make demands on the humans and their technologies to pre-cisely the same degree that the humans make demands on the animals. Otherwise, the cameras fall off and other bad things happen to waste everybody's time and resources. That part is "symmetrical," but the contents of the demands are not symmetrical at all. That asymmetry matters a great deal. Nothing is passive to the action of another, but all the infoldings can only occur in the fleshy detail of situated, material-semiotic beings. The privilege of people accompanying animals depends on getting these asym-metrical relationships right (*CT* 131–144).[8] Compound eyes use different refractive indices, different materials, different fluids, to get something in focus. There is no better place to learn such things than the immersive depths of earth's oceans.

Notes

1. Text from a 2004 brochure announcing the National Geographic Society's television series made up of thirteen half-hour episodes, *Crittercam*. Twelve featured ocean-going critters; and one tied its cameras to African lions, fruit of a three-year effort to develop crittercams for land-based studies as well as marine excursions. In this essay, I will not discuss the interesting land crittercams, attached so far, predictably, to lions, tigers, and bears. Crittercam research and the TV series are partially funded by the National Science Foundation, called on screen, "America's investment in the future." The promissory, futuristic, frontier orientations of the show are never out of frame on *Crittercam*; that is the nature of life in the era of Biocapital.

Beginning with National Geographic *Explorer* on TBS in 1993, as well as "Great White Shark" in 1995 on NBC, crittercam images had been seen on TV before the 2004 series.

2. Unless otherwise stated, quotations and descriptions throughout this paper come from various parts of www.nationalgeographic.com/crittercam.

3. Adapted from: http://animaldiversity.ummz.umich.edu/site/accounts/information/Remora_remora.html, the technical specifications for a remora are:

Remora remora is a short, thickset sucking fish with 28–37 long slender gillrakers, 21–27 dorsal fin rays, 20–24 anal fin rays, and 25–32 pectoral fin rays. The Remora has no swim bladder and uses a sucking disc on the top of its head to obtain rides from other animals such as large sharks and sea turtles. The Remora grows to about 18 inches. Near nothing is known about the Remora's breeding habits or larval development. The Remora is most often found offshore in the warmer parts of all oceans attached to sharks and other marine fishes and mammals. The Remora are considered to have a commensal relationship with their host, since they do not hurt the host and are just along for the ride. The Remora is of unique value to humans. The fish itself is not generally eaten, but is instead used as a means of catching large fish and sea turtles. Fishermen in countries around the world use them by attaching a line to their tails and then releasing them. The Remora will then swim off and attach itself to a large fish or turtle, which can then be pulled in by a careful fisherman. The Remora is not held in high esteem as a food fish, although the Australian aborigines are said to eat them after using them on fishing trips. On the other hand, aborigines from the West Indies never ate their "hunting fish" and instead sang songs of praise and reverence to them. The ancient Greeks and Romans had written widely about Remoras and had ascribed to them many magical powers such as the ability to cause an abortion if handled in a certain way. Shamans in Madagascar to this day attach portions of the Remora's suction disk to the necks of wives to assure faithfulness in their husbands' absence.

Following the remoras, Greg Marshall was in good company.

4. I take the term "reality engines" from Julian Blecker, *The Reality Effect of Technoscience* (University of California at Santa Cruz: PhD dissertation, 2004). Bleeker's dissertation is on computer graphics engineering and semiotics and the labor

it takes to build and sustain specific material realities. In this essay, I use a compound optical device, made up of lenses from a colleague, Don Ihde, and two of my graduate students from different cohorts, Julian Bleecker and Eva Shawn Hayward.

5. Donna Haraway, *The Companion Species Manifesto: Dogs, People and Significant Otherness* (Chicago: Prickly Paradigm Press, 2003).

6. Eva Shawn Hayward, "Inhabited Light: Refracting The Love Life of the Octopus," in *Envisioning Invertebrates: Immersion, Inhabitation, and Intimacy as Modes of Encounter in Marine TechnoArt* (Qualifying Essay, History of Consciousness Department, University of California at Santa Cruz, December 2003).

7. For the results of the crittercam team-whale biologist collaboration, see Fred Sharpe, Michael Heithaus, Lawrence Dill, Birgit Buhleier, Gregory Marshall, and Pieter Folkiens, "Variability in Foraging Tactics and Estimated Prey Intake by Socially Foraging Humpback Whales in Chatham Strait, Alaska," 15th Biennial Conference on the Biology of Marine Mammals: Greensboro. North Carolina, 2003.

8. As Ihde puts it, "an asymmetrical but post-phenomenological *relativity* gets its 'ontology' from the *interrelationship of human and non-human*" (*CT* 143).

13

Active and Passive Bodies: Don Ihde's Phenomenology of the Body

Andrew Feenberg

Don Ihde's *Bodies in Technology* explores the technical entanglements of the human body from a phenomenological standpoint. The essays in this book cover a wide range of topics, from virtual reality to growing up male in America.

Ihde's account of the body seems to me one-sided. Perhaps it is his orientation toward scientific perception and technical action that limits his focus. He is interested in the similarities and differences between the extension of the senses by scientific instrumentation, computer simulations, and virtual reality. This tilts the weight of his discussion toward activity, but activity is only one dimension of the body. I will introduce the complementary passive dimension in what follows. I find this dimension missing on the whole from Ihde's account, yet it is the essential correlate of the activities he analyzes insofar as we are finite beings in the world.

Let me begin by remarking on Ihde's distinction between what he calls "body one," the sensory body, and "body two," the body informed and shaped by culture. I like this multiplication of bodies. It corresponds to a phenomenological insight into the specificity of our lived experience. To body one and two I would like to add body three and four, which I will call the "dependent body" and the "extended body."

I discovered the dependent body in the course of coaching my son's elementary school soccer team. We had a very energetic but undisciplined team member named Gabriel who could not seem to learn the rules and codes of children's soccer. But he did understand one profound fact about the game: once when a team member was injured on the field, Gabriel shouted "parents!" at the top of his lungs and we all rushed over to help the fallen child.

189

Afterward I realized that Gabriel was giving us the body of this child: injured children's bodies belong to parents. All children know this. Several years later, long after Gabriel had left the team, he showed up one day at my doorstep with three comrades, one of whom had broken his collar bone in a fall from his bike. Gabriel handed over his friend Jose to me for care and I spent the rest of the afternoon finding Jose's parents and getting him fixed up at the local hospital.

Reflecting on these experiences I realized that we live our body not only as actors in the world, but also as beings who invite action on our bodies by others. This is most obvious in medical situations. We bring our body to the doctor to be poked at and examined. We, like little Gabriel, know to whom our pains belongs. Inside our dependent body, we attend to unexpected sensations we have solicited. Our time horizon shrinks as we no longer control or plan the next sensation, yet we remain exquisitely alert. This is a peculiar passivity since we have set the stage for our own inaction and can at any moment reverse the situation and take control again. In a modern context, it is also a highly technologized experience: we are operated on by a whole panoply of devices. From the user of tools we become the object of tools.

The phenomenological point is of course not just this objective reversal of perspective, visible to third parties, but the deeper import of our lived first-person experience of our own instrumentalized status. That this condition cannot be analyzed in instrumental terms should be obvious from its regressive quality: the dependent body belongs to our childhood, returning in the present in this peculiar voluntary form. A phenomenology of the patient experience would be needed to work out the implications of the dependent body in medicine.

The dependent body also makes its appearance in sexual behavior. Sartre and Merleau-Ponty have brilliantly analyzed this phenomenon.[1] The body as "*chair*" or "flesh" becomes the immediate form of consciousness, which hovers on the surface of the skin soaking up pleasurable sensations rather than watching as spectator from out of a situated identity in the world. Sartre rejects the notion that sex can be explained in terms of instincts or needs. Phenomenologically considered it is a relation between subjectivized bodies. He begins his analysis with the caress, which he treats as an incarnation of consciousness in the body of the subject attempting to achieve a parallel incarnation in the other. Sex is the construction of the dependent body of this other. Ritualized forms of passivity, which Sartre analyzes under the heading of masochism, carry the organization of subjective experience around the dependent body to the limit where consciousness dissolves in sensation and the person becomes a thing in the world of the other.

As in the medical example, the interesting question for phenomenology is the lived experience of being the object of action. This is quite different from the third personal relation to the body of the other, available to the physician in the medical situation or to the active sexual partner.

The example of sex appears at first sight to concern bodies stripped bare not only of clothes, but also of any relation at all to technology. Our normal technological involvements come under the phenomenological heading of situations, that is, contexts of use in which the subject is clearly distinguished from its instrumentalities. In the medical case, the subject situates itself as object of the technology of the other, and so reverses but also confirms this pattern. None of this applies in the phenomenological description of sex. Perhaps here we actually have the purified "humans" Latour decries in modernism. However, the apparent mutual exclusion of technology and sex is illusory. Consider the role of contraception in freeing the body from biology and history for the brief moment of the sexual encounter, which phenomenology takes as its essence. In the absence of contraceptive technology, descriptions like Sartre's are obviously partial and flawed.

I want to turn now to another more complex corporal phenomenon, which I will call the extended body. Like the dependent body, this is a form of bodily experience, which is characterized by a specific passivity. However, in this case the body uses instruments rather than being their object. I am not, however, concerned with the aspect of use but rather with its consequences for bodily objectivity and the subject's awareness of those consequences.

Let me begin by reflecting on one of Ihde's own examples, drawn from Merleau-Ponty. Ihde notes that the lived body is not identical with the physical object called the body. "Such a body experience is one that is not simply coextensive with a body outline or one's skin. The intentionality of bodily action goes beyond one's bodily limits . . . " (BT 6). Merleau-Ponty describes the blind man's cane as such an extension of the body. Indeed, the blind man senses the world through the cane and so is not directly conscious of the cane as such but rather of what it touches. The cane is a medium of perception not so different from eyeglasses in that respect. Merleau-Ponty thus describes it not as an instrument used by the blind man but as an extended sense organ: "To get used to a hat, a car or a stick is to be transplanted into them, or conversely, to incorporate them into the bulk of our own body. Habit expresses our power of dilating our being in the world . . . "[2]

However, the cane does more than sense the world; it also reveals the blind man as blind. His body is extended not only in the active dimension on which Ihde and Merleau-Ponty focus but also in the passive dimension of its own objectivity. Those around him recognize his blindness and are generally helpful. The blind man knows this is happening and has a nonspecific awareness of the helpfulness of those who perceive him as blind because of his cane.

Again, eyeglasses provide a more familiar example. In wearing them, I not only see better, but am seen as a wearer of eyeglasses, an experience that

I found very troublesome as a child attempting to keep up with the others in sports. We can clarify this with reference to Sartre's analysis of the three dimensions of the body, the body-subject, the body-object for the other, and the body-object for the other as perceived by the self. As a ten-year-old eyeglass wearer, I saw clearly as subject. But I also appeared as an object to others, as a particular kind of object, a boy handicapped by wearing glasses. As body-object for others, I lived my body as mine in this perceived deficient condition. I was aware of my added fragility—eyeglasses fall off in rough play—and the connotations of eyeglasses in connection to "braininess" and presumed incompetence at sports. Living this eyeglass-bound body I became cautious and hesitant in most sporting activities. Fortunately, we had a short soccer season, a few weeks out of the year, during which I could feel confident that the ball was likely to stay on the ground and the other players at a safe distance.

The extended body, then, is not only the body that acts through a technical mediation, but also a body that signifies itself through that mediation. I want to pursue this analysis further in relation to computer usage, a domain that is all too often analyzed, by Ihde too, in terms of the concept of disembodiment. This is a category that arises naturally from the contrast between what one can and cannot do in real and virtual bodies. But disembodiment does not adequately describe online self-presentation. I want to shift the focus from his example of virtual reality games to a far more familiar experience with computers that reveals another side of the extended body.

I have been engaged in online communication both personally and professionally since the early 1980s and have had plenty of occasions to observe the highly personal and engaging dynamics of written expression online. I am astonished that so many of my colleagues fail to recognize this aspect of online communication and criticize it as impersonal and atomizing. This observation is relevant in particular to the key notion of disembodiment. Am I disembodied in sending e-mail or participating in an online chat or forum? Certainly, in one sense I am. My physical body is not present to my interlocutors. From this fact, Hubert Dreyfus, among others, has drawn all sorts of drastic conclusions. Without bodily involvement, Dreyfus has argued, there can be no commitment and risk. Moral engagement is impossible under these tenuous circumstances. Human relations are abridged and trivialized. And so on.[3]

Such analyses are commonplace now and form a whole counter-literature to Internet hype. As such they are perhaps useful, but I would like to get away from the polemics and consider the experience of online presence phenomenologically. From that angle the picture looks quite different from both the critique and the hype.

Let us recall once again Sartre's analysis of the body for the other. Sartre notes that our objectivity before the gaze of the other extends beyond our skin out into the world of things by which our presence is signified. We are objects of the one from whom we are hiding in the cracking of a branch underfoot.[4] Our body extends to the glow of the cigarette that gives our presence away, or, to give a contemporary example, the ringing of the cell phone that embarrasses us in the middle of a lecture. This is the extended body in its simplest form.

On the Internet we experience our self as exposed to the gaze just as surely as the hiding subjects in Sartre's examples. Like them our physical body is invisible. But also, like them, our presence is signaled and our objectivity established through signs. In this case the signs are intentional and complex and consist in written messages.

Is this merely a metaphor? From the standpoint of objectivistic thought there can only be a figurative equivalence between our physical body and the extended body of our written expression. But, phenomenologically considered, the point is not the objective thinghood of our physical self but what we live in the first person as our self in situation. As Ihde notes, mediated human contact is always measured against full bodily copresence; however, the consequence of this situation is not simply a feeling of loss but evokes compensatory efforts to fill in the gaps, to enrich the "monosensory dimension" made available technically (*BT* 8). Ihde does not follow up this suggestion because he turns to what he concludes are fruitless attempts to overcome the reductive limitations of mediation through virtual reality. But there is much more to be said about the compensatory moves in relation to online writing.

Language is a way in which we objectify ourselves, and where this form of objectivity is our entire social being—as in the case of online expression— it calls forth extraordinary compensatory efforts. Online writing is a conscious self-presentation. It constitutes what Ihde calls "an editing or fashion style of existence" (*BT* 84). We could be said to "wear" language online in something like the sense in which we wear clothes in everyday life. It is a form of virtual embodiment as surely as what the fancy video goggles display. Others can often identify us from a few lines of our writing. We identify with it too as our extended bodily presence, in this case a strange kind of textual cyborg. Here Ihde's claim that "our bodies have an amazing plasticity and polymorphism" is confirmed (*BT* 138).

But like all forms of self-presentation, our writing reveals more than we intended and we are caught out by our interlocutors. Our role in an exchange or group is established before we know it by the expressions we use and such basic facts about our communications as their length and style. Our language shows us as neat or sloppy, formal or informal; we reveal our mood by our linguistic gestures as happy or sad, confident or timid. The fact that we can be proud or embarrassed, open or secretive, friendly or distant, all point to the complexity of this mode of technical mediation.

The role of written language can be analyzed in terms of Ihde's phenomenology of technology, specifically, his distinction between "embodiment"

relations and "hermeneutic" relations to the technical mediation of experience
(*TL 89*). In the embodiment relation, our experience is organized through a
technical mediation and our identity merges with it, as in the example of
eyeglasses. Self-expression through embodiment is a familiar experience from
speaking on the telephone. We do not feel the telephone to be an external
tool; it becomes an extension of ourselves as we talk through it to our interlocutor. For those who frequently use online communication, the same relationship prevails to the written means available in that technical environment.
However, Ihde does not develop the reciprocal of this embodiment relation
for such cases of mediated self-expression. Maria Bakardjieva points out that
on the other end of these embodiment relations, someone receives a message
that must be decoded in what Ihde calls a "hermeneutic" relation to technology.[5] In this relation the interpreted message stands in for the world, is in
effect a world. In the case of mediated communication, a person and the
social context of their presence is delivered in the message.

These observations bear on a controversial issue on which I have been
doing research for the last several years, the nature of online community. Is
an online community possible at all? There is a school of thought that argues
that community requires bodily copresence: by definition then, online community is a contradiction in terms. But I contend that community is a subjec-
tively constructed phenomenon. It exists not because we are physically present
to each other but because of the way we live our mutual connection, whatever
it may be. To confuse that imaginative engagement with the other, with simple
physical presence is to completely abandon phenomenology for a crude ob-
jectivism. As Gabriel Marcel pointed out, I am far more fully "with" certain
persons who are thousands of miles away than with the random individual
sitting next to me in the subway. Community needs to be interpreted from the
inside out, not as a geographical fact.

In that sense, the copresence of extended bodies, constructed out of language in the online world, is a potential basis of community just as much as
physical presence. Naturally, this will be a different type of community with
different problems and potentials. Ihde's analyses show the primacy of the
"real" body with respect to virtual extensions. However, he is not dismissive of
these extensions and rejects a reductionism that would sharply divide the human from the nonhuman, the real from the virtual. Here we are in agreement.
I too intend to occupy his "middle ground" between implausible claims of total
symmetry and a romantic refusal of all mediation (*BT* 96ff). Thus, admitting
various limitations of online community, I see no reason of principle to believe
that the basic moral qualities of commitment, respect, and solidarity we expect
in a face-to-face community cannot be achieved there too.[6]

Naturally, to say these qualities *can* be achieved is not to say that they
will be achieved because of the nature of the technology involved. We are

way beyond that sort of determinism, although it continually rears its ugly head in popular discussions of the Internet. On the contrary, this phenomenological interpretation of online community leads to a consideration of the variety of technical mediations that either obstruct it or make it possible. The boundaries and affordances of online community depend on such technical facts as software design. A community that is open to the world has different characteristics from one that is closed by a password provided only to qualified individuals. A community that can easily find traces of its own past interactions is different from one in which the past is erased as it advances forward in time. A community whose members are aware of each others' passive presence is different from one in which only active contributors are known to be present. Such technical aspects of online community shape the extended body of its members. Different types of software such as listservs, newsgroups, and Web-based forums offer a variety of possible structures, some more favorable to community building than others.

As Ihde argues, "the very structure of technologies is multistable, with respect to uses, to cultural embeddedness, and to politics as well. Multistability is not the same as neutrality. Within multistability there lie *trajectories*, not just any trajectory, but partially determined trajectories" (*BT* 106). The philosopher of technology can attempt to understand these trajectories in their human significance and to adapt technical design to ethical norms. This process is inevitably political.[7]

This discussion of extended bodies appears to take us away from Ihde's concerns. But in fact we have never left the subject of his book, "bodies in technology." I have attempted here to develop his argument in a way he may find complementary to his own concerns, moving from the active side of the subject to its passive dimension. Both aspects of subjectivity are technically mediated today. A full picture of the bodily subject must take into account not only the classic concerns of philosophy with the perceiving and acting subject set in a natural environment, but the social subject in a technically mediated world. As such we are perceiving and perceived, acting and acted upon in complex and unexpected ways that deserve the attention of philosophers.

Notes

1. Jean-Paul Sartre, *Being and Nothingness*, trans. H. Barnes (New York: Washington Square Press, 1966), part 3, chap. 2–3. Maurice Merleau-Ponty, *Phenomenology of Perception*, trans. C. Smith (London and Henley: Routledge & Kegan Paul, 1962), part 1, chap. 5.

2. Merleau-Ponty, *Phenomenology of Perception*, 143.

3. Hubert Dreyfus, *On the Internet* (London and New York: Routledge, 2001).

4. Sartre, *Being and Nothingness*, 346.

5. Maria Bakardjieva, "Virtual Togetherness: An Everyday Life Perspective," in *Community in the Digital Age: Philosophy and Practice*, eds. Andrew Feenberg and Darin Barney (Lanham: Rowman & Littlefield, 2004).

6. For a survey of the different positions in the debate on online community, and contributions from different standpoints, see Ibid.

7. Ihde advocates that philosophers should get involved in technical decisions and design. I have done precisely this in recognition of the significance of software for online community and more specifically for online education. For information on my software project, see www.textweaver.org.

14

Body and Machines

Donn Welton

Several of the most important discoveries of the German phenomenologist Edmund Husserl took place not in front of him but, so to speak, behind his back. In pursuing his account of the "teleological" structures of logical reason and the "archaeological" structures of transcendental, phenomenological method, he would often pause, sometimes for hundreds of pages, and write materials that illustrated or contributed to his larger account, but were not his primary focus. His analysis of passive synthesis, which he excluded from his systematic account of "logical reason" in *Formal and Transcendental Logic* (1929), is one example of this.[1] But perhaps the most important of his oblique discoveries, first developed in *Ideas II* (composed around 1912), was his account of the body.[2] In contrast to the treatment of the body in the tradition of Modern Philosophy since Hobbes and Descartes, Husserl argues for a distinction between *Körper* and *Leib*, between physical body and lived body.

The topic that I will be addressing in this paper is the relationship between the body and machines. But the distinction that Husserl introduced means that the topic is more complicated than we first thought. We must first sort out what we mean by body and then see if the way we are thinking of it gives us insight into how the body is involved with machines. Indeed, the term machines needs to be qualified as well, for I will not follow Don Ihde's unique trajectory of dealing with technologies in a broad sense but only attend to a certain set of machines that are directly used or incorporated into the body. One could, therefore, think of this essay as complementing Ihde's seminal work on technology. While he has studied the way in which perception may be "materially extended" through devices or artifacts that are worn or used by embodied subjects, he has yet to address the direct implanting of devices into the neuro-physical body. Toward the end of this essay we will look at two scenarios in which machines or devices not only extend but also transform the very material structure of the body.

***

It would require yet another paper to do justice to Husserl's provocative but laconic account of the difference between physical and lived body. Let me instead give a general description of the somewhat superficial way this contrast is often understood and suggest several problems with it, leaving aside the question as to whether my criticisms do justice to the full scope of Husserl's analysis.

The lived body is often analyzed as the body experienced "from the inside," while the physical body is treated as the body experienced "from the outside." This difference is then justified by a series of contrasts, some receiving more attention than others.

The first appeal is to two different kinds of sensations: kinaesthetic sensations, which convey information about the posture and position of the body, and "presentational sensations," which form the content of perceptual acts. Placing them in relation to each other, the kinaestheses account for our awareness of the movements of the body that attend acts of perception, while acts of perception proper employ a different type of sensation that contributes to the way in which an object is presented to consciousness. This difference in types of sensations was supported by a second difference in types of perceptions. In an effort to secure the strong contrast between physical body and lived body, the physical body is understood as what is experienced through "external" perception, while the lived body is taken as that same body but given in "internal" perception. As a consequence, *Körper* was characterized as "object" body while *Leib* was understood as "subject" body. In some existentialist versions this led to the identity of the ego and the body: I am my body.

But let me suggest difficulties in using phenomenal differences in types of sensations or types of perceptions as the sufficient criterion for the characterization of lived-body:

1. Defining the contrast between physical and lived-body by means of a classification of different types of sensations is thoroughly phenomenological in the sense that it appeals to different categories of experience. But it is thoroughly unphenomenological in the sense that it must assume that sensations are freestanding and internally differentiated entities that can be identified and brought under a description apart from an analysis of the act or actions in which they are involved. Let me briefly explain:

My first criticism does apply to Husserl's first and, I would argue, provisional account of sensations. In *Ideas I*[3] he understood sensations as "hyletic" contents that are then "animated" by an act of perception that gives these contents a determinate form (sense) and function. As a result of the perceptual act "animating" the data of sensation, the object is experienced as having certain visual, tactile, etc. features.[4] Even if this model works for "presentational" content, it is clear that kinesthetic sensations are not organized by a sense nor are they animated by acts since they do not present anything. Rather than accounting for the qualities of presented objects, these sensations are entirely noetic and account for the awareness we have of the act or the action itself. If so, the burden of the difference, then, would have to be borne by differences internal to the contents themselves, which itself assumes that the kinaestheses have a determinacy "before" being "animated" by the act. But this is precisely what they cannot have according to the form-content account. The use of an internal difference between kinaesthetic and presentational sensations seems to be more of a remnant of the empirical tradition than a phenomenological finding.

What I am suggesting, in this first criticism, is that even if there are different sensations in play—and I will agree that there are—they are not themselves internally differentiated, free standing complexes that can be studied "before" the act or action in which they are involved. As a consequence they cannot offer a sufficient criterion or explanation for the contrast between physical and lived body.

2. Any attempt to resolve these difficulties by moving beyond sensations to perception and the contrast between internal and external perception gets us no further. Husserl repeatedly argued that in the case of internal perception, there is no difference between act and object. In this domain "to be" (*esse*) is "to be perceived" (*percipi*). We might be able to understand how this works in the case of pain, for the perception of pain just is the pain itself that exists. But how does this criterion apply to kinaesthetic awareness? Is there an identity between the perception of the movement and the movement itself, that is; is having the internal perception of the movement the same as the performance of the movement? Obviously not, for any perceptions that would accompany the movement of the fingers do not themselves account for the pattern of that movement but only our awareness of that pattern.

Indeed, the very notion of consciousness of the body is troubling. We can understand how this "of" works in the case of physical bodies. They are intentional objects toward which conscious acts are directed and there is never confusion between the act and the object that is apprehended. But how does it work in the case of the lived-body? Is it also an object, but now one seen from the inside rather than the outside? Who, then, is doing the seeing? And how can such perceptions account for the set of gestures or movements that they are said to control? This leads to a third criticism.

3. The first two points challenge the thesis that a characterization of the lived body can be derived from a classification of types of sensations and perceptions. And if this is true, then it also indirectly challenges the thesis that such a path is capable of accounting for how the body contributes to intentional acts. But there may be a more serious issue. Even if we

grant that such sensations and perceptions give us an awareness of the body as the "organ of perception," can it also do justice to the body as the organ of actions?[5]

Husserl is careful to keep the kinaestheses tied to the posture and movement of the body and to even argue that one should understand the lived body in terms of "I can," of its ability to move, as when we reach for or walk around an object that we are observing. Unlike Plato in the Phaedrus, self-movement is not the sign of the presence of the soul but of the body as lived. But is the account of movements also an account of actions? Are actions just movements plus intentional acts? Until one sorts out the relationship between act and actions, we will not be able to say how the contrast between presentational and kinaesthetic sensations and then between different kinds of perceptions are to be situated in an account of the body.[6]

4. There is yet a fourth difficulty, which brings us to the topic of this lecture: how does one understand not just cases when we as embodied beings use machines but cases when machines become literally part of the body, when they are incorporated into my body and, perhaps, my consciousness. Can they be understood as part of the lived-body? But how can they since they lack sensations and are very physical in nature?

Our critical comments suggest, then, that an introspective inventory of types of experiences will not get us very far in our efforts to characterize the body phenomenologically. Different types of experiences might provide us with a point of access to the body as lived. In fact, Husserl was truly revolutionary in his emphasis upon touch as opposed to vision as the primary modality in and through which the lived-body is manifest.[7] But this starting point is not sufficient to carry the analysis. So where are we to turn? And how are we to think of the notion of lived-body phenomenologically yet beyond the appeal to internal experience? And can we develop a typology of various body-machine relations?

* * *

The first decisive advance in our effort to provide an adequate characterization of the notion of lived-body is found in the work of Merleau-Ponty. He understands the lived-body in terms of what he calls the body schema (*schema corporel*, not "body image" as the English translation has it),[8] a term that he took over from the British neurologist Henry Head but then modified appropriately.[9] Merleau-Ponty places the body schema within the structure of what he calls body intentionality, a notion that immediately sends the concept of consciousness into a dimension from which the tradition of Modern Philosophy had excluded it. The body schema consists of countless subschemata that account for the typical postures and movements of the body. They function on the basis of internal or "introceptive" sensations, what both Husserl and Merleau-Ponty called "kinaestheses" and what current researchers label "proprioception." The kinaestheses give us an awareness, sometimes explicit and sometimes implicit, of the positions of the limbs or the movements of various parts of the body. For Merleau-Ponty it is not just perceptual mechanisms or perceptual schemata, as suggested by *Gestalt* psychology, but also the body's motility, its powers, and its desires that contribute to the significance (*sens, Sinn*) that things have. At the outset of our analysis, then, it is important not to confuse body schemata with the kinaestheses that accompany them, and then both of them with perceptual schemata, which form, as Husserl would say, the "noematic" side of acts of (external) perception.

In Merleau-Ponty's account the body schema itself is not an object expressly known but only "tacitly understood."[10] It functions not as object of consciousness because it forms the basis of or the hidden "background" behind all explicit intentional acts.[11] To be more specific, the awareness that attends the body as it engages the world is not a "positional consciousness" and thus does not involve an explicit "representation" or "presentation" (*Vorstellung*) of the body.[12] Thus it is not a perception of the body. This contrast, central to Merleau-Ponty's analysis, has been codified and developed recently in the work of Gallagher, Cole, and Meltzoff, who argue for a distinction between "body schema" and "body image." While the two normally slide into each other and are part of a single whole at the level of our actions and our routine body-awareness, there is good reason to distinguish them conceptually.

Body images arise from an explicit perception of the body or, more generally, from our conceptions of the body and our feelings about our body. They are representations that arise when the body is taken as an object, for example, when I look at my body in a mirror or gaze at the body of others, or when I describe the body that I see in the language of my culture, or when I assume a certain emotional attitude toward my body.[13] By contrast, body schemata are not representations at all and serious errors arise when one uses the terms "body image" and "body schema" interchangeably. Body schemata consists of three elements:[14]

a. *Motor Programs.* The lived-body is an integrated system of motor capabilities; schemata are the programs or, better, different sets of processes that enable the movements and thereby the actions of the body. They are not merely codifications or products of actions that have taken place in the past but, rather, actions depend upon them for their style and their direction. They should not be thought of simply as patterns but also as conditions of action and, at another level of description, as based in our neuro-physiology. They do not consist of the "awareness" that we have of parts of the body but rather produce an "active integration" of the parts in view of a "value" established by the organism as a whole.[15] Bodily schemata, then, are systems of possible movement. As Merleau-Ponty, echoing Husserl, puts it, "consciousness is in the first place not a matter of 'I think that' but 'I can'."[16]

b. *Proprioception.* When we speak of the lived-body we are describing not so much the body as "seen from the inside" but the fact that its schemata functions on the basis of proprioceptive stimulation coming from the body itself. These sensations arise from kinetic, muscular, articular, and cutaneous sources.[17] Even when proprioceptive information does not cross the threshold of conscious awareness, the tacit presence of our body as well as the functioning of body schemata is entirely dependent upon it.

c. *Orientational Perceptions.* The ability to respond to cues from the horizon—from the shape of the room in which we are situated or from the movement of the boat in which we are standing, for example—also belong to body schemata.[18] These perceptions account not for the position of things in space but for the place and orientation of the body.

The difference between body image and body schema that I have just sketched leads to the pressing question as to what allows this conceptual distinction to be understood as a phenomenological distinction.

If it were Husserl's phenomenological reflections that taught us to trace the structures of "normal" or "unhindered" bodily life, it was Merleau-Ponty who suggested that our best path to an account of normality is through an analysis of abnormality. Perhaps it is not unitary but "broken" experience that gives us our richest clues to the structure of the body in general and to the relationship between body image and schema in particular. Merleau-Ponty's study of the patient Schneider was decisive for him but an even stronger case comes by looking at Gallagher and Cole's patient I.W.

As a result of a devastating illness in which large nerve fibers were destroyed, Ian has no proprioception and no sense of touch below the neck.[19] Proprioception, as we have seen, is the term used to describe sensations that come from within the body, from various joints and muscles and that produce or monitor posture and the movement of the limbs. Before his illness, which occurred at the age of 19, he was a mature, able-bodied male capable of normal movements. But after his illness and the loss of all proprioceptive and tactile information, he no longer had control of his limbs and was not even capable of sitting upright in bed. Unfortunately, the neurological damage was irreversible. During the course of his rehabilitation, however, he discovered that by visually looking at a limb he was able to gain control over it. As he concentrated on his arm, he could raise it and, eventually, feed himself. By keeping his legs in view, he relearned how to place one foot in front of another and to walk. But if he failed to concentrate or if the lights were turned out and the room become dark, he would fall to the ground. By looking at his hand he was able to pick up an egg but because of the lack of any tactile feedback, it took him some time before he could do so without crushing it.

Perhaps one of the most interesting skills he relearned was driving a car. Of course, he would not be able to drive if he sat in a standard automobile, for his legs would be invisible. In his car the controls are mounted in front of him on the steering wheel, where he can see them while also looking at the road. In fact, he very much enjoys driving, though getting out of the car to fill the gas tank is another matter.

Endless amounts of ink have been spent criticizing the Cartesian view of the relationship between mind and body but in the case of I.W. we have the body as an object that performs intentional action only because its movements are caused by the mind. The body is a natural object for Ian, and each of its movements is the result of an explicit intention involving direct awareness. He is the perfect Cartesian subject, a living demonstration of how our mind would be related to our body if Descartes' account were true.

Ian is a rare case in which bodily movements are being governed entirely by body images and it stands in striking contrast to Merleau-Ponty's own favorite case of Schneider, who suffered damage to the brain during the First World War. Schneider's body schemata functioned without hesitation but he lacked body images: he could blow his nose into a handkerchief but was incapable of pointing to the nose when asked to do so for no reason.[20] These cases, at opposite limits of the lived-body, allow us to do what might otherwise be impossible, namely, to pull apart body schema and body image.

* * *

The distinction between body schema and body image puts us in the position to speak about the first way that machines or tools are related to the body. Tools allow the body to become enlarged or extended. If we think of the body in terms of body image, then, of course, the body is one thing and the tool yet another. Talk of extension could only be metaphorical. But, in fact, learning to use a tool involves a transformation in which a tool that is "outside" the body becomes integrated into the body schema.

Learning to use a tool usually begins with visualizing how the tool is related to the body and thus involves body images. One becomes an apprentice and studies the correct way to hold the bat or ride a motorcycle. But the goal of the process is to assimilate the tool or the machine into the repertoire of the body. Once it becomes absorbed into a body schema, the schema becomes extended in new ways and, as a consequence, our perceptual relationship to the world also changes. The baseball player senses the ball he is hitting not in his hands but at the very end of the bat. The blind man, Merleau-Ponty says somewhere, feels the sidewalk at the tip of his cane. Tools allow for an elaboration and enlargement of the body schema and, thereby, an augmentation of perceptual schemata in ways that would otherwise be impossible. Let me call the tools' first relation to the body one of expansion and the resulting change in our perceptual relation to the world extension.

In principle, mechanical prosthetic devices also function like tools. The artificial arm, for example, is simply strapped on to the stump and serves to extend the reach of a person. Sometimes movement of the stump or the shoulder strap allows a claw at the end of the device to open and close, thus adding the ability to grasp something. In this case, I would suggest, the machine also expands the range of the actions of the body by a form of schematic extension and thus belongs to our first group.

But there is a second and closer relation to tools that we can uncover by looking at another striking case in which body schema and body image are at odds with each other. There are a number of people who, because of illness or an accident, have had one of their limbs amputated but who then have what is called a "phantom limb." Though it is literally nonexistent, they still have the experience of the limb. Sometimes the phantom limb is whole and continues to move, reaching for cups, gesturing when one speaks, waving at friends. While no longer a part of the body image, the limb is so much a part of the body schema that it continues to act and to be experienced as a limb even though it is no longer there. The fact that the phantom limb is more than mere wish fulfillment or mental projection is borne out by the many vexing cases in which the phantom limb is itself deformed or deficient in ways that one would never wish. It may be fixed in a certain awkward position or rest rigidly against the chest. It can also be very painful, causing a person endless distress. There are cases of fingers that are curled and dig into the palm of the hand and, even worse, the case of a soldier who had a grenade explode in his hand and continues to feel the excruciating pain.

Dealing with phantom limbs that are "frozen" or immobile has proven especially difficult. As the result of a motorcycle accident at the age of 25, Phillip had a paralyzed left arm that rested in a sling for a year. Since there was no chance of recovery, his arm was amputated. He soon developed a phantom arm but, unlike others, his phantom arm remained fixed in an awkward position and immobile for ten years. Even worse, there was terrible pain in his phantom elbow, wrist and fingers. It seems that the trauma and pain of the accident was fixed in what is now his phantom arm. But how can what does not exist be locked in one position and not another? How can it have pain? And is there a way of helping this patient?

A Dr. Ramachandran, whose analysis I am drawing from here, developed a simple machine whose application not only brought relief to Phillip but also provides us with crucial insight into the relationship between body schema and body image. He constructed a box with two holes in the front, large enough to insert an arm in each. Because it did not have a top, the patient could look into the box. Down the middle of the box he placed a vertical mirror so that Phillips right arm would be on the right side of the box. Even though there was nothing to insert, he was also told to put his left phantom arm into the other side of the box. By looking over the right side of the box and adjusting his line of sight, Phillip could see his real right arm and the mirror image of that arm. Once he placed his head correctly, the mirror image that he also saw seemed to occupy the place of his left arm. He had the perceptual illusion, then, of seeing both his right arm and an existing left arm. Phillip was then told to move both the real right and the phantom left arm simultaneously and in the same way as he looked at the real arm and its image. Phillip protested. His phantom arm had never moved. But as he observed the real arm and its image, his phantom arm suddenly sprang to life. He could feel his elbow and his wrist changing positions. No longer was the phantom arm fixed in one position but extended out in front of him and could move about in parallel with the right arm. As soon as he shut his eyes, however, the phantom would return to its fixed position and there was no movement.

I would suggest that this situation is best understood in terms of the distinction of body image and body schema. Before the introduction of the mirror box there was already a conflict between the experience of the fixed phantom limb, which was part of the body schema, and the body image from which the limb was completely absent. Even though the limb was a perfectly useless contributor, even a hindrance to the movements of the body, it seemed that the shock of the accident and what followed produced a kind of bodily fixation that no visual image was able to correct. But after the introduction of the mirror box everything changes. The mirror box, first of all, gave the phantom arm an image that it previously lacked. Now it even could be seen as moving. But there is also a second operation in play. The illusion of movement of the left arm that the mirror created also allowed for a transfer of proprioceptive sensations of movement from the right arm that suddenly changed the body schema of the phantom left arm. It was now alive and as long as it remained so both the original body image, from which the arm is missing, and the original body schema, in which the arm was frozen, were displaced. With the left arm now moving, a conflict was created between a first and a second schema and a first and a second image. The resolution was to suspend the initial schema of the fixed arm and the image of the missing arm, momentarily replacing them with the schema and then the image of a moving arm. It was a fragile resolution, however, for it worked only as long as Phillip kept his arms in the mirror box.

There is, however, an interesting conclusion to this case. Remember the agonizing pain he experienced? Phillip took the box home and was asked to practice with it every day in the hope that his phantom arm would become permanently mobile. But even after several weeks the phantom still required the mirror for it to move. After a few more weeks, however, he called Dr. Ramachandran, very excited.

"You know, my phantom arm, which I had for ten years. It does not exist anymore. All I have is my phantom fingers and palm dangling from my shoulder."[21]

As a result of ongoing experience with the mirror box, it seems that the discord between the first and the second schema only intensified. With a conflict raging between two incompatible schemata, a final resolution was forthcoming in which the phantom withdraws, moving safely out of sight. It is as if the phantom says "A plague on both your houses," packs its bags, and disappears. But now, since Phillip now longer has a phantom wrist or elbow, the aching pain in them disappeared as well![22]

While more needs to be added, we can draw a second type of machine-body relationship from the case of Phillip. We have known for a long time that those images that are linked to feelings will have the strongest possible effect upon the body and its actions. In the case of Phillip the power of the image goes much deeper for the image carries not just emotions associated with it but the actual proprioceptive sensations of the perceiver himself. This is a limiting case where the schemata of the body undergo modification as a result of an image that intervenes with the body's own sensing of itself. By producing an image that is laden with the proprioceptive sensations of bodily schemata, the mirror is able to change the body into that image. This intervention brings one part or one body into synchrony with another, thus bringing one's schemata and even one's desires into affective harmony with those carried by the image. This is the deepest level of schematic transformation that images can produce and, to generalize, the deepest reach that a visual culture can have into the life of an individual.

* * *

Thus far we have spoken of two modalities of our body's involvement with machines. The cane of the blind man, we saw, produces an augmentation of the body schema and, as a consequence, an extension of certain of its perceptual schemata. The second modality almost reverses the direction of influence, for in this case the mirror box introduces a perceptual image animated with proprioceptive sensations that then produces a modification of the schema. A third and fourth transformation are possible; in discussing them I can be much briefer for we have already laid the groundwork.

The most recent development in the field of artificial limbs (prosthetics) involves a surgical operation in which electrodes are attached to the nerve endings in the stump of a limb that has been amputated. The electric impulses from the nerves detected by these electrodes are read by a microprocessor that then activates certain movements or operations of the artificial limb. The Orthotics and Prosthetics Laboratory at Rutgers University, for example, has developed an artificial hand with such fine control in the individual fingers that it can type on a keyboard. What sets these bionic limbs apart from the earlier mechanical limbs is that they are neurologically joined into the body. As a result limbs that are bionically attached do not merely extend the body schema but they make possible schemata that might otherwise be missing from the body schema as a whole. While not themselves producing kinaesthetic sensations or sensations of touch, what Husserl called *Empfindnisse*,[23] they work with existing sensations and provide an elaboration of them. Schematic integration and kinaesthetic elaboration, then, are what we find with these machines.

While philosophers continue to worry about its dominance in our understanding of the nature of truth, there is little doubt that sight is our most treasured of senses. This is certainly the case of Jens who, as the result of two different accidents, lost sight in both his eyes. We have accounts of Jesus healing the blind man but it is only in the last couple of years that we have been able to approach anything like this through medical technology. One of the most interesting and complex machines to be developed recently is the Dobelle artificial vision system. On each side of Jens head there are two metal circular plates, about the size of a large coin, into which two computer jacks are plugged. Behind the plates inside the skull are two brain implants. Each is a platinum electrode array of about 50 electrodes encased in a plastic that is biocompatible.[24] Images from a digital camera, mounted as glasses Jens wears, are fed to a processor mounted on a belt, and then through the skull and into the visual cortex. The visual cortex is capable of detecting these signals. The interesting question is what happens next.

We have known for some time that electrical stimulation to the visual cortex causes subjects to perceive small points of light, called phosphenes.[25] A new patient like Jens goes through a learning process in which the relationships between different phosphenes are mapped and rendered meaningful. The goal is to produce "functional mobility," the ability to cross streets, ride the bus, and find one's way around in buildings.[26] The most recent Dobelle system allowed Jens as a new patient, after only a half-hour of training, to recognize a telephone and pick up the receiver within 10 seconds. Later in his first day of training Jens even drove an automobile in a parking lot.

Our imagination begins to spin. The camera being used is simple. Think about what could happen if the system became sophisticated enough to process signals from other kinds of optical devices such as night vision, X-ray vision, microscopic focus, and long-range focus.[27] Still, this system developed by Dobelle is rather crude. Another researcher, Dick Norman, suggests that progress can be made by using electrodes that do not simply rest on the surface of the visual cortex but penetrate it. They would be much smaller, use less current, and stimulate individual neurons, thus allowing for an increase in resolution.[28]

In this fourth and deepest relation between body and machine, which we can call bionic incorporation, there is full assimilation of the device into the central nervous system, which produces not a change in the movement of the body (except incidentally) but a radical and deep transformation, even transmutation of perception itself. Though the device relies on the natural circuitry of the body, the signals that it produces are of its own making. There is the question, then, as to whether we are seeing or the machine is seeing through us.

What I have suggested in this paper is that the interpretation of the body in terms of a difference between body schema and body image is both the best way of understanding the notion of lived-body (*Leib*) and the key to understanding four different modalities of the body's direct involvement with machines. My goal has been to provide a typology of four structurally differ- ent types of transformation. We end only by opening yet another question, the question of the risk involved when parts and systems of the body become replaced with their artificial counterparts, a risk that will only grow as our technologies continue to progress.

Notes

1. Edmund Husserl, *Formal and Transcendental Logic*, trans. Dorion Cairns (The Hague: Martinus Nijhoff, 1969).

2. Edmund Husserl, *Ideas Pertaining to a Pure Phenomenology and to a Phe- nomenological Philosophy*, Book 2: *Studies in the Phenomenology of Constitution*, trans. Richard Rojcewicz and Andre Schuwer (Dortrecht: Kluwer, 1989).

3. Edmund Husserl, *Ideas Pertaining to a Pure Phenomenology and to a Phe- nomenological Philosophy*. Book 1: *General Introduction to a Pure Phenomenology*, trans. F. Kersten (The Hague: Martinus Nijhoff, 1983).

4. Husserl, *Ideas I*, 85.

5. Edmund Husserl, *Analyses Concerning Passive and Active Synthesis: Lectures on Transcendental Logic*, trans. Anthony Steinbock (Dordrecht: Kluwer, 2001), 50.

6. Actions here should not be reduced to *Handlungen* as action is a much broader category that is difficult to get into German.

7. See Donn Welton, "Soft, Smooth Hands: Husserl's Phenomenology of the Body," in *The Body: Classic and Contemporary Readings*, ed. Donn Welton (Oxford: Blackwell, 1999), 44–48.

8. Maurice Merleau-Ponty, *Phénoménologie de la perception* (Paris: Gallimard, 1945), 114. See Maurice Merleau-Ponty, *Phenomenology of Perception*, trans. Colin Smith (London: Routledge & Keegan Paul, 1962).

9. Henry Head and Gordon Holmes, "Sensory Disturbances from Cerebral Lesions," *Brain*, 34 (1911): 102–254.

10. Merleau-Ponty, *Phenomenology of Perception*, 101.

11. Ibid., 102.

12. Ibid., 104. See also 124, 129, 132.

13. Shaun Gallagher and Jonathan Cole, "Body Image and Body Schema in a Differentiated Subject," in *Body and Flesh: A Philosophical Reader*, ed. Donn Welton (Oxford: Blackwell, 1998), 132.

14. See Ibid.,136–140 for an elaboration of these three elements.

15. Merleau-Ponty, *Phenomenology of Perception*, 100–101.

16. Merleau-Ponty, *Phenomenology of Perception*, 137.

17. Gallagher and Cole, "Body Image and Body Schema in a Differentiated Subject," 136.

18. James Gibson, *The Senses Considered as Perceptual Systems* (New York: Houghton Mifflin Co., 1966), 72–74.

19. Taken from Gallagher and Cole, "Body Image and Body Schema," 134–135.

20. Merleau-Ponty, *Phenomenology of Perception*, 103–104, 113–114, 122–124.

21. V.S. Ramachandran and Sandra Blakeslee, *Phantoms in the Brain: Probing the Mysteries of the Human Mind* (New York: William Morrow, 1998), 49.

22. Ibid., 47–50.

23. Husserl, *Ideas II*, 153.

24. Steven Kotler, "Vision Quest," *Wired* September, 2002: 96.

25. Ibid., 96.

26. Ibid.

27. Ibid., 100.

28. Ibid., 101.

15

Ontology Engines

Andrew Pickering

In the past few years I have had the chance to get to know Don Ihde and at least some of his works quite well—a very enjoyable experience in many ways, but also, more obliquely, a frustrating one. I have always had the feeling that I wanted to argue with some aspect of his writings, but have never been able to make the argument happen in person; we always seem to agree. Perhaps it will be easier in his absence. I take my contribution to this volume as an opportunity to discuss where our understandings diverge.

A good place to start is Ihde's recent essay, "You Can't Have It Both Ways: Situated or Symmetrical."[1] He remarks there that his interest in science studies grew out of his work in the philosophy of technology, and that within science studies his perspective resonates with what I call the "posthumanist" wing; he mentions the work of Donna Haraway, Bruno Latour, and myself as particularly interested in the materiality of science. Ihde wants to engage us in conversation on two important topics: the situatedness of scientific knowledge and a putative symmetry between the human and the nonhuman.

I would like to continue this conversation, and I can start by noting that at the level of verbal formulations of epistemological positions we seem to be in close agreement. Neither of us dispute that scientific knowledge is situated and somehow "relative," rather than simply and transcendentally true. But "symmetry" is an ontological question, and this is where we part company. I therefore want to sketch out what I take to be Ihde's ontology and then contrast it with my own.

Ihde lays out his position like this:

[W]hat is it to be situated? My answer will be in the form of a narrative from my preferred philosophical framing of existential and hermeneutic phenomenology. In this tradition, to be situated entails that the knower is always *embodied*, located, *is a body*, and this must

211

> be accounted for in any analysis of knowledge. . . In my narrative I
> shall attempt to show not only the invariant role of embodiment, but
> how 'the body' is merely hidden in those epistemologies that attempt
> disembodiment.[2]

I am not sure that Ihde does "show" any necessary role for embodiment. In
this essay he seems content simply to gesture toward some standard phenomenological arguments: "I will not bore you with the centuries of debate about
this, but will pull a simple existential phenomenological trick . . . Nor shall I
here take you through all the complicated steps Husserl took to show this, but
jump to the conclusion . . . The tactic that I have just displayed . . ." and so
on.[3] I am not concerned here with the propriety of this way of proceeding, but
I am concerned with Ihde's conclusion, which is indeed that any full analysis
of knowledge has to start with the human body: knowledge grows out of our
embodied experience of the world. And the first point I want to emphasize is
that this is indeed an ontological position: it is an image of the world and our
being in it, which is, as it happens, resolutely centered on the human. All that
we really have to work on philosophically is this experience we have of the
world as embodied beings. And one corollary of this is that, philosophically,
we can have no image of the world itself beyond that which appears in our
embodied experience. Like analytic philosophy, Ihde's phenomenology is,
and has to be, silent on the world itself.

Of course, Ihde's position calls forth a standard puzzle. If knowledge is
ultimately grounded in our bodies, how come scientists manage not to know
that? How is it that scientific knowledge itself usually does not refer us back
to the body? But here he wheels on his very attractive idea of an *epistemology
engine*. He argues that disembodied epistemologies are themselves grounded
in certain machines and instruments. He shows first how the *camera obscura*
has functioned historically as a model for a modern, dualist, epistemology, in
which our knowledge of the world figures as a direct representation of nature,
quite independently of our embodied being.[4] This is, in fact, the epistemology
he undermines by the phenomenological "trick" mentioned above, which
consists of asking: *"where is Descartes when he makes the claims about
knowledge that he makes?"*[5] The *camera obscura*, then, is an epistemology
engine that drove dualist epistemology by encouraging us not to see our own
situatedness. This is a very interesting and clever idea, and later in the same
essay, Ihde also discusses a second family of epistemology engines—video
games, the Internet, virtual-reality techniques—which he plausibly claims
power not a modern but a postmodern, fluid and constructivist, epistemology.[6]
Here, too, Ihde urges caution. We should not fall for postmodern epistemology any more than Cartesian dualism:

[W]hatever these new realities [of cyberspace] are they will emerge from the dance, the interrogation, the "foldings of the flesh" that Merleau-Ponty talked about . . . and they may be located by looking at the practices and in giving account of our bodily engagements and embodiments in that world.[7]

So in Ihde's phenomenology there is something we *can* talk about beyond our embodied experience, namely the machines that serve as intermediaries to, or even substitutes for, the world, but we need to be suspicious of them—they provide access beyond the domain of our naked senses, but they can also serve as epistemology engines that obscure the centrality of our embodied being. And this, then, is Ihde's ontology: at the center, the embodied human, immersed in a world that cannot be spoken of outside our experience of it, plus a set of representational instruments that efface our embodiment. And now we can see clearly what his title means: "situated or symmetrical: you can't have it both ways." For him, the situatedness of knowledge arises from the necessity of referring back to the human body (in both its specific brute materiality and as socially marked), and this centrality of the body itself constitutes an inescapable *asymmetry* between the human and the nonhuman in phenomenological enquiry.[8]

* * *

Ihde's ontology is not the same as mine, and I now want to pursue this topic of symmetry from a different angle. I want to clarify my own position and juxtapose it to Ihde's by transposing his notion of an epistemology engine into that of an *ontology engine* and reversing the sign. My idea is that certain machines can help us think about ontology, rather than deceiving us about epistemology. I have argued before[9] that one wing, at least, of cybernetics can be understood as a realization in many domains of practice of the ontology that I laid out in *The Mangle of Practice*,[10] and here I will focus on just one of the many cybernetic machines that I could invoke: the so-called homeostat built by Ross Ashby in the late 1940s.[11]

Figure 15.1 shows four interconnected homeostats, archetypal black boxes, Figure 15.2 the wiring diagram of a single homeostat. Without going into details, each homeostat unit took an electrical input and turned it into an output; the input current caused a needle on the top of each unit to rotate and the position of the needle in turn modulated the output current. Any unit in isolation was inert. But constellations of interconnected units displayed interesting properties. The whole assemblage might be *stable*, meaning that the needles on each unit would come to rest in their central positions and return there under small perturbations; or it might be *unstable*, meaning that the needles would be driven to the limits of their ranges. In the latter case, another bit of the homeostat's circuitry came into play. A relay would trip, causing a "uniselector" to rotate, changing the resistance of the unit's circuitry according to a table of random numbers. This might leave the assemblage still unstable, in which case the relays would continue tripping, until the assemblage eventually found a state of stability, at which point it would become quiescent. The homeostat was, in Ashby's terminology, an *ultrastable* machine: whatever state one started it off at, it would eventually achieve a state of dynamic equilibrium with its surroundings.

So what? Such homeostat assemblages can be understood as instructive ontological machines from several angles. We should note, first, that Ashby intended the homeostat as *a model of the brain*; not the representational brain, however, familiar to us from representationalist philosophy and computer-science artificial intelligence, but an adaptive brain, the organ that enables us to get along, cope and come into equilibrium with environments that we have not experienced before. Thus in the four-homeostat setup, one of the units could be regarded as a brain, while the other three constituted its material environment. And now I can make some observations:

First, the relation between the brain and its environment in such setups was a performative rather than a relational one. The homeostat-brain did something, emitting an electrical output, which would stimulate the environ-

Figure 15.1   (a) Four interconnected homeostats; (b) detail of the top of a homeostat unit, showing the rotating needle.[12] *Permission:* the Ashby family

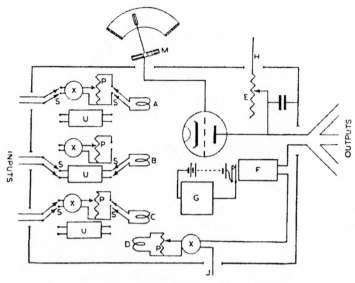

Figure 15.2   Homeostat wiring diagram.[13] *Permission:* the Ashby family.

ment homeostats to do something, convert that input to their own outputs, which in turn stimulated the brain, and so on, and so on, back and forth, until equilibrium was achieved. This is as nice an electromechanical exemplification of what I called the "dance of human and nonhuman agency" and the achievement of "interactive stabilization" as one could wish. And this is a primary sense in which I want to call such setups ontology engines. Contemplate them, and you can get the hang of the ontological vision I found myself arguing for in *The Mangle of Practice*.

What then of Ihde's phenomenological ontology? One point that strikes me is that in contrast to the performativity of the interconnected homeostats, Ihde's thinking always seems to run along representationalist lines, as if the point of our being in the world were to represent the world to ourselves, rather than the unavoidable project of getting along materially. One could doubt whether Ihde's *camera obscura*, video games, e-mail, and virtual reality, as well as quill pens, glasses, and word processors come near to spanning and typifying the overall range of embodied experience.[14] But beyond that, I want to note the utter *symmetry* of Ashby's assemblages. Exactly the same devices were used to model the environment of the brain as the brain itself. It is not that one could not reasonably designate one of the units to stand for a brain, an embodied brain at that, but that it would make no sense to see that unit as the foundation or organizing center of the whole setup. In Ashby's scheme brain and world both sites were of liveliness and agency, and the interesting action happened in the interconnection of the two. The Ashbyite ontology engine thus conjures up a symmmetric, decentered and mangle-ish ontology in which the human does not occupy a privileged position, in contrast with Ihde's asymmetric phenomenological humanism. This is the key divergence between Ihde's ontology and my own.

Having got that far, I can now enter a qualification. Ashby himself was keen to argue that there was nothing absolutely special about the brain—he wanted to show that adaptive behavior "is in no way special to living things."[15] Indeed, the homeostat was intended partly as a demonstration of that: some simple circuitry could mimic what he took to be the brain's key feature, its adaptability. But that did not prevent him arguing that there was a finite, down-to-earth difference between the human brain and lower level reflex circuits in the nervous system, let alone between the brain and a lump of coal: "The only other point to mention . . . is that the development of a nervous system will provide vastly greater opportunities both for the number of breaks available and also for complexity and variety of organization. Here I would emphasize that the difference . . . is solely one of degree and not of principle."[16] As a matter of fact, the brain can take on many more states than a lump of coal, and that is why it is the supreme organ of adaptation. In this sense one can say that there is only a partial symmetry between the brain and its environment—a sense analogous to what I had in mind in *The Mangle* when I said that there are aspects of human agency (e.g., plans and goals aimed at nonexistent future states) that I could not usefully impute to bubble chambers or machine tools. The point I need to stress here, however, is that remarking on this finite difference does not return us to Ihde's ontological humanism. The adaptive brain, whatever its complexity and however that is manifest, remains an integral part of a brain/environment system and not its organizing principle.

And, to make a similar point from another angle, although Ashby thought of the homeostat as a model of the brain, he did not think of it only as that. In Ashby's writings, the multihomeostat system stood just as readily for itself (a collection of inanimate electromechanical parts), an adaptive autopilot flying a plane, the British economy and the evolution of biological species.[17] Homeostat assemblages could, then, serve as models of all aspects of the world, including aspects from which humans were simply absent. Ashby's setups thus instantiated an ontological Theory of Everything, which could include or exclude the human as appropriate. This is just what I said of the mangle-ish ontology set out in my book, and it is profoundly different from Ihde's ontology.[18] The homeostat ontology engine drives us into a quite different place—a quite different understanding of the world and our place in it from Ihde's cozy but claustrophobic realm of human embodiment.

***

I have contrasted my ontological position with Ihde's by juxtaposing Ashby's exemplary ontology engine and Ihde's deceptively dehumanizing epistemology engines. The last question is: where does that leave us? Perhaps in a volume like this I should leave the question hanging, but I find it hard to be quite so symmetric. Let me pick up one last thread from Ihde's essay. To bolster his own human-centrism, Ihde invokes Haraway's remarks on the "god-trick," the "view from nowhere." [19] The view must be from somewhere, is the idea, and that must be the standpoint of embodied experience. I hate to argue with Donna; she's usually right about everything, and I can remember her calling me a "vampire" in just this spirit. I feel like saying: yes, I stand convicted; I did not situate myself in *The Mangle of Practice* and, oh no, I've just failed to do so again. Where did my (material and socially marked) body go this time? How careless can you get Pickering? But let me slow down and try not to panic. Is the "god-trick" necessarily quite so pernicious? It amounts to a degree of scholarly distancing of author and arguments, of course, but that can surely be a good thing. In *The Mangle* I did not say, you have to believe this because I say so, or because God told me so (or the Devil, according to some readers). I collected a lot of evidence from my own studies and others'; I worked through the best analysis I could make of it; and I discussed alternative explanations and why they struck me as inadequate. That, and that alone, put me in the position to write the way I did. I suppose I could be accused of delusions of grandeur, but more charitably I could be read as making the situated assertion: here's what I see and what I make of it; can you see the same things? What do you make of them?

And, of course, the "god-trick" is not so easy to get away from. How does Ihde persuade us of his existential phenomenology? Not by presenting us with Ihde the body. In the essay discussed, he does it with a self-acknowledged "trick," as I mentioned. No doubt, as he also indicated, Ihde, if anyone, could drag us through Husserl's arguments. But, of course, absent any quasi-theological faith in their validity, Husserl's arguments are just another variant of the distancing "god-trick." So here are the alternatives, two versions of the "god-trick": mine, which is based on evidence and argument, or an (absent) Ihde/Husserl *a priori* argument for "the invariant role of embodiment."[20] Mine opens out into an intense curiosity about humans and nonhumans in a world that endlessly becomes, and in which we humans are only, at most, a part; Ihde's takes us back to where we started, the lived human body. Contra Ihde, I think we can have it both ways—situated and symmetrical—and I think we should.

Notes

1. *BT* 67–87.

2. Ibid., 68.

3. Ibid., 74.

4. Ibid., 71–75.

5. Ibid, 74.

6. Ibid., 80–85.

7. Ibid., 86.

8. Ibid., 70.

9. Andrew Pickering, "Cybernetics and the Mangle: Ashby, Beer and Pask," *Social Studies of Science 32* (2002): 413–437.

10. Andrew Pickering, *The Mangle of Practice: Time, Agency, and Science* (Chicago: University of Chicago Press, 1995).

11. W. R. Ashby, *Design for a Brain* (London: Chapman & Hall, 2nd ed., 1960). See also: Andrew Pickering, "Psychiatry, Synthetic Brains and Cybernetics in the Work of W. Ross Ashby," in eds. P. Asaro, A. Pickering and J. Wedge (forthcoming).

12. W. R. Ashby, "Design for a Brain," *Electronic Engineering* 20 (Dec. 1948): 380.

13. Ibid., 381.

14. *BT* 88–100.

15. W. Ross Ashby, "The Physical Origin of Adaptation by Trial and Error," *Journal of General Psychology 32* (1945):13.

16. Ibid., 20.

17. W. R. Ashby, "Effect of Controls on Stability," *Nature* 155 (1945): 242–243.

18. Andrew Pickering, *The Mangle of Practice: Time, Agency, and Science*, 213–243.

19. *BT* 70–71.

20. Ibid., 68.

Part VI

Reframing Science

16

From Workbench to Cyberstage

Robert P. Crease

The philosophical account of experimentation long remained in a rudimentary state for lack of a suitably comprehensive framework in which to consider all its dimensions. Consider what such a framework would have to accommodate. It would have to allow experimentation to be treated both as interest-driven, that is, responding to and arising from changing human wants, needs, and utilities; and as event-driven, that is, responding to and arising out of concrete physical events in the laboratory. It would need to approach experimentation as a process of inquiry. It would need to show how experimentation is meaning-generating. It would have to describe how the experimental process adds phenomena to the lifeworld. It would have to distinguish between performances and demonstrations. It would have to explain the affective dimension of the practice of science. It would have to involve some reception theory. It would have to illuminate issues in science management. And it would need to incorporate a place for things like artistry, creativity, technique, and even beauty, among others.

The philosophical account of experimentation would have to allow us to see all these things within one framework, rather than adding them on subsequently as appendixes to some central main account. This is the path followed by many textbooks, which start with some allegedly central feature or restricted set of features that appears to the authors to be the "jugular" of science. Some authors see this jugular as wider than others, but they have traditionally generally conceived it as some version of the logic of confirmation, or the nature of laws or theory structure. Subjects like creativity, social impact, and ethics are then treated awkwardly as appendages, with little clue provided for showing how they tie in to the jugular. These textbooks thus see science as composed of two parts, its inner chambers and its anterooms, the main account and the add-ons. But we cannot abide add-ons in a truly philosophical account, one reason being that we could then never be sure they relate to the same phenomenon.

I have argued that a suitable framework for the philosophy of experimentation is provided by the concept of performance.[1] The word performance has a spectrum of meanings,[2] but the salient one here is the conception, production, and witnessing of material events, the experience of which is *meaning-generating* in that these events give us back more than what we put into them. When viewed in this way, I have argued, the structure of performance is not a metaphor extended merely suggestively from the theater arts into experimental science; it is the same in both. In both, the representation (theory, language, script . . .) used to program the performance does not completely determine the outcome (product, work, result . . .) but only assists in the encounter with the new. The world is wider, wilder, and richer than we can represent, and what appears in performance can exceed the program used to put it together, and it can even surprise and baffle us, get us to change our minds, and compel us to alter the very theories and representations that we used to program the performance in the first place.

Such a framework is necessary, too, for grounding one's work in the elements of the philosophical tradition. A philosophical account of a phenomenon can never simply start from scratch and pull concepts out of thin air. A scholar of any sort enters a field that has already been worked over and structured by other scholars, and this work and these structures have created a context in which discussions of an orderly sort can take place and develop, in which discoveries can be made and shared, and the field transformed. The arts and sciences are not different in this respect. Just as one would have no reason to trust a proposed new cancer cure that has not been shown to have a basis in contemporary practice, or that corrects or carries forward that practice, so one would have no reason to trust a philosophical account that did not benchmark itself with respect to existing work, however much it sought to transform that work. Philosophy needs to avoid the scholarly equivalent of cold-fusion episodes, in which lack of care in tying one's work to existing practices can produce something apparently fresh and innovative and world-changing—but which later turns out to have been merely sloppy. This can happen in many ways: if one is not comprehensive enough, if one is unaware of other work, if one is unaware of other phenomena, and so forth. An attempt at a framework also can be simply underdeveloped. Suppose, for instance, we refer to a goal-oriented practice such as experimentation as a "dance of agency."[3] This is poetically suggestive but demands greater precision, which the performance framework can certainly provide. What is a dance, after all, but . . . a species of performance? If we define further what that means as a "dialectic of resistance and accommodation," isn't that just the beginning of an attempt to outline features of performance?

As Don Ihde has demonstrated throughout his work, too, philosophical discussion of experimentation needs to be both hermeneutical and phenomenological. By a hermeneutical account, I mean one that describes how experimental intentions and practices arise and evolve out of an already existing involvement with, and understanding of, a concrete situation, leading to transformations of those involvements and understandings, and thus of the situation and our understanding of it, and so forth, in an unending process.[4] By a phenomenological account, I mean one that takes its point of departure from what is variously called embodiment, lived body, flesh, or animate form, the experiences of which are that of a unified being, and which cannot be understood apart from concrete human experience. Ihde regularly combines both approaches in his explorations of the materiality of instruments in the process of producing readable but also perceptual objects in the laboratory. Ihde's work, indeed, has helped to liberate hermeneutics from its preoccupations with textuality, and phenomenology from its preoccupations with experience.

Dimensions

The performance framework can help elucidate numerous dimensions of experimentation that are usually omitted, downplayed, or distorted by traditional versions of the philosophy of science and technology, such as artistry, creativity, and affect.[5] This framework can also help in understanding such key and ubiquitous features of technoscience as the role of simulations, the affective dimension of science, and the behavior of scientific institutions.

Simulations in science can raise new and difficult issues about knowledge-acquisition. The traditional use of instruments was to stage experimental performances that engaged the world to tell us something about or for it: using gnomons and shadows to determine the circumference of the earth, timers and balls rolling down a plane to describe how bodies fall, oil droplets moving at terminal velocity in the presence of an electromagnetic field to find the charge of an electron. In these examples, information was used to calibrate or program an instrument in such a way as to produce more information. Virtual-reality simulations, of the sort that create a "simulated, interactive, artificial, completely manipulable 'world'" do not do this exactly.[6] The fictional Holodeck from "Star Trek: The Next Generation," for instance, uses information essentially in the service of experience or entertainment—and military flight simulators such as those used in training for aircraft, which incorporate in their program not only information about the aircraft's weapons and flight capabilities but also information about the weapons and capabilities of enemy aircraft and tanks, utilize information for training purposes. While models and computer-controlled simulations have long played a role in assisting or guiding scientific inquiry (think of Monte Carlo simulations), a qualitatively new level has been reached with the use of supercomputers to simulate complex processes involving huge numbers of multiple variables over extended time periods. Instead of using information to calibrate or program an instrument to give back more information, the experiment uses information to produce a simulation—and the simulation then embodies answers to the questions posed by the experimenters. One might call this kind of experimental performance a *cyberstage*. The move from workbench to cyberstage not only represents an advanced stage in the transformation of certain fields (such as biology) into information sciences, but also raises questions arising from the use of a highly technological process to achieve a simulation of apparent transparency. It thus underscores the urgency of developing what Ihde has called a deep and critical analysis of precisely this instrumental, technological constructionism.

The performance framework also allows us to appreciate the *affective dimension* of science. Science is not a robotic process of hypothesis formation, testing, and hypothesis reformulation—an intellectual game. Nor is it a vast, ongoing, political negotiation whose participants swap interests like politicians or lawyers. Science is an existential activity, a form of life that its practitioners carry out with their whole bodies, and it therefore has an extensive, structured, and highly nuanced affective dimension. There is, of course, the celebratory joy that is a natural concomitant to a new discovery or to the acquisition of a new performance ability, to the forging of a new way of being-in-the-world; this belongs to the psychodynamics of creativity and is anything but the detached and impersonal triumph that accompanies success at a project of domination and control. Anyone whose attraction to science depends only on such few-and-far-between moments of success does not last long in the field. The affective dimension in science extends much further and involves a pleasurable dimension. Science involves embodied individuals aware of themselves in action, in an experienced, dynamically unfolding, qualitative flow. The qualities and affective feelings of this flow are always present, not deeply hidden, often overlooked, but available whenever we want to direct our attention to them. As Nobel Prize winning physicist Leon Lederman recently wrote, to pin one's hopes on making a discovery that will bring fame and fortune "is not a life." He continued, "The fun and excitement must be daily—in the challenge of creating an instrument and seeing it work, the joy of communicating to colleagues and students, the pleasure of learning something new, in lectures, corridors, and journals."[7] Any account of science that leaves out this obvious but extremely important existential dimension is guilty of sheer ignorance or gross distortion. To explore it requires redirecting our attention from science as performative to science as performance.

Performance is also important to the *behavior of scientific institutions* such as laboratories and high-technology companies. Management theory dates back to the work of "efficiency experts" such as Frederick Taylor who analyzed the conditions under which workers perform. In the 1960s, management theory underwent a radical change when the focus on the ways the activities of the individual worker contribute to company performance began to be supplemented by a focus on the corporation and the ways its activities contribute to individual performance. The result was the emergence of the field of "performance management," concerned with the interaction between the performance of individual workers and the company. The management of scientific institutions such as laboratories and companies with a strong scientific-technological emphasis poses still more complex interactional problems. In his intriguing book *Perform Or Else*, Jon McKenzie distinguishes three different domains of performance—cultural (involving effectiveness at making cultural change), organizational (effectiveness at making groups of humans function), and technological (effectiveness in a given task)—and develops the concept of performance in a way that can help to elucidate the process by which scientific institutions such as laboratories and high-technology companies respond to the pressures and risks arising from changing uses, technological breakthroughs, and emerging competitors.[8]

Cyberstage

The framework provided by the concept of performance allows us to address highly complex developments in technoscience without resorting to anterooms and add-ons.

Consider, for instance, IBM's "Blue Gene" project, to construct a computer able to simulate protein folding, an effort that yokes together three very different cultures: experimental protein biologists, physicists and computer engineers, and corporate planners.

Proteins are the interface where the microworld of atoms and molecules turns into the macroworld of living, animate beings. Proteins are pieced together, atom by atom, at the instructions of strands of DNA: genes. Each protein emerges from this process as a long, more or less linear chain of molecules that then twists up or folds into a complicated final or "native" shape that governs the protein's functions. The word "folding" sounds like a simple process—like folding up a map, card table, or piece of origami. But figuring out how to fold up a chain of tens of thousands of atoms is highly—and until recently, almost insolubly—complex. The decoding of the structure of DNA in 1953—perhaps the most important single scientific event in the second half of the twentieth century—made many scientists confident that they at last understood the "secret of life." But in the intervening years, the breakthroughs failed to keep pace with expectations. A major hurdle was the failure to understand the protein folding process, for knowing the protein's genetic code did not help much. It was like being asked to build an automobile when all one has is a list of parts—or better, parts of parts—without even knowing what these parts look like. Protein folding remains the still mysterious bridge between structure and function, between physics and biology—between the microscopic world of atoms and molecules governed by elementary forces, and the "real" world of living organisms, governed by interactions with environments. It is also the interface where the culture of experimental protein biologists meets that of physicists and computer engineers.

To appreciate the polarity of this difference, consider the computational biology class taught at Stony Brook by computer engineer Steve Skiena. From the very first time that he taught the course, Skiena experienced the divide. The biologists and the physicists/computer scientists among the students had different interests, background, and even educational attitudes. The biology students took for granted the existence of a strict hierarchical pecking order that leads from professor to postdocs to grad students to lab assistants to undergraduates, and assumed that they must start at the bottom and work up. The computer students, by contrast, saw no such hierarchy, described themselves simply as working in the "Skiena lab," and treated everyone as peers, including Skiena himself. The biology students tended to feel violated if asked to program a computer, and computer engineers tended to feel likewise if asked to learn something about proteins. Skiena's challenge in the class is to teach these groups to at least mingle intellectually. Exasperated, he now begins his first class by mirroring back the cultural difference, in an attempt to diffuse it or at least have the students question it. He shows the following slide:

There are many fundamental cultural differences between computational/life scientists:

- Nothing is ever completely true or false in biology, where everything is either true or false in computer science/mathematics.

- Biologists strive to understand the very complicated, very messy natural world; computer scientists seek to build their own clean and organized virtual worlds.

- Biologists are data driven; while computer scientists are algorithm driven. One consequence is CS WWW pages have fancier graphics while Biology WWW pages have more content. . . .

- The Platonic ideal of a biologist runs a big laboratory with many people. The Platonic ideal of a computer scientists is a hacker in garage.

These cultures have adopted two contrasting ways of approaching the protein folding problem. The experimental biologists tended to adopt a method called *threading*. Threading is a comparison method based on the data you already have about other proteins. If you have a new sequence, you seek out similar sequences among those whose shapes you already know, and see if you can adjust or "thread" the new sequence into the others. The insight is that you can often "move" the knowledge you have about one organism or organic molecule to another. You understand a new organism by picking out something that it's "like" and tinkering with it. This approach might be called "metaphorical bootstrapping," for you are slowly growing more knowledge about the world by saying that it's a form of what you already know and adapting that knowledge. This approach works for the most part, but it's slow and laborious. It involves the traditional kind of workbench experimentation that can be described in terms of experimental performance.

Computer scientists and physicists tended to adopt the contrasting *ab initio* approach: you don't seek to move knowledge from one organism or organic molecule to another, but build it up from scratch. This seems conceptually simple enough: since biologists know all of the atoms that make up the proteins, and all of the forces that bind the atoms to each other, why not just use that knowledge to calculate the shape they will end up in as they get jostled about after their sequence is produced? You set down all the initial conditions, and simply find out what happens by simulating the protein-folding process from the ground up. This is also known as molecular dynamics, for it seeks to solve the protein-folding problem by understanding the basic molecular units and the dynamics of the forces that push or pull them into shape. It is, in short, performance on a cyberstage. The vision behind this approach is powerful and ambitious: in a sense, it is a biological version of Laplace's determinism. If you know the positions and speeds and forces governing all the particles in the universe, in Laplacian determinism, you could calculate everything that ever took place or ever will take place. In the twenty-first century, biological version, if you know the atoms that comprise a protein and the charges affecting them, you can use that information to simulate the protein's folding process, thereby determining its shape—and therefore its role in cellular life.

Simple and direct in theory, the *ab initio* approach involved many variables and numerous iterative steps—requiring a seemingly hopeless amount of computational ability and time, and depended on numerous assumptions about the behavior of organic molecules that made practiced protein biologists wary. Thus for years these two groups—computationally savvy protein biologists who threaded, and biologically inclined computer engineers who modeled—argued about how best to fold proteins. A biologically inclined computer scientist such as Peter Kollman would announce at a conference that "We have solved the folding problem," only to run into more difficulties when the experiments were actually carried out. As an article in *Scientific*

American put it in 1991, "In theory, all one needs to know in order to fold a protein into its biologically active shape is the sequence of its constituent amino acids. Why has nobody been able to put theory into practice?" Our twenty-first century biological Laplace would answer, "because they haven't yet tried supercomputers."

Enter IBM. IBM's struggles in the computing field illustrate many of the pressures and risks to which high-technology companies are exposed, and the company has pioneered strategies of performance management. One of them is the "grand challenge," in which one sets a goal that is daring and ambitious enough to inspire the individuals in the company at all levels, but achievable enough so that the risk of becoming saddled with a white elephant, though present, is not great. One of IBM's most famous grand challenges was the "Deep Blue" project to develop a computer with enough ability to play chess on a world-champion level. Deep Blue, capable of a teraflop, or one trillion operations per second, was a resounding success and made headlines when it defeated world chess champion Gary Kasparov in 1997. (IBM's nickname "Big Blue" had been coined by business writers in the 1960s from the blue covers of its mainframes and other products, and IBM soon incorporated it into its names for its supercomputers.) And in December 1999, IBM launched its first post–Deep Blue grand challenge: to develop, in six years, a petaflop supercomputer able to simulate protein folding. They called it "Blue Gene."

In tackling Blue Gene, IBM is interested in more than proteins, of course—just as, in tackling Deep Blue, it had more on its mind than grand-master-level chess. The company is betting that the ability to simulate folding would also transform computer technology. While computers are already improving at a torrid rate, building one with Blue Gene's capabilities would require extensive improvements in hardware, software, and computer architecture. Success would break Moore's law—that the number of transistors on a chip doubles each year—the infamous predictor of chip evolution. Success would also generate new kinds of large-scale, interdisciplinary collaborations among scientists, especially mathematicians and computer engineers. Its impact would be ecological, affecting the intellectual environment in profound ways by opening up possibilities and discouraging others. Finally, as IBM was keenly aware when it debated the project, success with Blue Gene would transform the computing industry. The ability to simulate protein folding would make supercomputers of Blue Gene's capabilities indispensable for cutting-edge work in the life sciences, meteorology, weapons research (which has led to collaborations between IBM and the Department of Energy to develop prototypes) and other fields that depend upon evaluating huge numbers of multiple variables over extended time frames—and would tend to foster experimentation that could be structured in that way.

IBM's Blue Gene project exhibits the intersecting dimensions of contemporary technoscience, from conventional workbench experimentation and personal motivation to computer-driven cyberstages to capitalist survival strategies and governmental involvements. The project is but one illustration of the need for a framework flexible enough to accommodate all of these dimensions, exhibiting the way these different performance dimensions open up certain possibilities while closing off others, and thus laying the groundwork for the "deep and critical analysis" of technoscience that Don Ihde has so insistently and persuasively urged.

Notes

1. Robert P. Crease, *The Play of Nature: Experimentation as Performance* (Bloomington: Indiana University Press, 1993).

2. Bert O. States, "Performance as Metaphor," *Theatre Journal* 48 (1996):1.

3. Andrew Pickering, *The Mangle of Practice: Time, Agency, & Science* (Chicago: University of Chicago Press, 1995).

4. See also Robert P. Crease, "Introduction," in *Hermeneutics and the Natural Sciences*, ed. Robert P. Crease (Dordrecht: Kluwer, 1997).

5. Robert P. Crease, "Inquiry and Performance: Analogies and Identities Between The Arts and the Sciences," *Interdisciplinary Science Reviews* (1 December 2003): 266–272.

6. Robert Scharff and Val Dusek, "Introduction" to the section on "Technology and Cyberspace," in *Philosophy of Technology: The Technological Condition.* (Oxford: Blackwell, 2003), 537.

7. Leon Lederman, "The Pleasure of Learning," *Nature* 430, 5 (August 2004): 617.

8. Jon McKenzie, *Perform Or Else: From Discipline to Performance* (New York: Routledge, 2001).

17

Technological Mediation and Embodied Health-Care Practices

Finn Olesen

Introduction

Don Ihde's far-reaching philosophy of technology, particularly his account of technical mediation, provides a useful framework for addressing questions concerning how research on high-tech solutions in the health-care services can be linked with philosophical ideas about human nature, knowledge, and experience. Whereas earlier philosophies of technology have inquired abstractly into technological conditions, Ihde's philosophy is concerned with what a particular technology *does* in a specific setting, and how subjects and artifacts *constitute* each other in praxis.

The prominent efforts being made today in Denmark (and elsewhere) to establish nationwide, standardized computer solutions to efficiency problems in health-care systems, will advance a move away from *clinical knowledge*—based on situated knowledge and embodied practical experiences—toward increased *scholastic* knowledge—based on explicit knowledge and rule-based actions. This kind of move will involve altered environments for interactions between health professionals and for their communication with patients, and it will imply both premeditated and unexpected transformations of particular work tasks in the health domains involved. Thus, the effective range of "do-able" problems for the health professionals will be altered in a number of ways that goes beyond rational planning. These changes pose questions for how to study such altered conditions and their alleged consequences. On what level of observation should such alterations be studied? What theoretical framework is able to grasp the magnitude of the issue? As stated above, Ihde's philosophy of technology offers a beneficial set of tools and methods to investigate these questions.

Health Care and Digital Efficiency

The Public Health Services in Denmark face a number of challenges these years, mostly a result of political determination to improve the effectiveness of the domain with the help of computer-based information technology (IT). At present the magnitude of these challenges is arguably most visible in the various attempts to develop and implement a nationwide Electronic Patient Record (EPR). The overall goal of that undertaking is to make basic functions and activities in the national health services more rational. They are to be made more efficient and economical in order to improve the treatments of patients and upgrade the organization of health-care work.

For these ambitions to be fulfilled, a shared set of *standards* is required. They are of different kinds: There need to be interchangeable standards for database structure, search hierarchies, programming languages, and hardware capacity. These standards are all, predominately, of a highly formalized kind. Furthermore, there needs to be a unifying focus on professional language and terminology, for instance on classification and definition of key words, and how to structure communication processes. This is all about *semantic* standards, and the National Board of Health has already introduced a set of semantic standards to be used by all parties in the national quest. Moreover, job performance will have to be coordinated by the various groups of health professionals, both internally in particular wards, and externally in accordance with outside groups and domains. It appears to be generally recognized among the central players that, without tending to all levels of the standardization work, it is highly unlikely that Denmark will gain computer-supported health services on a national scale and the consequent improvement in efficiency.

Crucial to the further spread of IT *as an instrument of standardization* is the expression of professional language and work processes in the health sector in unambiguous, clear definitions and concepts. During the last decade this kind of standardization work has increased on both national and on organizational levels. Such politically and economically motivated visions of IT-based solutions to improve the efficiency of work and communication in the health-care system are strongly influenced by certain culturally inherited presumptions regarding relationships between technology and humans. One such predominant assumption that seems rather hard-lived, concerns the alleged *neutrality* of technological artifacts. It is those who use technology who are to blame or praise for technology-related changes, not the artifact or system itself.

Ihde, among others, has rejected this view and demonstrated its shortcomings. He has made the case for *postphenomenology* as a separate perspective, from where it is meaningful to claim that humans and technology coconstitute each other (*PP*). Hence, both humans and artifacts are shaped by the labor of the other. The immediate merits of this view is that one needs to depart from macrosocial theory—where technological neutrality may seem reasonable—and move to microsocial studies of situated praxes. At the latter altitude "technological mediation" is no longer about ideals of efficiency and clear communication. Instead it is about heterogeneous relationships between individual human beings and the world, including the artifacts used for mediations. As Ihde has forcefully demonstrated in several books, we are embodied, engaged, and interpreting beings, who are firmly situated in the world (*TL BT*). One does need to distinguish between embodied microlevel relations and cultural macrorelations, but in the phenomenological tradition the microlevel is the most profound level of analysis—and for several good reasons.

The remainder of the chapter asks how technology can mediate between health professionals and the world on an individual, microperceptual level of experience. A key concern will be to study the non-neutral, or transformative effects of technological artifacts.

The Stethoscope: A Window into the Thoracic Cavity

First, I wish to address a conception of technology that demonstrates the strong relations between technology, communication, and professional work practices in the health-care system. The well-known historical example to be used may seem somewhat simple in respect to the current high-tech possibilities in health-care practices. Yet, it serves as an exemplary illustration of why it is reductive to conceive of technological devices and systems as neutral aids to human intentional actions. Such devices often serve as active contributors to *transforming the content* of communication and work. The example will also serve to substantiate the initial question if philosophy of technology is useful.

The kind of technology to exemplify non-neutral technology is *stethoscopy* invented around 1816 by the French medical doctor René Laënnec. Historically, he belongs to the so-called French school from the beginning of the nineteenth century. Its followers saw the *diagnosis* as an attempt to localize illnesses anatomically in the living body.[1] Until the end of the eighteenth century the medical profession tended to emphasize the *symptoms*, so that all the symptoms of a disease were considered equally important. With the development of the French school, special importance was instead placed on symptoms with a diagnostic relevance. At the same time, physical signs were assigned primary importance for diagnosis and prognosis, evident in the development of nosology, that is, the classification of diseases.[2]

The turn toward the clinical and pathological dimensions involved a weighting of different physical methods of diagnosis, first of all *palpation* (examination by touch) and *percussion* (examination by tapping the surface of a body part). Especially the emphasis on the physical, *observable* body in pathology led to the invention of a number of medical visualization techniques and artifacts, among these various endoscopes, ophthalmoscopes, and specula, later in the nineteenth century.

While examining a young girl with heart problems, Laënnec attempted to trace internal anomalies in her thoracic cavity by means of percussion and palpation. However, the patient's obesity made it impossible to apply these demonstrable techniques in any satisfactory way. Instead, he considered carrying out direct *auscultation,* that is, placing his ear against her chest and listening to her heart. He stopped doing this, however, ". . . because he found it inconvenient and distasteful to move his ear over the patient's chest, and the procedure embarrassed the patient."[3] Her age and gender, and his own dislike of this sort of intimate contact stood therefore in the way of a successful examination by means of direct auscultation.

Laënnec remembered reading that sounds moving through solid bodies achieve acoustic amplification. Therefore, he placed a tube made of firmly rolled paper between the patient's chest above the heart and one of his own ears. Now he could suddenly hear a whole new range of sounds that had been inaccessible till now due to practical, psychological, and moral reasons. With this discovery, a *gestalt shift* occurred in Laënnec's outlook on diagnosing and exploring the human chest area: "From this moment . . . I imagined that the circumstance might furnish means for enabling us to ascertain the character, not only of the action of the heart, but of every species of sound produced by the motion of all the *thoracic viscera.*"[4]

One could say that the acoustic amplification also caused a significant diagnostic amplification. Laënnec began to gradually develop his listening device, and it took the shape of a thin, approximately 30-centimeter-long, hollow wooden cylinder (a similar device is still used by Danish midwives labeled a "listening tube"). Laënnec ended up naming his device a "stethoscope," derived from the Greek *stéthos* "chest" and *skopein* "I see/examine." As simple as it may seem today, his device and the techniques involved, soon turned out to be most effective, first of all in diagnosing a number of lung diseases and examining cardiac sounds. Stethoscopy was thus well-suited for uncovering *internal indications* of disease, in cases where, for example, percussion had demonstrated its inadequacy. In other words, the method offered radically new knowledge about inner signs of a particular disease.

Laënnec's many examinations of and experiments with acoustic differences in healthy and sick bodies led to the publication of his dissertation *On Mediated Auscultation* in 1819. As implied by the title, Laënnec would make a radical distinction between listening that is mediated and intensified through a device, and listening that is done with the ear placed directly on the patient's chest.

In broad terms, the task of the medical profession could now be defined as the endeavor to make a diagnosis based on the doctor's own audible experiences with the patient's body. The sounds thus registered were conceived as *objectively accessible signs* by Laënnec and his followers, that is independent of the patient's subjective descriptions of his or her illness. Just as importantly, this conception meant that the doctor himself—on a par with the stethoscope—was *objectified* by acting as a functionally determined element in a successful auscultation. Only highly disciplined behavior on the part of the doctor could ensure the objective, instrument mediated diagnosis. Through mediated auscultation the diagnosis of symptoms in the chest area had shifted from subjective opinion to objective analysis.

Objectifying the Medical Body

The doctor and historian, Stanley Reiser has compared the effect of the stethoscope on the medical profession with that of letterpress printing on Western culture.[5] The product of the printing press—accessible, mass-produced, typeset books—contributed to foster the detached, objective individual, who sits calmly in his study, reading and reflecting on other people's thoughts. This detached dwelling is not possible in an oral culture, where any exchange of ideas is normally linked to embodied presence in a particular setting. Likewise, the stethoscope contributed to fostering the objective doctor, who is able to remain detached from his patient and avoid becoming influenced by the latter's subjective ideas about illness. Instead the doctor is now able to establish a more discontinuous relationship with the patient—not so much with the patient as a subjective interpreter of what is wrong as with the disease-revealing sounds emerging from the patient's body.

Mediated auscultation, or stethoscopy, strengthened contemporary hopes of transforming medicine from an art to a science. At the core of these expectations was a conviction that stethoscopy made it possible to establish *causal relations* between the sounds of the thoracic cavity and anatomic lesions. Until then it had not been possible to show unequivocal connections between, on the one hand, the patient's narrative presentations and outer physical signs of a disease and, on the other, the inner, anatomical defects. On the basis of stethoscopy, medical doctors were now able to carry out systematic, experimental verification and control of any hypothesis about signs of disease. In other words, it was possible to carry out premeditated experiments with auscultatory sounds and thereby demonstrate regular connections between certain sounds and specific diseases of the chest organs.

Concepts like "certainty" and "precision" along with "causal, constant relations" were soon associated with stethoscopy by virtue of experimental verification and evidence. All that served to emphasize the scientific foundation of the method. At the same time it emphasized the shift away from a situated conversation with the patient toward universal, reproducible diagnosis of a medical case.

It is important to note that Laënnec's method and instrument cannot be seen independently of each other. On the contrary, they are best seen as co-constituting each other. Without an instrument there is no sound-amplification to bring about objective signs of disease and thus confirm the certainty of the method; without a method there is no convincing reason to use the stethoscope in diagnostic praxis. The stethoscope and stethoscopy depend on each other.

The interdependence between the stethoscope and its method of use underscores, I believe, a general point about technology—that no device by itself guarantees better work practices. Built into "technology" is a "logos" entailing some sort of knowledge about the operations of the device. This unites the instrument with an array of thoughts in a context. On the one hand, the instrument acquires some kind of theoretical motivation to function in an orderly manner. On the other hand, the actual interplay with a technical device is a materialization of deliberation.

Hence, there are two conclusions to be drawn from the development of stethoscopy in the early nineteenth century, both emphasizing the transformative consequences of technology for medical practice and theory. First, with the stethoscope medical science came to be more concerned with diseases than with patients. Second, the patient's knowledge is particular and subjective while instrument-driven knowledge is general and objective. The latter knowledge may thus serve as a basis for scientific experience in medicine.

Instrument-Mediated Diseases and Patients

Thanks to the stethoscope a device had been placed *between* the doctor and the patient, and this new element would transform medical practice and theory in a number of decisive ways. Instrumental mediation indicated certain methods and understandings that had not been accessible previously in either theory or practice. The inner organs and the functioning of the living body were no longer hidden to the doctor, and technological mediation was the instrument that opened up the new landscape. The further development of medical devices in the nineteenth century contributed to strengthening the professionals' beliefs in technologically mediated diagnosis and conception of disease. This belief is also found in the development of the ophthalmoscope, the laryngoscope, and early X-ray apparatuses.

Three stages of medico-historical development must be referenced in regard to this chapter's topic: (1) direct communication with the patient;

(2) direct communication with the patient's *body* through physical examinations, and (3) indirect communication with the patient and his experiences and body by means of technical aids.

In the third, instrument mediated stage, where current medicine is to be found, new specialties have appeared. Among these are pathology and radiology, both defined by decoding the meaning of technically produced information. These areas of expertise have contact with tissue samples and X-ray photographs, but not with patients. There are also other features of the current health sector that show its dependence on technological mediation. For example, the laboratory technicians are indispensable at the modern hospital; their absence would make diagnosis and interpretation practically impossible because technologically mediated laboratory results are an integrated part of the diagnostic process.

In the process outlined above, the doctor—and in a broader sense the clinical personnel—abandoned an inadequate dependence on subjective evaluations, that is, the patient's statements, in favor of a new kind of dependence on technologically based evaluations. One partial view of disease was replaced by another partial view.

Decisively, many traditional methods were transformed with the introduction of stethoscopy. The doctor's questioning of the patient, which had previously been of primary importance to the interpretive work and successful treatment, was made less relevant. Gradually, the thorough observation of outer symptoms of disease also lost its fundamental significance concurrently with the growing trust in apparatuses and machines. In this way, stethoscopy, more than so many other medico-historical examples, symbolizes the shift in the medical profession away from being an art toward being a technology-driven science. Traditional faith in the healing power of nature was replaced by a new faith in the healing powers of technology.

As will become clear below, the technological conditions for doing health-care work tend to create a distance, not just between doctor and patient, but also between professional clinical work and personal judgment.

Human-Instrument-World Relations

As the following example suggests, there are often contradictions between direct and instrumentally mediated experiences. At a large Danish hospital a doctor was sent for by a nurse because a patient was discovered to suffer from *bradycardia,* that is, his pulse was slow. The nurse had discovered his condition because a sphygmograph was connected to the patient and a digital display on the device showed the current pulse rate. Upon arriving in the room the doctor observed an unaffected patient whose skin color and breathing was normal.

Hence, to the doctor, the patient did not appear to be in the critical condition otherwise indicated by the display. The doctor volunteered to hand-count the patient's pulse for 15 seconds and was able to establish that the beat was normal indeed. The nurse nevertheless insisted that the patient had the slow pulse evidenced by the display. Not until the doctor counted the patient's pulse for a full 60 seconds and still found it to be perfectly normal did the nurse agree that the patient's condition was not critical—and consequently drew the conclusion that the sphygmograph was broken.

The nurse experienced a *Gestalt shift* in her interpretation of the situation from the "patient is in crisis" to the "device is broken." The important thing was not so much that the gestalt shift took place but rather *how* it happened. It turned out that the faith in the measurement value of the device kept her in a certain technology-mediated interpretation of the situation *in spite of* her own clinical experiences and the doctor's assurance that the interpretation was wrong. The doctor had to intensify, as it were, her demonstrable arguments by counting for a longer time period before the nurse's faith in the human evaluation became greater than her faith in the technological assessment. Presumably, it was decisive for the nurse's change of mind that she also had tactile experiences from measuring the pulse beat with her fingertip; that is, she knew what it meant to feel the pulse in a wrist and to count the beats.

This example shows that conflicts between direct, personal experiences of the world and technologically mediated experiences frequently occur. The outcome of such conflicts is not certain. It very much depends on the ability of the persons involved to judge correctly. However, in most mundane work practices there is no neutral place from where one can make judgments. In the following outline of Ihde's phenomenological understanding of technological mediation it will be evident that our understanding of ourselves and our praxis is largely shaped by the experiential relations and situations in which technological mediation is a factor.

Ihde's Postphenomenology of Technology

The following description of technological mediation aims at showing how technology can advantageously be studied as constituent part of embodied experience. In his books, Ihde has argued that a phenomenological analysis of the relations between humans, technology, and world must strive to point out some of the structural features of the symbiotic, or co-constitutive relations between humans and technology in a praxis. Over the years he has developed a very helpful notation, based on the *human-technology-world* schemata, to capture the structure in different types of experiential situations.

This has been developed most rigorously in his key work *Technology and the Lifeworld,* especially chapter five.

Some of our experiences are characterized by a direct human—world relations, for example, doctor-patient, where the doctor verbally questions the patient about his illness, or palpates his chest. In most cases, however, we are experiencing the world through mediations. This is where Ihde's human-technology-world schemata has proven most suggestive as a means, or method to grasp the active processes of technological mediation. The method suggests a continuum of technologically mediated relations starting from embodiment relations, over hermeneutic relations, and ending with alterity relations. Following this range one can also discern an increased polarity between the subject position and the object (the technological artifact) beginning with the almost unified embodiment relation and ending in the nearly intersubjective relationship of alterity relations.

In a recent publication Ihde has stated that: "postphenomenology, I contend, substitutes embodiment for subjectivity . . . if there is a "subject" at all, it is the actional "subject" of bodily action." (CT 11–12). The point of departure for the postphenomenological analysis of technologically mediated experiences is thus found in the study of the experiential characteristics of our embodied interaction with technology. Hence, embodiment relations seems particular viable to demonstrate the usefulness of philosophy for research on the design and use of computer-based technology in everyday life.

Embodied experiences of the world through/with technological artifacts possess an existential quality. Individual tools like the hammer, the knife, the pickaxe, the loom, and so on, has been an integrated part of our lived, practical life long before we obtained scientific institutions and began to produce abstract images of the world. Therefore, much of our basic understanding of life is linked to these kinds of embodied relations with technological artifacts. Without them the world would be experienced and understood quite differently.

Such existential technological relations are characterized by Ihde as embodiment relations. That is because the relations are tied to practical situations of use where technological instruments are implicated in the individual's world of experience in a particular way. The world is thus sensed *through* the instrument, while a concurrent reflexive transformation of perceptual and bodily experiences occurs. The transformation is reflexive because I am influenced by the impressions continuously thrown back on me from the world while I use the instrument.

Let me return to the example of mediated auscultation. In phenomenological terms one can now say that the introduction and implementation of the stethoscope involved a shift in the doctor's diagnostic practice and sensory experience, from: doctor hears-thorax, to: doctor hears-through sound-amplifying instrument-the thorax.

Relations of this kind between instrument and human are distinguished as embodiment relations because the doctor embodies the instrument in *her* experience in a certain way. First, by sensing *through* the stethoscope and, second, through a gradual, reflexive transformation of her perceptual and embodied perception of the patient's body. The stethoscope is placed in a mediating position between the listening doctor and the object of her listening. It is because the doctor is listening *through* the device that the referent, the patient body, is put on the other side of the stethoscope. In this context the patient is separated from the doctor and will mainly be perceived through the stethoscope. The doctor's primary experience of disease will, in other words, be mediated in an interactive relationship with the instrument.

Following Ihde's postphenomenology, this is not enough to point out the relation between a human and technology as an embodiment relation. First, one must determine where and how the instrument is experienced by the doctor. The stethoscope must be technically suitable as an instrument through which she can listen. It must possess certain material qualities before it can be said to be *transparent* or obvious. If it is not transparent to the doctor she cannot listen through it as an obvious part of her work. Not until it is sufficiently transparent, that is, at a minimum approximates a "pure" form of transparency, is it possible to embody the stethoscope. This is the material condition for embodiment.

Embodiment, in the sense of an activity, must be learned, which in phenomenological terms means *constituted*. If it is a technological product of a decent quality, that will not pose great problems; take, for instance, a pair of well-fitting glasses. When the necessary adjustments to the new glasses have been made and the user no longer "sees through a pair of glasses" but simply "sees," one can say about the embodiment relations that the technological transparency is optimal. Another example of this is the blind man's cane, which contributes to his motor skills. Here it is also true that the cane—as a cane—withdraws, becomes background, and through the cane-extended hand the blind man feels the world, that is (the blind man-cane-) world. It has become transparent.

In a somewhat similar fashion a well-constructed stethoscope becomes assimilated in the doctor's perceptual-bodily experience so that stethoscopy becomes a natural part of her diagnostic ability, that is (doctor-stethoscope)-body. This means that the stethoscope becomes internalized in the way the doctor will normally experience, for instance, the thorax. In phenomenological terms one would say that stethoscopy has moved from foreground to background in the doctor's world of experience, now an obvious part of her everyday medical work practice.

How well or how poorly the technological design is done is, in other words, decisive for the success of embodiment relations—as, for example, expressed by the precision involved in measuring the refraction of the eyes, grinding the eyeglass lenses, and fitting the frame. The better these processes are carried out, the more easily the glasses disappear in the background, that is, are internalized in the user's bodily and visual experiences of the world. In everyday terms, the closer a given instrument comes to invisibility, transparency, and extending one's own bodily senses, the better its design. This involves the important point that optimal design is only in part about the instrument. It is far more about the *combination* of instrument and human.

In addition, the examples show that our embodied sensual perception is not given once and for all. On the contrary, it is flexible and can be reduced or expanded depending on the qualities of the particular embodied mediations. Our experience of our own body's extension cannot be reduced to a narrow idea of bodily limits. Rather we possess, in Ihde's words, a *polymorphous* experience of bodily extensions.

The examples of technological mediation thus far have been *monosensorial*. Driving a car is noteworthy as a more complex example that involves whole-body motility. Driving involves several senses at once, that is, *plurisensorial* mediation. The joy of driving is normally connected to the total range of embodiment relations. The driver experiences the road and the surroundings *through* the activity of driving the car, the movement being the focal activity. The bodily experience is expanded to include what that can be experienced by a (driver-in-a-car) body. In respect to several other kinds of experiences, many instruments, technologies, and a more composite learning process are involved here, but the involved knowledge is fundamentally embodied.

Ultrasound examinations involves, for instance, a large degree of embodied relations between apparatus and doctor. It is an embodiment relation: (the doctor sees—with the ultrasound scanner)—the patient. Through proficient use of the ultrasound scanner, the scanner's probe work essentially like an extension of the arm's tactile qualities as it is moved over the patient's abdomen. The relation is plurisensorial due to the interaction between touch and sight (and sometimes sound); for example, the screen image of the embryo in the uterus can be made more clear by a "suitable" turn of the wrist. This relation to the patient's body is in a sense opposed to, for instance, CT scanning. Scanning based on computer tomography does not take place by virtue of continual, embodied relations between doctor and apparatus. Rather it involves discontinued relationships, and CT scanning constitutes a different kind of instrumentally mediated relation to the patient: the doctor sees—(with the CT scanner, the patient). This is evidently what Ihde calls a hermeneutic relation, that is, a relation in which the world is mediated to the individual as a "text" for the doctor to read in order to know about a particular part of the world: The doctor sees—(with the CT scanner, the patient).

All this should emphasize the fact that our sense of our own body is polymorphous: our body experiences are not predetermined but rather malleable and reducible in correlation to those technological mediations the body is able to take in. The sensing body may just as well be a (listen-with-the-stethoscope) body as a (drive-in-the-car) body, or something entirely different. It depends on the situation and the already constituted technologically mediated relations. The body can thus be described as *multistable*.

What is crucial here is that the degree of embodiment relations to the patient is reflected in a particular health practitioner's total repertoire of notions about her patient's condition. In general terms this means that the less embodiment relations are part of clinical work, the less the patient will appear to the health practitioner as an independent, living person.

Visual Noises and Knowledge

In this chapter I will speculate on one significant aspect of the above mentioned shift from embodiment to hermeneutic relations to the patient and the world.

While developing stethoscopy in the nineteenth century the method was described metaphorically as "an open window into the thorax." To listen to the sounds coming from the patient's chest was, in other words, construed as "seeing" the patient's disease. Mediated auscultation is ". . . a window in the breast through which we can see the state of things within," as proclaimed by a contemporary supporter.[6] This view accentuates quite nicely a common attitude in Western intellectual history to make visualization the principal sense (*EH*). This inclination to tie intellect and vision together has been portrayed as occularcentrism.[7] In the present example, auditory impressions are metaphorically redescribed as visual images, and the symptoms of the patient are represented as visual experiences.

I emphasize this cultural penchant, known at least since Plato's cave, in order to point out a typical phenomenological feature of technology-driven human practices. Constantly we strive to get at clear picture of, or "get insight into" the sensual world through visual (re-) descriptions. In health-care work this fondness for the visual shows itself in the great number of medical scanning techniques: X-ray, ultrasound, MRI, CT, and CAT.[8] I find it reasonable to think that the current development of the computer is closely connected with strong, culturally based efforts to establish "a view from nowhere" on the world, e.g. on the many activities and relations in the health care systems. Donna Haraway has aptly identified such effort as "the god trick."[9]

These attempts have motivated numerous plans and project to augment our limited sensual capacity by the help of computer power. And in order to do so we generally lean on augmented vision.

The Scholastic and the Clinical Attitude

In the introduction I claimed that the continued production of formal tools like imaging technologies and the EPR will intensify a general move away from what I choose to term as *clinical knowledge* toward *scholastic* knowledge; or better, a move from a clinical toward a scholastic *attitude* to health-care work. This kind of move will involve an altered environment for interactions between health-care professionals, and for their communication with patients. It will imply planned, as well as unanticipated transformations of specific work tasks in actual health-care practices. Let me expand on this classification and claim:

A scholastic attitude to health care work encompasses theoretical knowledge, that is, explicit knowledge, which is accessible through books used in medical schools, nursing schools, etc. Theoretical knowledge can always be made explicit and turned into precise, literal expressions about factual phenomena and conditions. Only what can be turned into literal language counts as significant components in treatment and care. This points to a certain normativity in the scholastic attitude. To put it crudely: relevant, well-defined problems of health-care work *ought to be* solved by using appropriate, scientific knowledge according to predetermined rules. The scholastic attitude thus assumes that health professionals are able to solve problems most efficiently by *rule-following use of explicit knowledge*. This is the core of professional competency in health-care work, according to the scholastic attitude.

By adapting this core, it will seem obvious to choose highly formalized devices and systems to increase rational planning and efficiency. Hence, the scholastic attitude will go hand-in-hand with high-tech solutions to improve the quality of work, etc. What is easily overlooked is that the *standards* to settle what counts as "problems" and "solutions" are not neutral, universally given definitions, but rather culturally inherited ideals, which are typically associated with the very means, for example, computer-based systems that define the range of possible solutions.

It was once said as a joke that "the computer is the solution, what is the problem?" But, if there are no work tasks in want of formal protocols, or no skills to be standardized according to the logic of computational procedures, it is not obvious to define the computer as the right means to ensure efficient solutions in health-care work. The non-neutrality of technology needs to be integrated in a viable stance toward health-care work, as well as its transformative qualities.

Following Ihde we need to develop an awareness about the co-constitutional labor of humans and technology in real-world situations.

The clinical attitude to work and communication embraces theoretical knowledge and rule-based skills, as well as ruleless skills and tacit knowledge. Tacit knowledge is obtained through long-term observation of, and participation in everyday work.[10] Ruleless skills are likewise achieved through experiences in clinical praxis. To make a proficient interpretation of an X-ray picture, to discern the patient's present condition correctly, to carry out a successful counseling of a nervous patient, or to work well as a team on a heart attack, all presupposes tacit knowledge, know-how, and previous experience as much as theoretical knowledge and explicit rules, if not more.

Hence, if the clinical attitude is accepted, embodied work experiences cannot straightforwardly be described in terms compatible with computational operations. Consequently, it is not obvious for a whole range of tasks performed in health-care work to be enhanced by the application of computer solutions, certainly not if these tasks rest on embodied performances of the practitioners.

More thoroughgoing field studies and concern for the situated character of everyday work thus seem necessary if future design of standardized technologies are to be a true improvement of health-care work. If technologically mediated embodiment relations are not taken into account, it seems highly unlikely that the efforts will succeed.

Conclusion

The predominant view that in order to establish IT-based health services nationwide we need to standardize several basic tasks and competencies, represents a certain set of philosophical ideas about dealing with everyday work tasks. To put it in broad terms, this view reflects a modernist stance toward human beings, technology, and how they are related. The logical core of IT systems has been made the focal point, and task handling is seen in entrepreneurial terms as a matter of problem-solving. This view is embraced by the scholastic attitude.

From the perspective argued here, however, there is more to the case than autonomous subjects operating standardized tools in intentional actions. Both things and people are transformed during processes of change. It is precisely the dynamic, interdependent evolving of things and embodied humans, which makes it possible to stabilize particular relations over time. Ihde's postphenomenology has offered some important philosophical handles to get a grip on these issues.

Based on the philosophical support from Ihde's work I venture to predict that we must expect intended technology-based improvement of health-care practices to be counteracted by unexpected transformations of work and competencies. Incorporating new technology can not just be seen as neutral augmentation of existing clinical experiences. Rather, it is likely to prompt a move away from plurisensorial embodied experiences toward specialized, monosensorial representations thanks to advanced imaging technologies and an increasing number of hermeneutic relations. This is a reminder of the contention, stated in the introduction: The effective range of "do-able" problems for health professionals in a work context will be altered in a number of ways that goes beyond rational planning due to the introduction of new high-tech solutions to improve clinical work efficiency.

Ihde has done philosophers of technology a great favor by fleshing out the trajectory from classical phenomenology to postphenomenology. Hopefully, we will be able to bring his arguments forward to designers, executives, and politicians.

Notes

1. Stanley Joel Reiser, *Medicine and the Reign of Technology* (Cambridge: Cambridge University Press 1978).

2. Erwin H. Ackernecht, *A Short History of Medicine* (Baltimore: Johns Hopkins University Press, 1982).

3. Reiser, *Medicine and the Reign of Technology*, 25.

4. Ibid.

5. Reiser, *Medicine and the Reign of Technology.*

6. Ibid., 30.

7. David M. Levin, *Modernity and the Hegemony of Vision* (Berkeley: University of California, 1993).

8. Stuart S. Blume, *Insight and Industry – On the Dynamics of Technological Change in Medicine* (Cambridge, MIT Press, 1992). See also Bettyan Holtzmann Kevels, *Naked to the Bone – Medical Imaging in the Twentieth Century* (New Brunswick, NJ: Rutgers University Press, 1997).

9. Donna Haraway, *Modest_Witness@Second_Millennium FemaleMan©Meets_OncoMouse™—Feminism and Technoscience* (New York: Routledge, 1997).

10. Michael Polanyi, *Personal Knowledge – Towards a Post Critical Philosophy* (New York: Harper Torchbook, 1964).

18

Mediating Between
Science and Technology

Albert Borgmann

Don Ihde is the great mediator of contemporary philosophy. He has connected phenomenology with postmodernism, philosophy of technology with philosophy of science, Continental philosophy with analytic philosophy. He has tirelessly mediated across oceans, and he has widely explained himself through his prolific writing.

Mediation for Ihde is more than scuttling back and forth between opposing schools and pleading for mutual understanding. There is a center to his mediations, a distinctive position first sketched in his *Experimental Phenomenology* of 1977, clearly outlined in the classic *Technics and Praxis* of 1979, expanded and refined in many ways since, and summarized for the time being in *Chasing Technoscience* of 2003.

Mediation, accordingly, can be used to name not only the energy that has flowed from Ihde's central position across disciplines and continents, but to characterize that central position. From the start Ihde has been interested in what mediates between reality and humanity, more particularly how the materiality of the world comes across to the bodily beings we are.

One way of bringing Ihde's mediations into relief is to set them in between two of the outstanding, perhaps *the* outstanding intellectual challenges of the early twenty-first century. The first, I suggest, is finding the theory of everything, a consistent account of the physical lawfulness of the world.[1] More specifically it is the reconciliation of the inconsistent twin pillars of contemporary physics—relativity theory and quantum theory. The other, I propose, is getting insight into the drift of contemporary culture.

There are theorists of physics and culture who would disagree. Freeman Dyson for one thinks that a unified theory of physics is neither possible nor desirable, and Ihde might be considered critical of the view that there is

247

something like *the* drift of something like *the* contemporary culture.[2] So let me start with what can be said on behalf of the two challenges:

We see reality in light of physical theory. We do not see the world in this light only, to be sure, but the light of theory is distinctive for our time and uniquely revealing. The force of theory comes to light against the conceivable alternative. A world that did not instantiate physical lawfulness would be capricious and troubling in a more profound sense that it is now. Grievous surprises assault us as it is, but underlying them is the assurance that things hang together and can in principle be grasped in their regularity and coherence if not controlled in practice.

The underlying regularity of reality allows us to occupy, or at least aspire to, a restful position in a luminous world. Rest and light must have been what premodern people missed most. At any rate eternal rest and light perpetual is what Christians wish for their departed. Today we get to feel the mischief of darkness and unrest from those who represent irrationalism in religion and culture and threaten oppression and wantonness on the rest of us.

Einstein, to the contrary, likened the vision of scientific lawfulness to "the silence of high mountains, where the eye ranges freely through the still, pure air and fondly traces out the restful contours apparently built for eternity."[3] Other physicists have put it differently, but agree that beauty and elegance are intrinsic if insufficient features of physical theories.[4] Inconclusiveness and incisiveness, the capacity to reveal underlying universality, is a crucial ingredient of a theory's aesthetic charm. It would come into its own in a theory of quantum gravity.

Contemporary culture has nothing of this fundamental cohesion and unity. Its variety and instability have been rightly celebrated by Ihde. It exhibits none the less striking global features as Ihde also notes (*IR*, 139–140). One is global warming, which, though it is not caused by everyone, affects everyone. Another is obesity, which is becoming a global epidemic.[5]

There are still more striking features of contemporary culture if you agree that the culture of the advanced industrial countries is paradigmatic and represents the type that most other cultures tend or aspire to. One might take this one final step and propose that the United States is the paradigm of paradigms, the oldest technological society in that, like the oldest sibling, it was first to move through the stages of technological development since the late nineteenth century.

What is remarkable about American society, given its prosperity and opportunities, is its ignorance of the world and its indifference to the world's misery. To illustrate, Americans on average vastly overestimate the share of the federal budget that is devoted to foreign aid. It's in fact less than one percent and makes this the most callous in the community of prosperous countries.[6]

In 2002 a psychologist shared the Nobel Prize in economics. It was Daniel Kahneman who was cited "for having integrated insights from psychological research into economic science, especially concerning human judgment and decision-making under uncertainty."[7] Kahneman demonstrated that human judgment typically misjudges the effect that pleasures have on happiness.[8] His investigations converged with research showing that a person's or a society's happiness can be validly and reliably determined. It was found, not surprisingly given Kahneman's research, that growing prosperity from a certain point on leaves happiness flat or makes it decline.[9]

The drift of contemporary culture, it seems to me, points to a conjunction of material success and moral failure. The force of this drift or the drift itself constitutes a form of life, one that, following Langdon Winner, we can call technology.[10] Material success in this kind of life is the conquest of hunger, disease, and cultural confinement. Moral failure means indifference to environmental stewardship and global justice and sullenness when it comes to human flourishing.

More pleasure—less happiness, more information technology—less knowledge, more food—less health, greater ability to help—less willingness to share, this is not what most of us expected. These are not the sunny uplands of global liberty and authentic prosperity, of rich diversity and vigorous self-realization, of ecological harmony and cultural creativity. But if the technophiles and optimists had it wrong, so did the dystopians. Life may be flat and sullen, but it is far from grim and oppressive.

We are facing a paradox, *The American Paradox: Spiritual Hunger in an Age of Plenty* as one recent book title has it, *The Progress Paradox: How Life Gets Better While People Feel Worse* as another puts it.[11] Is the paradox an antinomy in Kant's sense, an inconsistency that would be resolved if only we could locate a fundamental but unwarranted assumption everyone is making?[12] Or is it an antinomy in Quine's sense, an inconsistency that will only be resolved if we find fundamentally new ways of understanding?[13]

A resolution in either case might help us to direct the drift of contemporary culture in a more compassionate, responsible, and engaging direction. That theory can aid practice is a widely held axiom of contemporary culture. At a minimum, a resolution would give us a steadier and more penetrating vision of the world—sometimes the only consolation of philosophy. A harmonious vision of science and technology, moreover, would not lead to a life of terminal ease. It might disclose, however, what labors and pains are truly worth the effort.

If the paradoxes of technology and science constitute crucial intellectual challenges, there is at least one other—how do these inconsistencies consist with one another? Is there a connection between them? This is where Ihde's mediation, his work on technoscience, comes into play. What distinguishes

Ihde's approach is its openness to theoretical science on one side and to the concreteness of the technological culture on the other. Thus it contrasts favorably with the strong program of technoscience that turned out to be self-absorbed and worse. On the science side it has displayed lamentable ignorance and arrogance or at least unwarranted social constructivism.[14] On the wider cultural side it has been largely silent.

Ihde has maintained the fundamental realism of the early stage of phenomenology. It is of course a sophisticated and circumspect sort of realism, and current astrophysics illustrates well Ihde's celebrated shift from the embodiment relation of scientific instruments to the hermeneutic relation. The telescope is incorporated into our bodily visual being. Not so the instruments of astrophysics, ranging from cyclotrons to the Hubble Space Telescope and the recent Gravity Probe B. They produce texts that need to be interpreted, and without technology none of them would be available. Important information, moreover, was not just searched for by technological means but first came to the scientists' attention through technology. The cosmic background radiation is the leading case in point.[15]

Ihde agrees with the technoscience people that social conditions influence the whether, the when, the who, and the how of scientific research. But he does not let reality slip from his grasp. As he puts it, "we know a lot because we are making the things speak."[16] He pleads "partially guilty" to being a realist. "If you can interact with the thing you are investigating," he has said, "in such a way that you can determine, to use Merleau-Pontyian language, that it is questioning you back, then you have something real" (*CT* 126).

On the side of contemporary culture, technoscience faintly embodies the ethos of liberation that has become part of modern society and has remained an unfinished task. The theorists of technoscience clearly want to free us from the oppression of a philosophy of science that champions theory and propositions to the exclusion of social conditions and practices. But this liberation does not reach into everyday life except for the consonance of its feminist professions with women's liberation.

Ihde has seen that technoscience, both as a philosophy of science and as a philosophy of technology is "unavoidably linked to social-political and ethical philosophies" and "must turn its focus to issues of daily life, to the ethical impacts of philosophy" (*IR* 139, 140).

Ihde's technoscience, then, opens up on astrophysics as the powerful and indispensable instruments that mediate between humans and cosmic lawfulness, and it opens up on daily life through the technologies that mediate the lifeworld and human interaction. But I find still deeper lineaments in Ihde's mediations though I am not sure Ihde himself would recognize them. At any rate they point toward the resolution of the inconsistencies I began with.

Ihde uses multiperspectivalism and multistability as roughly subjective and objective correlates, both coming into relief through his variational method (*BT* 33 and *CT* 133–135). I want to firm up the correlation in one sense by distinguishing between multiperspectivalism as an epistemological issue and multiculturalism as an ontological issue, and to modify the correlation in another sense by suggesting that the ontology that corresponds to the epistemology of multiperspectivalism differs from the ontology of multistability, and so, analogously, for the epistemology that goes with the ontology of multistability.

The possibility of multiple perspectives on one and the same object is a necessary condition of empirical realism. Consider the two alternatives. One is Platonic or absolute realism where supposedly the entire essence of an object is disclosed to the eye of the mind. Perspectival knowledge in this view is partial and deficient knowledge, that is, opinion. The other alternative is subjectivism. Every perspective discloses its own unique state of affairs. There is no one world that is shared by different perspectives.

The cosmic structure is the invariant that is disclosed by the variations of hermeneutic texts, mediated by the technologies of investigation. The intellectual challenge is to penetrate and integrate the seemingly disparate texts and to see through them the one lawful theory of everything. Ihde's work shows how many layers and kinds the variants will have. The greatest challenge, of course, is to learn how to see relativity theory and quantum theory as variants or special cases of one theory. The great technological question is whether for the hypomicroscopic level of, for example, strings, at which a theory of everything can be articulated, there can be hermeneutic texts that will decide among competing versions of the theory.

The telos, at any rate, of current astrophysics is a univocal theory, cast in the language of mathematics, while the epistemology will be multiple, at least in the phase of discovery. If or when it is found, Ihde's mediational epistemology will face a new task, and it will be as well prepared as any I know. The task is this. How do you make an abstract and prohibitively difficult mathematical theory palpable in its cognitive power and aesthetic appeal to bodily humans generally and to lay people particularly? Dozens of popularizers have tried, of course.[17] Here lies a wide field awaiting careful work—how do we judge and perhaps improve these efforts in light of Ihde's mediations?

The multistability of everyday culture is primarily an ontological rather than epistemological issue. To be sure, it is introduced as an epistemological phenomenon in the ingenious investigations of *Experimental Phenomenology*, but it is later extended to cultural circumstances, most impressively in *Technology and the Lifeworld*. One example is the Acheulean hand ax. What is it? A sculpture? An ax? A projectile? A paperweight? A mineral? We can, of course, give a "neutral" description of it as Ihde does. It is "a symmetrically shaped stone. It is ovaloid in form with one end more pointed than the other, flattened by chipping and flaking such that a sharp edge runs around the entire circumference"(*TL* 68).

One might cast and dismiss this issue in Fregean terms and say that the "neutral" description gives us the referent; the questions suggest the many senses the referent may have. But any naming of an object gives some sense and never the referent as such. The Fregean referent or denotation is like the Kantian thing-in-itself, unknowable as such, accessible only in its appearance or sense. Thus the "neutral" description gives the sense of a Neolithic tool, Frege's *Venus* as the referent of the Evening Star and the Morning Star invokes Roman mythology, etc.[18]

The important contribution Ihde makes is to show that this multiplicity of senses reflects an irreducible ontological multistability. Ihde takes pleasure in disclosing it where we did not suspect it, and he often celebrates the richness that comes to the fore in multistability. It's a reflection of Ihde's sunny disposition, and his affirmative views of the bright side of technology are a much needed counterweight to the dystopianism he often complains about.

The ontological significance of multistability comes further into relief and perhaps more impressively so, when considering cases where it reveals conflict as well as richness. Consider for example the Front in Montana. What is it? "The Front runs 100 miles from U.S. Highway 200, north to Glacier National Park, along the eastern edge of the Rocky Mountains. On a map, that's where you will find it."[19] This is the artfully impoverished geographical designation that we are inclined to mistake for the thing in itself. In actuality this is plains Grizzly habitat, sacred territory of the Blackfeet, working ranch land, prime real estate for trophy ranches, a deposit of oil and natural gas, a tourist destination, an American Serengeti, a source of lumber, and more.

The crucial point is that the Front *is* in fact all this. The mill workers who say that there is timber in the foothills are not just imagining this. The oil and gas companies are not deluded in claiming that there is oil and gas below the prairie. In an absolute ontology, modeled on Fregean semantics, we could dismiss the multistable character of the Front as so many properties of one and the same thing. In the absolute ontology of the intrinsic-value-of-nature school, the Front is just one thing—untouchable wilderness.[20] Not so in Ihde's relational phenomenology, which is theoretically more illuminating and culturally more realistic. Contrary to "Fregean" ontology, Ihde's "core ontology" requires us to face up to the "interrelations of humans and environments" (*CT* 133). Contrary to the-intrinsic-value-of-nature ontology, Ihde's variational method discloses that there are interrelations other than humans respecting the intrinsic value of nature.

This leaves us with a problem Ihde only touches on. The multistability of the Front and its relational complement lead to conflict. Not all the relations can be acted on. Some are compatible with one another—current ranching practices and respect for sacred Native American sites. But respect for nature and drilling are not. Ihde responds in two ways to this conflict, the first powerful and implicit, the second explicit and merely illustrative.

Consider the bistability of the body of water known as the Long Island Sound. It is not only an enchanting world of wind and water, but also a site for a gigantic wind farm where tens of thousands of wind generators on towers many hundreds of feet tall could generate a third of the electricity needed in New England. When alerted to this bistability, would Ihde be indifferent? He is a passionate sailor and has referred to that body of water as "my own Long Island Sound" (*TL* 163–164).

To appreciate Ihde's explicit response to conflicted relations we need to see the connection between multistability and pluriculture. Ihde sometimes seems to suggest such a connection though he rejects it on other occasions (*TL* 150, 160). In any case, the Front at one time was just hunting grounds and sacred ground for the Blackfeet. For the first settlers in the second half of the nineteenth century, it was simply homesteading land. But for an impartial observer, the arrival of the homesteaders had already fractured the univocal relation to the land, and in the course of the twentieth century the land began to speak in still more voices.

So also with culture. Today in this country there is no longer a local cuisine anywhere that is so exclusive and taken for granted that it is just *the* cuisine. Instead there are "multiple cuisines," Ihde says. But there is a normative boundary to multiplicity. Ihde puts it this way. "There is no way that one could phenomenologically establish that there is a best cuisine. On the other hand, I am equally clear that one can tell the difference between good and bad Cantonese cooking, and good and bad nouvelle French cuisine"(*CT* 129–130).

Perhaps these "normative dimensions in phenomenology" can be extended to the Front. We might say that one cannot establish a best way of being concerned with the Front, whether as a geologist, a botanist, a zoologist, a historian, a sociologist, or a land manager, but that one can tell the difference between good and bad geology, good and bad history, and good and bad land management. But this may be getting the right normative regions by gerrymandering.

Be that as it may, what in any case we can take from Ihde's multistability and variational method toward the resolution of the paradox of technology is the need to make the richness of contemporary culture more vivid to society at large, to bring out the normative dimensions that are consistent with that richness, and to encourage the full-bodied engagement with the world that is at the heart of Ihde's work.

Notes

1. Steven Weinberg, *Dreams of a Final Theory* (New York: Pantheon, 1992).

2. Freeman Dyson, "The World on a String," *New York Review of Books* (May 13, 2003): 16–19.

3. Albert Einstein, "Principles of Research (1918)," available June 2, 2004: http://www.cs.ucla.edu/~slu/on_research/einstein_essay2.html.

4. Weinberg, *Dreams of a Final Theory*, 132–65. See also Brian Greene, *The Elegant Universe* (New York: Norton, 2000), 75, 130, 135, 146, 166–67, 169, 212, 227, 255, 347, 368, 386.

5. World Health Organization, "Controlling the Global Obesity Epidemic," available June 3, 2004: http://www.who.int/nut/obs.htm.

6. Martin Gilens, "Political Ignorance and Collective Policy Preferences," *American Political Science Review* 95 (June 2001): 379–396.

7. Nobel Prize Internet Archive, available June 2, 2004: http://almaz.com/nobel/economics/2002a.html.

8. Daniel Kahneman, "Objective Happiness," in *Well-Being*, eds. Daniel Kahneman, Ed Diener, and Norbert Schwarz (New York: Russell Sage, 1999), 3–25.

9. Robert E. Lane, *The Loss of Happiness in Market Democracies* (New Haven, CT: Yale University Press, 2000), 3–137.

10. Langdon Winner, *The Whale and the Reactor* (Chicago: Chicago University Press, 1986), 3–18. With greater caution, Winner speaks of "Technologies as Forms of Life."

11. David G. Myers, *The American Paradox: Spiritual Hunger in an Age of Plenty* (New Haven, CT: Yale University Press, 2000). Gregg Easterbrook, *The Progress Paradox: How Life Gets Better While People Feel Worse* (New York: Random House, 2003).

12. Immanuel Kant, *Kritik der reinen Vernunft* (Hamburg: Felix Meiner, 1956), 491–496.

13. W.V. Quine, "The Ways of Paradox," *The Ways of Paradox and Other Essays* (New York: Random House, 1966), 3–20.

14. Criticisms of various kinds have been leveled against all three companions of Ihde's in *Chasing Technoscience*. On Pickering, see Alan Franklin, "Do Mutants Die of Natural Causes? The Case of Atomic Parity Violations," in *A House Built on Sand*, ed. Noretta Koertge (New York: Oxford University Press, 1998), 166–80. A minor criticism of Haraway is given by Meera Nand in *Prophets Facing Backward: Postmodernism, Science, and Hindu Nationalism* (Delhi: Permanent Black, 2004), 308, note 32. Criticisms of Latour are given by John Huth, "Labour's Relativity," in

Koertge, *A House Built on Sand*, 181–94 and can be found in Alan Sokal and Jean Bricmont, *Fashionable Nonsense* (New York: Picador, 1999), 124–33.

15. Weinberg, *Dreams of a Final Theory*, 129; Greene, *The Elegant Universe*, 348–349.

16. Anders Albrechtslund's "Interview With Don Ihde," 7–8, available June 9, 2002: www.filosofi.net/artilker/douihole/pdf7.

17. Weinberg and Greene are both first-rate physicists and popular writers.

18. Gottlob Frege, "Sinn und Bedeutung," and "Begriff und Gegenstand," in *Funktion, Begriff, Bedeutung*, ed. Günther Patzig (Göttingen: Vandenhook & Ruprecht, 1962), 38–78.

19. "Wild Montana" (Spring 2004), 12.

20. J. Baird Callicott, "Intrinsic Value in Nature: A Metaethical Analysis," available July 5, 2000: http://ejap.louisiana.edu/EJAP/1995.spring/callicott.abs.html.

19

Toward a Practice-Oriented Methodology and Philosophy of Technoscience

Hans Lenk

As pertains to the topic "philosophy of science and technology," I would like to address some mutual influences and interactions that link the philosophy of science with the philosophy of technology. The main thesis is that the philosophy of science might profit from interfacing better with technology-oriented methodologies and an action-oriented reorientation of the concept of "knowledge," what can, in a wider sense, be called "grasping."[1] The concept of "grasping" implies that the active dimension of acquiring knowledge is a genuinely constructive activity and not primarily a representational task of trying to represent external structures. Grasping should not only be interpreted in the literal sense of "gripping something"; it should also be understood in the figurative senses of "understanding," "knowing," and "getting inside." Knowledge in this sense is understood to be a kind of activity or even interactivity between partial systems that it relies upon agents, be they even, among others, "software agents."

In the last decades an interesting and new emphasis in the philosophies of technology and science has arisen from the school of "New Experimentalism" initiated by Gooding, Pickering, and others. It deals mainly with the development of instruments and experiments, as well as with the respective technologies and potentialities that are opened up by the development of ever-improving instruments and procedures for measuring. The approaches by Ian Hacking, Ronald Giere, and Don Ihde (*TP*, *IR*) are particularly important. These authors have demonstrated that scientific work and progress cannot be reduced to theoretical claims (as, for example, analytic philosophy of a traditional provenance would have it). Instead, it is a process that essentially relies on: (1) the development of experimental techniques and instruments;

(2) on the "embedding" of these instruments in the respective scientific and experimental contexts; (3) and on the "embodying" of scientific enterprises in the practices that involve technological instrumentation (*IR*).

The core of this movement centers on Hacking's idea that the theoretical entities which are postulated initially are, in a certain sense, set only by instruments, experimental appliances, and measuring devices that allow for the experimenter to enter into a quasi-"direct" epistemological relation to reality. Hacking's thesis can be illustrated *via* the example of electrons: By using electron rays and electrons in our experimental and measuring instruments in order to solve other problems, (e.g., to prove the existence of the Z-boson or the top-quark), it becomes clear that technologically mediated experimental activity allows for electrons to be hypostatized as "*real*"; they change their status from being just theoretical entities to becoming real "instruments" (i.e., technologically effective real entities).

Giere developed this idea into a theory of the role of models in science. [2] He depicts a theory as a set of models that are connected by hypotheses and real systems. In this context, what is important is the relation of similarity between that which is presented in the models and that which appears in real systems: "There is . . . no direct relationship between sets of statements in the real world. The relationship is indirect through the intermediary of a theoretical model."[3] "A real system," Giere contends, "is *identified* as being similar to one of the models."[4] Furthermore, "the notion of *similarity* between models and real systems provides the much needed resource for understanding approximation in science."[5]

In short, Giere depicts theories as "a set" or "a family" of models; they are, "still better, a family of families of models."[6] Theories in this sense should not be understood as linguistic entities or frameworks for formulae; they are heterogeneous sets of abstract constructs (the theoretical models) and hypotheses (formulated in ordinary language). *Prima facie*, this view might appear to be "modellistic." However, it is crucial to note that technology plays a decisive role in connecting theoretical models and the real systems to be grasped. In this context, Giere's modelistic-constructive realism is comparable to Hacking's experimental-manipulative realism, both accounts appeal to experimental techniques in order to explain how theoretical entities come to be proven as real and how researchers are inspired to develop new models. For example, if we routinely use electron rays (cathode rays and beams) in an electron-microscope in order to solve successfully other scientific problems, then the postulated electrons count as *real* entities.

The parallels between Giere and Hacking include the further contention that scientists are more or less successful constructive realists: they use technological instruments to intervene into reality and, despite their theoretical constructions, end up disseminating in the scientific community an experimentalist-realist interpretation of models in the sense of relative "*satisficing*" (after H.A. Simon). Scientists, according to Giere, are thus "satisficers" or "optimizers," but not absolute "maximizers" regarding the degree of similarity that they expect from their models with reality. In fact, several models may fit in a certain sense; one need and could not talk of *the* unique optimum theory alone, but we must deal with a certain kind of fit or fitting (i.e., "satificing") of the models of which perhaps several ones might fit equally and relatively well to fulfill the required function of explanation, prediction, etc.

Instead of just talking of models, Giere further proposes an analogy of going "from maps to the kind of models one finds in many sciences": "The fit between a model and the world may be thought of like the fit between a map and the region it represents."[7] Ultimately, Giere calls his approach a "perspectival realism," which "is a later development of constructive realism."[8] The constructive element remains as before:

> The categories we use are, to some extent, constructed by us. Nevertheless, scientists can sometimes legitimately claim similarity between their logical constructs and aspects of reality . . . our theories do not ever capture the totality of reality, but provide us only with perspectives on limited aspects of reality. Scientific knowledge is not absolute, but perspectival.[9]

> Realism need not require that we be in possession of a perfect model that exactly mirrors the structure of the world in all respects and to a perfect degree of accuracy.[10]

As the language of these (and other) passages suggests, despite its many benefits, Giere's account of models remains within a cognitive and theory-laden vocabulary.

Turning explicitly against the general *methodological theoreticism*, Ihde has tried for decades to integrate phenomenological-epistemological approaches to "instrumental realist" perspectives in the philosophy of science and technology, what he calls "technoscience" (*IR* 138ff). He was certainly not the first author to stress the interconnections and the integration of technology in science, in methodology and actual experimentation as well as world formations diagnosing a "design of an artificial environment as whole" as a progressing substitution of the natural environment by a "men-created cultural world." (As early as 1970, I addressed the transition from the so-called "scientific age" toward "the *information- and systems technological age*."[11] Rapp and I also compared methods of science and technology and highlighted the ever-expanding technicalization of scientific experimentation and the scientification of technology.[12]) But what Ihde has developed successfully is an integrated methodology and an epistemology of technoscience. Indeed, since 1979 Ihde has discussed technology and science as embedded in social *praxis* and emphasized the "technological embodiment of science" in "its instrumentation" (which differed crucially in the modern and ancient periods). He has thus drawn attention to the need to study the interface between the philosophy of science and the philosophy of technology as well between science and technology themselves.

In 1991 Ihde attended to the American discussion of five Anglo-American philosophers and phenomenologically oriented Euro-American philosophers of technology and science (Hubert Dreyfus, Ian Hacking, Patrick Heelan, Robert Ackermann, and himself) who criticize the classical positivist philosophy of science for studying science without attending to perception, technology, or experimental instruments.[13] Some of these representatives differed on the problem of perception (i.e., seeing by, through, or *via* instruments) and on the role of social "praxis" (i.e., the social embedding of technological practice). But they all agreed about "the *technological embodiment* of science" *via* the role of instruments in experiments. (Interestingly enough, some unmentioned Continental philosophers of technology—including Rapp, Ropohl, and myself—clearly saw the accumulating integration and interconnection between technology, science, society, and economy.)

Despite the value of Ihde's accounts of instrumentation and perception, he seems to overstate his case a little bit when he claims that at the "heart of instrumental realism" the "theoretical" becomes replaced with the instrumentally "observable." If not obedient to what I call "the reading paradigm," "the text metaphor" (*IR* 113) seems prone to overstating the "reading" and/or "seeing" metaphor—as Ihde himself would acknowledge in criticizing Heelan's collapsing of the "difference between embodiment and hermeneutic relation through technologies" (*IR* 106). Ihde seems to somewhat underestimate the "action-impregnatedness" or "activity-ladenness" of experimentation besides the instruments by tendentially overaccentuating "perception." The extant theories of action and the activities of model designing, structuring, or schematization of action—also in forming knowledge and perceiving—seem to have been underestimated to some degree, although implicitly all this is certainly somehow involved and unnoticeably accounted for.

With all of this, we are at the point of reaching an approach, which I had developed three decades ago, namely a realism of what I call methodological interpretationist provenance, or methodological scheme-interpretationism. In short, we may say: We conceive of the world as being real, hypostatize it, for practical and theoretical reasons, as real; the world is real, but any grasping of it or of parts of it or entities in it is always impregnated by or bound to interpretational perspectives, that is, is interpretative, schematized, "theory-impregnated," or "theory-laden," etc. Any "grasping" (in the double sense mentioned) whatsoever is to be understood from a scheme-interpretationist approach and is beyond that to a large extent also shaped and structured by actions, action-forms, or presuppositions. This is the main idea.

We need knowledge and action *as well as* experimentation and instrumentation. We know that gaining knowledge is a sort of *action*; at times it is a higher-level activity, namely acting with models, preparations, or experimental arrangements (e.g., quantum theory and its "measurement problem"). All of our "graspings" are structured, schematized, and to a large extent "constructive"; but it is equally true that knowledge and insights in experimental science are not merely constructions and interpretations that will fit into arbitrary models; as Giere rightly stresses, the models and their fit are *not* relativistic or arbitrary. Indeed, they are bound to strict and stringent requirements of experimentation, objectivity, repeatability, etc., according to the traditional rules and norms of "good" scientific practice. This is the element of realism in the otherwise rather perspectival and constructivist model-making and theory-building activity of the scientist or group of scientists frequently described by using a certain Kuhnian *"paradigm."* As I have stressed time and again, gaining knowledge, constructing, acting and intervening as well as interpreting necessarily go together.[14] Instead of just misleadingly introducing and highlighting models and falling victim to some kind of dichotomizing strategies, the philosophy of science has to take seriously the insights that we need models and laws *as well as* theories. With regard to the traditional approaches of philosophy of science, it is true that the propositional approach often interprets theories and hypotheses incorrectly by treating them as linguistic entities.[15] It is certainly an interesting problem to analyze and discuss how these analytic differentiations hang together with the real world or the respective evidences, resistances, or make-ups ("preparations") in the situation of experiments. I think the idea raised by quantum mechanics—that the initial preparation is very much of import—may even be or feature as the *general case* (i.e., there usually is a certain kind of interplay generally not to be neglected between questioning, preparing experiments and relevant perspectives in order to deal with experimental reactions from a perspectival approach).

The pragmatic technology-oriented approaches by Hacking, Giere, and Ihde as well as the action-theoretic interpretation delineate a route to avoid such one-sided exaggerations or even dichotomizations that distort the relational interpretation and interplay between cognitive models, "intended models of theories," technological realizations and actions (i.e., operation-theoretical sequences of operations and experiments).[16] Thanks to these contributions, theoreticians may now relate their methodologies (or metamethodological conceptions of operative principles) to the conceptualization of theories, concepts, and hypotheses without relying on absolute truth claims; instead, relativized concepts (e.g., the degree of fitting, optimizing as "satisficing") that apply to designs, plans, constructions of all kinds can be favored. A pragmatic philosophy of science can, therefore, learn from technological and action-theoretic approaches; likewise the methodology found in the engineering disciplines (or even what Ropohl calls "general technology") may benefit from considering the refinements and novel developments of philosophy of science under the auspices of general methodologies including theories of action. These methodological approaches, however, still to be integrated into a rather general theory and methodology of scheme-interpretation, one that includes a set of perspectives, employs teleo-functional requirements, theoretical approaches, and practical action-routines, as well as accounts for temporally and geographically situated social conventions and institutional rules.[17] A new "unity" of the sciences and technologies might well evolve and cover the access to the world by action and action-orientation by applying theoretical and interpretive as well as experimental models. The cooperation of philosophers of science, philosophers of technology, and philosophers of action theories should (and I believe will) set the stage for future developments in philosophy of science proper.

Notes

1. Hans Lenk, *Grasping Reality. An Interpretation-realistic Epistemology* (Singapore: World Scientific, 2003).

2. Ronald Giere, *Explaining Science: The Cognitive Approach* (Chicago: Chicago University Press, 1988).

3. Ibid., 82.

4. Ibid., 86.

5. Ibid., 106.

6. Ibid., 80.

7. Ibid., 82.

8. Ronald Giere, *Science Without Laws* (Chicago: Chicago University Press, 1999).

9. Ibid., 150.

10. Ibid., 241.

11. Hans Lenk, *Philosophie im technologischen Zeitalter* (Stuttgart: Kohlhammer, 1971).

12. *Techne – Technik – Technologie,* ed. Hans Lenk and Simon Moser (Pullach and Munich: Dokumentation Saur, 1973),180f, 206ff.

13. Whereas Dreyfus and Heelan as well as Ihde himself are considered the Euro-American (i.e., phenomenological) subgroup as a loosely working collaboration arriving at parallel results, Hacking and Ackermann are representatives of the more analytically minded Anglo-American representatives of this new American "school" of the "Philosophy of Technoscience," which Ihde explicitly calls "'The school' of instrumental Realists" (*IR* 97). (Surprisingly, Ihde did not integrate Giere into this discussion.)

14. Hans Lenk, *Einführung in die Erkenntnistheorie. Interpretation—Interaktion —Intervention* (Munich: Fink, 1998); see also Hans Lenk, *Grasping Reality. An Interpretation-realistic Epistemology*.

15. Theories, generally speaking, are methodical and methodological concepts as well as normative structurings of actions and procedures that are guided by interpretations and schematizations.The methodological scheme-interpretationism developed by the present author is indeed a higher-level methodological and epistemological conception covering from a methodological point of a metatheoretical provenance the special cases of scientific theories, technological developments and designs, procedures of structuring in everyday knowledge and perception as well as all kinds of action-forming and mental representation. See Hans Lenk, "Handlung als Interpretationskonstrukt," in *Handlungstheorien interdisziplinär* II, ed. Hans Lenk (Munich: Fink, 1978), 279–250; also see Hans Lenk, "Zu einem methodologischen Interpretationskonstruktionismus," *Zeitschrift für allgemeine Wissenschaftstheorie* 22 (1991): 283–302.

16. Hans Lenk, *Einführung in die Erkenntnistheorie. Interpretation – Interaktion –Intervention* (Munich: Fink, 1998).

17. Hans Lenk, *Interpretationskonstrukte* (Frankfurt am Main: Suhrkamp, 1993). Hans Lenk, *Über Schemainterpretationen und Interpretationskonstrukte* (Frankfurt am Main: Suhrkamp, 1995). Hans Lenk, *Einführung in die Erkenntnistheorie. Interpretation—Interaktion—Intervention*. Hans Lenk, *Grasping Reality. An Interpretation-realistic Epistemology*.

Part VII

Ihdeology

20

Forty Years in the Wilderness

Don Ihde

Here I am, faced with nineteen essays by former students, colleagues, and peers. They deal with forty years of work, 1964–2004. To respond is a daunting task since the limits dealt me simply do not allow each person to be given justice. In reading these essays, I was struck by an irreal experience: On the one hand to "hear" good things, I felt maybe I have done some good philosophy after all; but the downside is the question: now at age 70 (2004), obituary-like? Or will I, like Paul Ricoeur, two decades my senior, recently dead at 92, or Hans-Georg Gadamer, who died at 102, three decades my senior, have time to make this a two-thirds work report?

With my title phrase above, I do not mean to claim any Moses-like, heroic attributes, but neither I do expect to see any promised land. Actually, were I to retrospectively imagine being in that ancient scene, I would find my own *persona,* associated more with Aaron than Moses. The Bible, of course, gives Aaron a *bad rap;* he is blamed for yielding to the Israelites' demand for a false idol and fabricates a golden calf, a religious *technology,* or artifact. Its construction takes its raw material from the gold items the Israelites had brought with them from the higher-tech Egyptian culture; this gold, Aaron then makes into yet another culture's sacred bull-calf (bull worship was Canaanite—which today's minimalist archaeologists claim was the actual culture of the Israelites all along.[1]) Arnold Schoenberg, assuming a latter-day role of a Talmudic-like commentator, did a reconstruction of Aaron in his unfinished, two-act opera, "Moses and Aaron." The operatic Moses, the purist iconoclast, discovers the Golden Calf; dashes the tables upon the ground; demands the calf be ground up and the powdered gold be drunk by the Israelites. The true G-d cannot be imaged, perceived, and is totally invisible, imperceptible, Schoenberg's Moses claims. (Never mind that the actual text of the Book of Exodus is full of sightings, hinder-parts, even face-to-faces, let alone YHWH's auditory appearance in a Loud Voice.) In the opera, Aaron has the last word when he points out Moses' own hypocrisy, for he, too, cannot communicate without the mediations of "images" and artifacts—*materialities*—and asks Moses what are burned bushes, snake-rod transformations, and *the inscriptions on the tablets themselves?* As a gloss, I note not long after destroying the calf, the presumably formerly lost gold reappears and is described in biblical verses almost identical to those used earlier; it is recycled into a new fabrication, the Ark of the Convenant. It is clad with gold, to be the new religious artifact or *technology* to be carried into the Promised Land. This transformation of isomorphic image (calf) to nonisomorphic image (inscriptions) follow the pattern Bruno Latour points out in *Iconoclash.* Icon-breakers inevitably re-create new icons.[2]

As I claimed in *Technology and the Lifeworld,* humans have never been without their technologies, and the antiquity of that association clearly precedes *homo sapiens sapiens.* The 32,000 BP bear bone flute discovered not too many years ago, can be shown to have played to a five-tone tuning scale not too different from the Greek's scale, which of course was very different from Schoenberg's twelve-tone, atonal scale. I mentioned this musical technology in a conference in Bergen, Norway last year, and Friedrich Kittler, avid Heideggerian and German romantic, responded with the proper conclusion for his perspective: this means the Greeks really had discovered the proper proportion of tuning. I drew a different conclusion. So, we are off and running for *expanding postphenomenology.*

Listening to Voices

Looking back over the forty years of published work, I took an early lesson from Paul Ricoeur, whose work was the subject of my first book, *Hermeneutic Phenomenology: The Philosophy of Paul Ricoeur* (1971). In a conversation he told me that once a book is published, "it belongs to the world." This theme reappears in his trilogy, *Time and Narrative.* Not only does an author not control interpretation, nor do meanings reduce to author intention, but readers belong to interpretation as well. In some ways, authors may be their own *worst* interpreters.

So, I shall stick to minimals: Once at a SPEP book exhibit, a friend, pointing to one of my books on display, said, "Oh, that's 'early Ihde.' " "Early Ihde" might be thought of as the "phenomenological Ihde" whose themes were phenomenology-analytic philosophy comparisons, "doing phenomenology," particularly perceptual studies, *Listening and Voice* (1976) and *Experimental Phenomenology* (1976). Yet, even earlier, *Sense and Significance* (1973) is already alluding to pragmatism as a family resemblant philosophy of experience and "Vision and Objectification" (1973) contains a technology analysis and an illustration, which looks like multistability.

Technics and Praxis (1979), however, is full-blown philosophy of technology, which followed by *Existential Technics* (1983) and *Technology and the Lifeworld* (1990), might be "middle or philosophy-of-technology Ihde." Toward the end of this period, I had begun to encounter people like Bruno Latour, Donna Haraway, Peter Galison, and the instrument-sensitive philosophers of science. *Instrumental Realism* (1991) begins the trajectory into science studies or *technoscience,* which occupies "recent Ihde." This same period is that of "nonfoundational phenomenology" into "postphenomenology"—all themes that must occupy this response to conversational companions encountered along the way.

Now to my reader-critics: I must begin with an expression of my immense gratitude and satisfaction related to this project. It would not have happened at all had not Evan Selinger invented it and taken on the heavy burden of formulating and following through with the work that results in *Postphenomenology.* Although he did not try to keep the project secret, the persons included here are by his invitation. Evan arrived at Stony Brook at exactly the time I had begun what is known as the Technoscience Research Group. This group, with its affiliated, interdisciplinary seminar, has today evolved into a distinctively styled research program, which reads in the areas of philosophy of science, philosophy of technology, and science and cultural studies. We read only living authors and annually bring at least one for a "roast" to respond to our questions about the roastee's work.

Knowledges are situated, Donna Haraway reminds us, and Evan arrived at that newly situated time. I think he came, wanting to be a good "Continental" philosopher, albeit one who read philosophy of technology. But it was not long before he got into the action of a new network of living thinkers, all engaged in a lively, issue-oriented-style of philosophy. The result was a unique dissertation on a very contemporary topic, "expertise." He was the very model of a "technoscience" participant and his dissertation set a pattern now being followed by others. His living referents, including Hubert Dreyfus, Harry Collins, Steve Fuller, and others, were soon engaged by e-mail, in discussions, and in publications, with each claiming that Evan's criticisms and points had caused them to rethink positions. This is very unlike, if I may use my older term, "generic continentalism," which tends to focus upon figure-texts and those usually of dead authors. (Deconstruction and feminism movements did include living authors and thus provided some living, contemporary conversation.)

I had first thought to identify each of the contributors here according to good "actor network" associations, but then I changed my mind and will leave the reader to guess who fits what category. Five thinkers here were my former doctoral students, each now with distinguished careers; six persons have been hosted and roasted in my technoscience research seminar; three others are longtime European interlocutors; three are university colleagues; and the rest are very long-term peers with whom some of the arguments reflect spanned decades.

How do I respond to each? I have decided to begin from what a number of interlocutors have identified as distinctive aspects of my writing style. That style includes autobiographical references, anecdotes, and example sets dealing with *variations*. Trevor Pinch likes my "low church" approach, "Just compare what Ihde was doing back then with what philosophers of science were doing. Most were focused on the high church of physics. The beauty of sound and Ihde's approach to it is that there is no high church." Pinch also recognizes that the experiential examples are an opening to empirical and science studies on auditory experience and structures. And I particularly liked Vivian Sobchack, who, with a warmly personal and personable analysis, most astutely analyzes my use of "autobiography" and the role it plays to open, but then to lead into the unfamiliar. She clearly recognizes the aim, to provide a rigorous, but nonfoundationalist postphenomenology for which variational practice is the key method. "While variational method forms the core of his phenomenological investigations, what enlivens it . . . is an underlying—and rare—sense of existential *presence*." I have never regarded my style of doing "phenomenology" to be subjective. The only comment I would add for my interlocutors, is that I also have always admired Kierkegaard's ironic, sometimes sarcastic or provocative style. And so in what follows I highlight some ironic provocation.

Mordor and Heidegger's Dark Shadow

Open Court Press now has a philosophy and popular culture series with titles like: *The Matrix and Philosophy,* and *Philosophy and the Simpsons.* Running through one group of conversations here, one can see the *dark shadow* of Heidegger—the literary allusion here should be *The Lord of the Rings* and my title would be *Mordor and Heidegger's Dark Shadow.*

As Evan Selinger points out in the introduction, in both my early and middle periods, I published about a half dozen articles on Heidegger and most of these have been reprinted and/or translated. I have sometimes been identified as a "neo-Heideggerian" along with Albert Borgmann and Hubert Dreyfus. And, if one does philosophy of technology, Heidegger's dark shadow is unavoidable. While most of the best-known European philosophers began to deal with technology between the World Wars: Ortega y Gasset, Karl Jaspers, Nicolas Berdyaev, Friedrich Dessauer—the list could go on—it was Heidegger whose work soon overshadowed all the others. In their recently published, massive collection, *Philosophy of Technology: The Technological Condition* (Blackwell, 2003), Robert Scharff and Val Dusek devote an entire section to Heidegger (including reprints of some of my earlier articles). And, if I am to be self-critical, I have to remind myself that I dedicated my *Tech-*

nics and Praxis (1979) to the memory of Martin Heidegger who had died only three years earlier. I have come to regret that dedication.

My already growing disaffection peaked when I first read the infamous interview in which Heidegger equated the Holocaust with modern agriculture—all fall under *Bestand* and *Gestell*—put in the vernacular, human victims of the gas chambers and engineered tomatoes are all part of the "resource well" for modern Technology with the capital "T." My aversion, however, was not only because of the moral discrepancy, which does arise by equating gas chamber victims and biotechnological corn, but also because I saw that for Heidegger, *every technology ended up with exactly the same output or analysis.* This also is evidence that he views technology under a kind of metaphysics. As a pragmatist and a rigorous phenomenologist, I realized this meant, simply, that such an analysis was *useless* since it could not discriminate between the results of playing a musical instrument, also a technological mediation, and the process of genetic manipulation! Actually, the disaffection had begun earlier, and even more narrowly over the realization that the later Heidegger in particular, got too much wrong—much of it related to the histories of both technology and science, histories not being part of his intellectual *forte*.

So, if early I got tagged as a neo-Heideggerian, now, by moving away, I cannot escape him. The Heidegger dark shadow continues to be cast in this collection—he repeatedly appears, but perhaps fortunately for me, in very different guises. Richard Cohen and Robert Scharff are the two critics who most concentrate upon *die Frage nach Heidegger*. Cohen, at least implicitly, thinks I have not been negative enough regarding Heidegger. Cohen correctly sees my project as one always avoiding both utopian and dystopian views of Technology [with the transcendental capital "T"]. He sees that

> Heidegger, . . . undermines his own effort to understand technology
> by locating it . . . contrary to his own claims, a metaphysically total-
> izing context . . . what specifically is the distinctive characteristic that
> orders and permeates our epoch as technological in essence?
> Heidegger's answer is purely negative.

Cohen's counterclaim is that technology must be understood under the *ethical,* in this sense he follows Levinas. Heidegger's *essentialism,* rather than taking technology within the imperative of the ethical, derives it from the essential, the ontological. This gives it an implicitly "determinist" trajectory. In short, an ontological essentialism is the cause of occluding the ethical—this theme will return again.

Scharff's equally intense analysis of Heidegger comes to a different conclusion and he suggests I should reconsider my critique of Heidegger and give more credit where credit is due. Scharff holds that my . . . "dismissiveness of Heidegger's allegedly 'pessimistic totalizing' is off the mark." But, it is also clear that Heidegger's analysis, Scharff believes, is also on the mark:

> The widespread . . . presence of technology in our lives—so deserv-ing of Ihde's kind of concrete phenomenological analysis—*is also . . . existentially dominant* . . . In fact . . . my (and I believe Heidegger's) complaint about technoscientific hegemony goes pre-cisely into the same space as Ihde's technoscientific studies . . . Ihde and Heidegger both understand themselves to be thinking and acting 'in the midst of' the pervasive technoscientific character of life . . . "
> Yes, I do my thinking there, but I also must have tools that can do the job—and Heidegger does not provide these.

Still another voice comes from Paul Thompson. Thompson's main issue is, again, ethics, but it is cast with the "Heidegger question." The thrust of Thompson's often subtle analysis is that the very style of analysis I undertake remains under the dark shadow of Heidegger, noting my appreciation of the early Heidegger—hammer and embodiment, also noted by others, and yes, it's true, I prefer the early Heidegger—my later dismissal of romanticizing handcraft tools over industrial technologies by Heidegger is not enough. " . . . It is not enough to dismiss these views as forms of romanticism, for while they may share many dissatisfaction with the romantics, the dark views of the twentieth century have far more detailed and ontologically sophisticated discussions of *how* technology comes to be problematic than did anyone in the nineteenth century." Although I maintain that much of Heidegger's strategy is "romantic," I think the more biting criticism, noted above, is that it has *no utility*. Here I express my gratitude to Finn Olesen in this collection. He begins with the question of whether philosophy is useful, and noting my postphenomenology as an approach in which technologies and humans constitute themselves inter-actively, "enables questions about how to study such altered conditions and their alleged consequences." Moreover, the usefulness produces"

> immediate merits. . . . [when] one needs to depart from the macrosocial theory—where technological neutrality may seem rea-sonable—to move to microsocial studies of situated praxes. At the latter altitude "technological mediation" is no longer about ideals of efficiency and clear communication. Instead it is about heteroge-neous relationships between individual human beings and the world, including the artifacts used for mediations.

I also have come to agree with Jaron Lanier who thinks Heidegger's notion of technology is largely a nineteenth-century one dominated by Big

Military-Industrial technologies, which are not only being transcended by information and biotechnological ones, but are being transformed by quite different approaches. My laptop uses far less energy than a hair dryer and for several years I ran it off a portable solar unit designed for field anthropologists—even a Heideggerian ought to be able to appreciate that.

Heidegger receives note and mention by others in this collection, but he comes into play again in a more complicated way in a surprise from Peter Galison. Galison has long had an interest in technological breakdown. My first experience of this was at a workshop he organized at Harvard and MIT, spring 2002. Sixteen of us from different disciplines went over some case studies, primarily Flight 800 over Long Island, with a view to accident analysis. His piece here, on the Columbia shuttle, echoes themes of that workshop as well. He frames it with comments on Heidegger, again under the dark shadow. Galison joins what by now is the long phenomenological tradition of taking something that had usually taken for granted, which then under breakdown conditions, now gets revealed in a new way. "Heidegger wrote much about the *breakdown*, that sudden changeover, in which failure turned the invisibility of the hammer suddenly to an irreducible." Heidegger's hammer, later, becomes Merleau-Ponty's Schneider with his brain lesion a bodily breakdown, and, again in this collection, Donn Welton turns to missing anatomies, breakdowns to be replaced with bionic implants.

While I respect these now standard examples, I have long argued that while dramatic, breakdown that can produce revelatory function is not the only way to forefront new gestalts—rather, I have favored my radical use of *variations,* which move from the more mundane to the more radical, something Vivian Sobchack recognized in her contribution. Galison raises the "hammer" or breakdown to a new level of complexity, for, surely the Columbia reveals the ambivalence and ambiguity of technological breakdown and with it the many dimensions of social and technical systems implicated—yet, he cautions us this complexity of breakdown in "Global climate change, groundwater draining, species extinctions . . . we know these things and don't know them. . . . we gasp at disaster and continue to work . . . " and he comes down, in spite of Heidegger's dark shadow, with a conclusion, which resonates with the rejection of my rejected utopian/dystopian extremes. "Our world stars us in the midst of powerful effective, and failing technology—here we are, neither as tragic hero, broken hammer in hand, nor as Enlightenment scientist, laboratory at the ready."

Pigs and Bells

In medieval times, animals could be tried, convicted, and executed. For example, in cases of bestiality, both the human and the animal could be hanged if found guilty, and, at least for the human, torture might be used for gaining a confession—I do not know if the sheep or pig had to undergo torture. The capital sin of bestiality was embedded in a different social-moral-religious stability—or *episteme,* if we borrow from Foucault—than that of modernity or postmodernity. Back then, sexual practice always carried some meaning linkage with the Sin of Adam, tainted, when compared with celibacy, but acceptable if heterosexual and marital, and sexuality was also close-linked to procreation, not dissociated from it, or linked to entertainment or recreation. No doubt part of the fear was that a pig-human relation might well produce a monster, another foregrounded evil character of Medieval thought. Women, for example, who gave birth to deformed offspring, were thought to have been impregnated by that which the monster most resembled. They were, after all, only the receptacle, the *matrix,* for the formative male principle.

Early modernity, with Leeuwenhoek's microscope began to change all that. He was the first to observe sperm (1677). Questions arose as to how he could do this "ethically," since engaging in masturbation would also have been sinful, so he defended himself by claiming what he observed was "fresh from the marriage bed." (How he defended his observations of dog sperm, which he also examined, I do not know!) But even the microscope did not resolve the preformation/epigenesis controversy, although it did resolve that both sperm and egg were needed for reproduction.[3] Eventually modernity realized that hybrid *sexual* reproduction by copulation with animals was impossible as well.

But the story does not end there. Donna Haraway reminds us of the biotechnologically engineered tomato, which contains flounder genes to lower the temperature at which the tomato might freeze![4] This "hybrid" was produced by biogenetic manipulation. Nor are the pig heart valve transplants into humans that recognize the closeness of human/pig genomes, produced sexually. If these are "monsters" in the medieval sense, they do not result from beastiality. Here is an entirely different stability or *episteme.* Haraway celebrates hybrids, although always acknowledging "noninnocence"; we know where Heidegger would stand.

Similarly, cast bells in city towers, pealed the hours, called to arms—and with more frequency than I realized—could also summon rebellions against the duke or lord of medieval cities. At first, such an illicit use of bell technology could result in kings or popes decreeing the destruction of the bell tower and with it the stature of the city involved. Later, after such waste seemed questionable, there emerged instead, the practice of *flogging the bells,* which were whipped and chastised after being implicated in an uprising thus shaming both rebels and bells and ritually diminishing the stature of the city. In passing, I also want to note that an echo of the calf/tabernacle gold transformation can also be heard in this example. "The bells went to war," was a term used after the introduction of cannon, and bronze bells could be recycled into bronze cannons used in the beginnings of castle destruction that raged through Europe from the fourteenth century—from a golden to a bronze age?[5]

Bruno Latour claims *We Were Never Modern*. Modernity, he argues, depends upon a "settlement" whereby a clear and sharp distinction is drawn between *society* and *nature*. This distinction, however, functions to obscure the proliferation of *hybrids*, entities that are both cultural and natural. Clearly, material technologies, that are both "real" and "constructed" are good examples of hybrids. Peter Paul Verbeek, in his contribution wants to push me toward a morality of things, much closer to Latour. Can there be a "morality of things? . . . To what extent can the mediating role of things be described in ethical terms?" Donna Haraway also calls for a somewhat more intimate set of relations between humans, animals, and technologies, "technologies are not mediations, something in between us and another bit of the world. Rather technologies are organs, full partners, in what Merleau-Ponty called 'infoldings of the flesh . . . ' " Andy Pickering wants me to abandon not only subjectivistic, but *human centered* relations. Referring to my most recent emphasis upon the role of embodiment in science, Pickering asks, "If knowledge is ultimately grounded in our bodies, how come scientists manage not to know that ? how is it that scientific knowledge itself usually does not refer us back to the body?"

All of these pushes and pulls revolve around what I shall call variations upon interrelational or *relativistic ontologies*. Such ontologies are not relativisms, rather, they take into account both the context and the observer's positionality. I will locate my own first: All the interlocutors here recognize my self-admitted debts to the phenomenological-hermeneutic traditions and to three of its primary figures: Husserl, Heidegger, and Merleau-Ponty. I would argue each has a variant upon what I am calling a *relativistic ontology,* or interrelational ontology. Husserl's is cast in egological language, *ego-cogito-cogitatum,* and is called *intentionality;* Heidegger's becomes more historicized and existentialized as *Being-in-the-World;* and Merleau-Ponty's early is *etre-au-monde,* later, nuanced into *chiasm,* foldings of the flesh, etc. Relativistic ontology notes that the patterns of interrelation between the kinds of beings we are, always take place within a multidimensional environment or "world" and each part of the interrelation is mutually depend upon the others for the emergence of understanding. From "middle Ihde" on, I have focused upon the role of materiality, technology, and the role it plays within a relativistic ontology. Technologies are in "mediating positions" was my claim. Human-technology-world relations became the ontological framework within which I developed my "phenomenology of technics," with various continuous, for gradedly different human-technology-world variants. These are noted by many of the interlocutors, with their embodiment, hermeneutic, alterity, etc. differentiations.

From Husserl on, there was a marked difference between such a relativistic-interrelational ontology and early modern "Cartesian" metaphysics, the metaphysics of "subject-object," "body-mind," "internal-external," etc. I was aware of the anti-Cartesian and foundationalist thrust of classical pragmatism as well. But not until the eighties did I begin to discover, in the beginnings of my interest in science studies, that there were others who held to very similar ontologies, which were also relativistic and interrelational. Those most sensitive to materiality within such a context, became the conversation group of *Chasing Technoscience; Matrix of Materiality* (with Selinger, 2003). I have come to realize that what can be called the *symmetry* problem, arises from the nuances within relativistic ontology. I shall focus here on the role of "symmetry" between humans and technologies, material technologies.

What these interrelational, relativistic ontologies share is the notion that there is interaction and mutual "non-neutral" and "noninnocent" productive and emergent shaping, between humans and technologies, animals, etc. And, these ontologies share the notion that knowledge is "situated" and particular, not "transcendentally" true. Thus Pickering can agree that, "Neither of us dispute that scientific knowledge is situated and somehow "relative" rather than simply and transcendentally true "and that there is some kind of "putative symmetry between the human and nonhuman." Similarly, Haraway, "Don Ihde and I share a basic commitment. As Ihde puts it, 'Insofar as I use or employ a technology, I am used by and employed by that technology as well . . . We are bodies in technologies.' " But, if we use the four principals from *Chasing Technoscience,* we disagree on some fronts.

Latour wants to maintain a full symmetry: both humans and nonhumans, he declares, are *actants* (have some kind of agency). His common examples are artifacts like speed bumps, door openers, seat belts, and the like. Humans interact with these nonhumans, and, depending upon what concrete differences there are on each side of the relationship, actions are modified. Speed bumps in relation with drivers, produce slower speeds in the locale of the speed bump. Some seat belts automatically attach themselves and/or are connected to either ignition or gears before motion can occur, etc. It is the human plus the non-human interrelation that produces the action pattern that results. Now, I have to admit, I think this analysis is demonstrably superior to any Heideggerian analysis because one can differentiate between the actions resultant accordingly. [As it turns out, Latour and I used the *same examples* on several occasions—and our analyses are compared in *Chasing Technoscience.*]

Verbeek, who also enters this conversation, sees in Latourean symmetry, the opportunity to extend ethical considerations to "things." He correctly notes the expansion of ethical dimensions and often "rights" historically—from the free males only of ancient Greece, to twentieth-century emancipation and voting rights to former slaves and women, to the late twentieth-century considerations of animal and even environmental rights—why not technologies? But, as he himself worries, how radical can this symmetry be? That is precisely the point of my pig example! Clearly the pig, even though tried in a court for bestiality in earlier times, or in later times, sacrificed for a heart-valve transplant, did not give "informed consent" in either case! But this, too, remains too subjectivistic since rights talk is tied to modernism and its notion of autonomous subjects. Rather, my worry is in the type of *stability* evidenced by the pig example—bestiality *is* interrelational, but it is embedded in what has to appear to us today as an antiquated or surpassed stability. If bestiality remains a sin, its justification as such and reason for such has to be radically rethought.

Albert Borgmann is yet another person who emphasizes how this works. "Ihde uses multiperspectivalism and multistability as roughly subjective and objective correlates, both coming into relief through his variational method." Borgmann says, "multiperspectivalism [is] an epistemological issue and . . . [an] ontology of multistability . . . For Borgmann, this keeps me within the "condition of empirical realism." This, however, is not yet full embodiment.

Pickering demurs from situatedness being focused in embodiment. He wants to replace the Merleau-Pontean notion that embodiment is the location of all intelligent behavior—a view I share with Merleau-Ponty and Dreyfus, for example—and replace it with a *cybernetic* or *self-organizing* set of, for example, thermostats. These would be "situated" in some sense, but not embodied. I, however, am not so sure science doesn't implicitly include embodiment factors.

As Pinch noted, until very recently I have eschewed the "high church" of physics. But Albert Borgmann in this collection, reads me across the science-technology mediation, sees relevance in phenomenological variations for both relativistic and quantum physics. It turns out, serendipitously, that I spent the last summer reading Galison's *Einstein's Clocks, Poincare's Maps,* Brian Greene's *Fabric of the Universe,* and Thomas Levenson's *Einstein in Berlin.* All during this process, I, like Borgmann, discerned that the notion of multistability has strong relevance for quantum phenomena, and embodiment for relativity. I was excited to learn how many of Einstein's *Gedanken-experimenten* actually employed kinesthetic-tactile body experiences in his notions of the equivalence of gravity and acceleration, as well as other perceptual experience in relative train movement and clock watching in different space-time particularities. I point this out as a counter-example to Pickering, and would also refer to my many Galileo analyses of telescope use. My current work on imaging technologies even more strongly argues for the necessary perceptual *translation* practices to bring non-perceptible phenomena into perceptibility, or put more strongly, the reference has to be back to what our "opening to the world" allows.

Paradoxical Prognoses

From ontology to ethics, many of my interlocuters here—Selinger, Cohen, Thompson, more tangentially Scharff and Borgmann, too—demand I face the problem of normativity. Some of the issues raised revolve around the old notion that phenomenology is primarily *descriptive,* not *prescriptive.* Now, between philosophers primarily interested in epistemology and those interested in ethics, I do discern a bit of nonsymmetry. Normativists, I believe, are more likely to demand that descriptivists pay attention to prescription, than epistemologists are to demand that ethicists have detailed epistemologies! Wonder why?

My pragmatist self, however, agrees with Rorty that fact/value distinctions are not strong and epistemology and ethics are intertwined in complex ways. And, I have been interweaving the ethical with the epistemic as my poor victimized pig story showed as well. So much of the problem with normativity is that it is relative to the cultural-epistemic stabilities, which mark histories and locations. Paul Durbin, long ago in a review of *Technology and the Lifeworld,* also complained about my minimalism regarding ethics— but went on to admit that by highlighting the outcomes for the contemporary world, in which problems of the environment were recognized as "foundational" for our era that I did include ethical considerations in my work.

That I do not quite see how to undergo the conversion Cohen wishes for, to actually situate all epistemology within or under the ethical, I admit. But neither do I wish to be simply defensive. Thompson and Selinger both point to my taste for some kind of neo-enlightenment ethics, and to the problems associated with such an ethic. Yes, I do favor a contemporary ethics of a cosmopolitan, pluricultural, tolerant sort. The older, secular, and modernist attainment of laws of toleration were won only after centuries of religious wars, and in the process religions themselves had to be modified. What had been the absolutisms of politically incarnated groups, had to transform absolute beliefs into "private" ones, believed and practiced only within the confines of located churches, temples, mosques, and cathedrals, and taken off the streets and battlegrounds. These old battles seem to be reviving today, and ascendant fundamentalisms return, and, for me, this is a big worry.

Thompson, for example, thinks that my style of analysis is situated more comfortably with postmodernism—which usually rejects the Enlightenment, particularly its metaphysics—and even Heideggerian ontology, than with critical theory and the philosophical movements which explicitly embraced democracy or socialism. On politics, this means I should side with Carnap over Heidegger—and politically I would have—except, Carnap and his kin, once out of the grips of Fascism and the anti-semitism of mid-twentieth-century Europe, went about ideologically depluralizing and dedemocritizing the entire face of philosophy in America! Nor did many of the particulars of the Frankfort School look appealing for what I was doing—I could not well incline toward a philosophy of technology even *more dystopian* than Heidegger's with Marcuse, or take my "low church" approach noted by Pinch toward the frustrated elitism expressed by Adorno, and while more sympathetic to the context of lifeworld and communication in Habermas, the lack of sensitivity to materiality, showed little promise for one interested in technoscience.

Instead, as Selinger indicates so well, whatever "ethics" I could develop would have to come out of and be commensurate with my postphenomenology. Two recent themes of mine do just that: The *paradox of prognosis* in philosophy of technology and technoscience, arises precisely because if I am right about all technologies being *multistable, having unpredictable side-effects, and embeddable in different ways in different cultures,* then prognosis becomes either impossible or at the least, highly problematic. Faced with this complexity, what Selinger recognizes as my *significant nudges* or the pragmatic rules of thumb, which I refer to in "Prognostic Predicaments" (first published in the UK, later translated into several languages, and then placed in *Bodies in Technology)* is probably the best I can do for now. The other theme is one that implies resituating where some philosophers do their work.

For more than a decade now, I have been advocating that philosophers seek "R & D" (research and development) locations. While not wanting to eliminate or lessen the roles of philosophers in "applied ethics" positions, such as medical ethics boards, doing business ethics and the like, I have argued that these positions function somewhat like an ambulance corps after a battle. They have to go in after the technologies are in place and have affected the sites of employment, and do triage: who is dead or will die, who is treatable, etc. Olesen's claim about my move to the microanalysis where "Ihde's philosophy is concerned with what a particular technology *does* in a specific setting . . . [is] a frame that allows for the inclusion of abstract philosophical reflects as well as mundane work practices." He ends by affirming my recommendation for "R & D" positioning.

Instead, an "R & D" placement is located where technologies are being invented, dreamed up, being developed. I have previously described some of these roles—for example, Dreyfus has had an enormous impact upon the community of computer designers and, more recently, upon robotics, and that from a phenomenology of the body approach. Thompson himself has been working on the growing set of issues connected with GM (genetically modified) foods, the new agricultural practices and the like, as has Bart Gremmen who has been officially designated to bring together the Dutch participants in a national reflection upon GM food development in Europe. I, too, have played a critical role in a number of interdisciplinary research developments ranging from instrument design to learning laboratories. Maybe it is from "hanged pigs," to "pigs-in-space"?

Finally, those who have suggested that I might be inclined more to a Winner-like or Latour-like approach are surely right. Winner's artifactual politics of Long Island bridges and Latour's 'sleeping policeman' speed bumps do embed and incarnate a material agency-ethic close to what Verbeek hopes for. *But* even so, all these examples also worry me as did the pig and bell, because each material artifact-ethic is itself multistable and can belong to any number of contexts. In addition, there is also the question of defeasibility: My Tundra truck, at certain higher speeds rather than slower ones, barely recognizes a speed bump; gummy bears "fool" fingerprint scanners; and laser pointers disable surveillance video cameras—and I have not mentioned the various terrorist strategies, which have turned our world so upside down. No heroes with broken hammers or scientists with labs at the ready here.

So, let us cut to the quick and begin a meditation upon embodiment.

Bodies, Again

Imagine my delight when I found I had four "auditors," listeners, who reflected upon my interests in the auditory (Langsdorf, Lochhead, Olesen, and Pinch). The "early Ihde" works, *Listening and Voice* and *Experimental Phenomenology*, emphasizing the auditory and the visual, respectively, also can be seen as harbingers of later embodiment theses. Langsdorf correctly recognizes the primacy of "whole body" perception, since even in listening, one hears with one's whole body, from bone conduction to "ears." And one hears shapes, surfaces, and interiors. Lochhead takes this in a different and very original direction by undertaking a project of visualization of the musical object. Pinch appreciates my "low church" or widely variant, mundane approach to listening to music—and the role technologies play in music construction and presentation. I would point out that my earliest published attention to instruments is reflected in "From Bach to Rock" in *Technics and Praxis,* and more recently the role of instrumentation, particularly the saxophone, in jazz.[6] Pinch's work on analog synthesizers rekindled my interests more recently, since my son, Mark, did work on digital synthesizers. We did a one-day, intensive conference with Pinch at Stony Brook, complete with demonstrations of the Moog and Buchla analog machines and then digital machines.

Olesen, the second European here to accept my style of phenomenology as a *postphenomenology,* intererestingly illustrates his use of this type of analysis by examining the stethoscope, a nineteenth-century and very successful auditory medical instrument. He, too, recognizes the interrelational ontology noted above, "Traditional phenomenology is concerned with establishing that humans and technology are related. Don Ihde's postphenomenology is more radical in asking how subjects and artifacts *constitute* each other in a praxis." He later quotes *Bodies in Technology,* "Postphenomenology, I contend, substitutes embodiment for subjectivity . . . If there is a 'subject' at all, it is the actional 'subject' of bodily action." Langsdorf points out that my earlier work moves toward a "second phenomenology," more hermeneutic and existential than Husserl and closer to Heidegger and Merleau-Ponty. In the end it is even more "Merleau-Ponty" although later connected also to Foucault. So, the "auditors" deal both with bodily, active perception, and with musical and scientific instruments.

I add to this group two others who take up the body theme: Andrew Feenberg and "passive bodies" and Donn Welton with bionic and implanted technologies for living bodies. Both recall the role "breakdown" frequently plays in phenomenological literature. As in the previous sections, I will begin with a rough sketch of my own position first, then move to the alternative and critical issues.

I have always held that what I more consistently call "embodiment" today has both an organic, bodily-sensory dimension and a hermeneutic or social-cultural dimension. Situatedness is locatable, the here-body, the actional, perceiving body. This echoes the approach to the incarnate body of Merleau-Ponty as many of the interlocutors have pointed out. The hermeneutic and social dimension of body, somewhat more distantly, echoes Foucault. *Bodies in Technology,* roughly identifies these as "body one" and "body two" except they are, of course, *equiprimordial,* to borrow a Heideggerian term. Without the organic, sensory body there can be no body at all, but it is never found without already being within the dimension of world and others. To go way back to beginnings, I was one of the first to argue that even the developing fetus is *present to language,* that is embodied language. Mothers speaking and singing are already embodying the rhythms and "singing the world" patterns of meaningful sounds. Loud sounds also penetrate the mother's body and the prenatal baby can be startled by sudden sounds. Psychological studies about these phenomena began to be developed later and occasionally *Science,* which I read religiously, carries articles about such language development. *Technology and the Lifeworld* developed the language of micro- and macroperception to describe these interrelated dimensions of embodiment. But, in addition, embodiment is *not* simply confined to the limits of one's skin, or body image, it, like its world, is multidimensional and polymorphic—interrelational. Interestingly, cognitive scientists and neurologists today are, in effect, rediscovering this phenomenon as Welton recognizes. Again, Merleau-Ponty's later language is appropriate here: folding of the flesh, the mutual interrogation of the world and ourselves, the *chiasm.*

Langsdorf, Lochhead and Pinch, on this section on bodies, each concentrate upon *Listening and Voice* and relate it to their own, original projects. Note the interdisciplinarity here: Langsdorf does communication theory out of a communication department; Lochhead is a musicologist; and Pinch a pioneer in science studies and now engaged in "sound studies." In Langsdorf's case, the adaptation she undertakes toward an ontological investigation of social things, wants to move phenomenology into the discussion, "as supporting interpretive modes of inquiry, rather than . . . as requiring empiricistic and even positivistic methodologies." She emphasized my "second phenomenology" for that goal and, like Sobchack, notes that this second phenomenology is an "extension and deepening" of first phenomenology "by being 'opened outwards' toward limits and horizons as it expands analysis from the static to the active." She utilizes the concreteness of bodily perceptual activity as "demonstrations [which] display the function of communicative interaction in making both auditory and visual things present and in enabling, as well as revealing limits to, their variation." In all this, she also emphasizes the role of whole body perception—I hear with my whole body, and "dealing with vision in isolation is phenomenologically suspect."

Lochhead takes the same whole body emphasis in a different direction—she examines the role of vision and visualization in a highly original direction into making sound "visible." Again, the interpenetration of sight and sound motivates her study and "Thus, the project of visualizing music recognizes that sight plays an important role in defining sonic meaning." Her analysis of the function and role of notation, and recognition of its antiquity is informative, but what catches my attention most is the way in which she links this to the changes of musical technologies, particularly in contemporary times. The interrelationship of new types of musical visualizations relates as well to new technologies of sound production—particularly electronic and synthesizer technologies. What I discovered was that she and I, independently, are moving in to the analogues of visualization, and I would say imaging, is a map-like processing. I have been arguing that contemporary, often dominantly computer processed or produced science imaging has a result much more map-like than either a picture or a code.

Pinch follows a similar trajectory. "The most important move which Ihde makes in *Listening and Voice* is his rejection of the Cartesian perspective. Listening and voice, according to Ihde, are always part of our world. Sound in inseparable from language and culture." He then moves to relate this phenomenological perspective to the new field (in which he plays a major role), to "sound studies." And, parallel to Lochhead, devotes the remainder of his paper to his work on analog synthesizers. He produces a "science studies" analysis of the development of the Moog synthesizer, and discusses the unique and new sonic qualities produced thereby, but also shows the embeddedness in a new musical culture. "This approach meshes well with Ihde's research program. The specific empirical focus on technology and voice and hence upon specific gropus of actors in a specific temporal context seems to be a natural extension of *Listening and Voice*." I agree.

Finn Olesen, I have also grouped here, due to an interesting part of his paper on the stethoscope. He undertakes, in parallel with Pinch's Moog analysis, the "science studies"–styled analysis of the stethoscope. It was situated in a "paradigm shift" in medical modeling and diagnosis whereby diagnosis and symptoms helped define a disease. But, it was also a shift in perceptual observation since palpation and percussion (tactile techniques) were replaced by *auscultation* (auditory instrument). Sounds from the body were amplified and one could learn to hear very subtle phenomena not noticeable by palpation. It also was an excellent example of what I call an embodiment relation with the instrument in mediational position between patient and doctor. In this case, the sounds were, "Through mediated auscultation the diagnosis of symptoms in the chest area had shifted from subjective opinion to objective analysis." And although at this same time, other instruments were being invented for visual examinations (endoscopes, ophthalmoscopes, and speculum), the stethoscope was thought to be the most accurate. I have frequently noted how science seems to prefer visualization, and that increasingly with recent imaging technologies, there are interesting periods when the auditory style of observation prevails—Bettyann Kevles has also noted this.[7]

Shifting now to a different set of embodiment issues, Andrew Feenberg, in a response to *Bodies in Technology,* accuses me of being too biased toward embodiment as *active.* "Ihde's account of the body seems to me one-sided. Perhaps it is his orientation toward scientific perception and technical action that limits his focus. . . . This tilts the weight of his discussion toward activity, but activity is only one dimension of the body." I admit the bias, but I think it was probably inherited from Merleau-Ponty. I have argued that his implicit body is a sort of "sports body, active and transparent in action." Feminists have caught this as a bias of Merleau-Ponty, such as Iris Young in "Throwing like a Girl" where she argues that a certain double awareness existed for her as a young girl. Feenberg gives a variant upon Young's description with his illustration of being a young boy wearing glasses—his fringe awareness of wearing glasses in sports activities, for example, are accompanied by a consciousness of being a boy who wears glasses as seen by others. All of this is compatible with my "body one-body two" account, although I may be guilty of the overemphasis Feenberg mentions. And I simply compliment him on "dependent" and "extended" bodies since he largely does a phenomenology of these facets of experiencing one's embodiment. And I guess I would add, now at my age, that the increasingly "recalcitrant" body is yet another facet in the phenomenon of relative passivity. Schneider is the Merleau-Pontean equivalent of a broken hammer for Heidegger, but a sluggish hammer is harder to describe.

I also like his application to sexual activity—but in this case I would argue that there is indeed an indirect role for technologies. Sexual activity freed from the fears of conception, sexual activity in the age of AIDS technologically protected, is socially experienced differently than in other stabilities of time and culture. I argued in *Technology in the Lifeworld,* that the entire context of sexuality switches when effective contraception is introduced—modern societies tend to switch responsibility to deciding when or whether to procreate from other stabilities in which the main purpose of sex is procreation. His application of passivity to the repeated blind man's cane is also novel—it reveals the cane user *as* blind, although I have also spoken of "echo focus," which is the simultaneous awareness of touch at the end of the cane, but the echo awareness of the cane does not disappear, it only recedes to a background. In short, Feenberg enriches our sense of embodiment by pointing up these features.

In Donn Welton's case the persistence of the missing hammer tradition takes yet a different twist. Welton is a major Husserl scholar and while his latest book, *The Other Husserl*, tries to extricate Husserl from his residual Cartesianism and push him in the direction of a more dynamic, genetic phenomenology, his analysis here of *Leib* and *Körper* only reconfirms Husserl's vestigial Cartesianism. The analysis of inner and outer perception, of intro- and extro-spection only serves to keep one's sense of one's body in the *camera obscura* model of an ego inside a body. If there is "sensation"—and I have my doubts, since this, too, is a hangover from British empiricism—it doesn't occur with inner and outer discriminations, all of which Welton criticizes. He then recognizes the more nuanced role of Merleau-Ponty and the notion of a body schema. I would actually stress more his sense of "I am already outside myself in the world." Phenomenological bodily perception of one's own body is both/ and, not either or, and both are equally phenomenological.

The vestige problem is actually exacerbated by drawing primarily from current cognitive and neurological sciences. These sciences are probably the *most Cartesian* of extant practicing sciences, whereas many other sciences can be seen as downright "postmodernist." "Brains in vats" and the brain-as-homunculus models revert to a controlling mind acting through *visual* command-like actions—neurology seems thus to fall right back under Haraway's claim that controlling vision, predatory and commanding, is science's heritage.

Welton examines newer, high-tech electronic, bionic developments that show promise, all of which first provide a *visualization* of phantom limbs or brain hook-ups with other visualization devices. I do not have space here to analyze in detail how these actually fit into a kind of constitutive process similar to learning external movement, but as a good pragmatist and multistablilist, I would simply say "there's more than one way to raise and arm." One can, imaginatively speaking, also imagine technologies that do the job through voice command, or as in Steven Hawking's case by a mouth held device to punch computer keys. The question is one of how far into the embodied skill described by Dreyfus, can this go? The skills of visual command back toward embodiment remain low on the Dreyfus scale, but as with all prostheses, it's better than a total Feenbergian passivity.

Welton has helped me realize how distant I have become from Husserl's sense of embodiment, while remaining closer to Merleau-Ponty. Actually this distancing can also be discerned in some of my Galileo work, as in "Husserl's Galileo needed a Telescope." The whole sense of plenary perception in the *Crisis* misses both the "body two" sense of hermeneutic-cultural body, let alone the embodiment through technologies. Welton, and now the cognitivists and neurologists, however well recognize the blind man's cane phenomenon, which clearly places one sense of one's own body "at a distance," thus exceeding any body "image" or limitation inside one's skin. Andy Clark in *Natural Born Cyborgs* calls this being beyond the skin bag.[8]

Beyond Late Modern Science

I now return to my recent preoccupations with the recasting of how we may understand science. Hans Lenk undertakes a careful analysis of contemporary recasting within the philosophy of science—and of my role therein. Science now is often seen as intervention and grasping. "The concept of 'grasping' implies that the active dimension of acquiring knowledge is a genuinely contstructive activity and not primarily a representational task of trying to represent external structures." Lenk clearly agrees with Pickering on this— whom he cites—but he extends this praxis interpretation of science to those, again like Pickerng, who also focus upon experiment and instruments. Ian Hacking, Pickering, me, and then adding Ronald Giere. "These authors have demonstrated that scientific work and progress cannot be reduced to theoretical claims." He characterizes this as, "Hacking's experimental-manipulative realism, Giere's modelistic constructive realism and Ihde's instrumental realism all appeal to experimental techniques in order to explain how theoretical entities come to be proven as real and how researchers are inspired to develop new models." Lenk's own work should be noted here. (I have only recently become acquainted with his *Grasping Reality: An Interpretation-Realistic Epistemology*.) He also notes that German philosophers of technology earlier contributed to this constructive, praxis focused understanding of science, including himself, Friedrich Rapp, and Gunter Ropohl—and I would add, Walther Zimmerli. (I, in fact, know all these folk and have collaborated in conferences on occasion since the 1981 German-American philosophy of technology meeting in Bad Homburg. However, much of this work appears only in German. Thus I may have missed Lenk and Rapp's early insights, just as they apparently missed mine, which appear in journals in English in 1973 and 1974 from presentations in 1972.)

Robert Crease actually pushes this actional intepretation of science farther and captures it under his notion of *performance*. He sees particularly large contemporary science experiments, as parallel to theatrical performances and provides a detailed analysis of what is required to set up, perform, and evaluate such productions. Performance includes "the conception, production, and witnessing of material events, the experience of which is *meaning generating* in that these events give us back more than what we put into them." And, echoing the move away from representation alone:

> The world is wider, wilder, and richer than we can represent, and what appears in performance can exceed the program used to put it together, and it can even surprise and baffle us, get us to change our minds, and compel us to alter the very theories and representations that we used to program the performance in the first place.

Here, too, is another voice recognizing the praxis and concreteness of science in action. His original development relating to simulation takes science even further into *cyberstage.* I suggest that this new conversation community is also beginning to see that process in science and art, particularly with the new sets of instruments available, are tending to converge around instrumental constructivity. Crease notes that my own work notes that

> philosophical discussion of experimentation needs to be both hermeneutical and phenomenological . . . hermeneutical describes who experimental intentions and practices arise and evolve out of and already existing involvement with, and understanding of a concrete situation . . . and phenomenology, [taking] its point of departure from what is . . . called embodiment . . . the experiences [of] . . . a unified being . . . which cannot be understood apart from concrete human experience.

What seems to have emerged here is something like a consensus, very different from early, but also late-modern philosophy of science, in which even an expositivist like Giere can agree that "Scientific knowledge is not absolute, but perspectival." Interestingly, these relativistic ontologies today spring from a variety of sources, not simply my own traditions of phenomenology and hermeneutics.

My Place in History

This ironic, concluding subtitle takes its place because the remaining interlocutor is Carl Mitcham who is simply acknowledgeable as *the* most prominent "historian" of philosophy of technology. His book, *Thinking through*

Technology (1994) is internationally recognized as such and I am grateful for the treatment he gives to me in comparison to John Dewey in that book, and in the interesting supplement undertaken here. What Mitcham does for this volume is to undertake another examination of my relations with and to pragmatism. As I indicated earlier, I think my first published recognition of kinship was in *Sense and Significance* (1973), but repeated thereafter. In his remarks here, Mitcham traces some historical ways in which pragmatism relates to later phenomenology and particularly to the pragmatist strains in American philosophy of technology. He returns to an above-mentioned theme—American pragmatism incorporated a social and progressive program, clearly normative, into its notion of an "instrumentalism." After noting a number of interrelationships, there are two conclusions I find particularly suggestive: "The challenge to pragmatism is to consider what Ihde's phenomenology of human-instrument relations might imply for pragmatist instrumentalism. The challenge from pragmatism is to consider in what ways Ihde's phenomenology might be a basis for societal, political and technological reform."

This observation and recommendation returns to the normativity question that has been repeatedly raised. Selinger indicates that some of my critics claim my "philosophy of technoscience putatively lacks normative sensitivity." Selinger then goes on and examines how I differ from Dreyfus and Borgmann, with whom I am so frequently associated (as neo-Heideggerian). In the context of American pragmatism, however, an interesting twist develops. Selinger observes that, "Despite the diminished public role of the 'intellectual,' philosophers present themselves regularly as 'values experts,' " and then are expected to fit into various applied ethics contexts.

I suspect part of this expectation reverts back to our pragmatist heritage. John Dewey, particularly in education, was the proponent of various reform and progressive developments, which characterized much of the early-twentieth-century American experience of philosophers. This is very different from the Heideggerian heritage that has marked most of philosophy of technology arising out of more European sources. This comes forth in Selinger's analysis of Dreyfus and Borgmann, both of whom retain a much more "Heideggerian" cast to their understanding of both technologies and normativity. Dreyfus's retention of vestigial technological autonomy (in the Deep Blue example) and the vestigial nostalgia found in Borgmann's "focal practices" are evidence of this.

If one then recalls my own sympathies with "neo-enlightenment" directions, one should be able to see that the implicit trajectory of my normativity sensibility is more in the *direction* of American pragmatist progressiveness. This necessarily produces a tension with the "dark shadow." I reject a normativity that is predetermined by a dystopian (or utopian) cast.

Mitcham notes that,

> Unlike many phenomenologists, Ihde has been in regular dialogue
> with pragmatism, and has on more than one occasion challenged its
> late-twentieth-century manifestations. By weaning phenomenology
> from any residual foundationalist pretensions as well as bringing it
> out of the more purely philosophical traditions and introducing it
> into the scientific laboratories and their heavily instrumented prac-
> tices, Ihde has created a post-phenomenology that is in effect a
> pragmatic phenomenology.

How could I not like this positioning? Many of the interlocutors have
noted my notion of *multistability*. Borgmann has been particularly insightful in seeing this as my 'ontology"—indeed, multistability, in effect, replaces the notion of "essences" in classical phenomenology, just as
embodiment replaces the notion of "subjectivity" in classical phenomenology. So, I shall conclude with a simple example of phenomenological
multistability with relations to a *post*phenomenology.

The famous "duck/rabbit" of both Wittenstein and Kuhn fame, taken
phenomenologically, turns out to have a more fecund multistability than simply Gestalt Psychology grants. Here is the duck/rabbit, but I now enhance the
stabilities by simply using additional orientations:

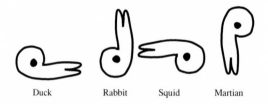

Duck   Rabbit   Squid   Martian

As one can see, there are now four, rather than two, variations. In this particular example, the key to each—which uses the same drawing—lies in the
orientation of the figure. Going back to *Experimental Phenomenology,* by
"naming" each, I have told a minimal, hermeneutic story which allows the
figure to be seen *as*, duck/rabbit/squid/martian. But within the story there lies
the implicitness of figure and background, our seeing as perspectival, and
from both our embodiment positional and our familiarity of the positionality
of the other, there is orientation, and while this is visually gestalted, it also
carries with it the kinesthesis of interrelational positionality.

And, there is something more—I contend that this *phenomenological
example*, which lets one see something new and different, carries with it
an asymmetrical trajectory. I challenge the prephenomenologist to go back

and regain the bistable configurational possibilities only; I hold that once seen, the retrogression to "only duck/rabbit" has been superseded. This is a simple illustration of what Langsdorf, Sobchack, Borgmann, and others have noted, that postphenomenology begins with what is familiar, but then begins to move beyond that into more radical variational possibility. And this is my answer to those interlocutors who ask, from what stance do I make my claims—this includes most explicitly Scharff, but also Pickering, and others. Or, if one allows a reversion to Husserl's old motto, paraphrased, "let the things speak for themselves" (after they have been critically interrogated).

Epilogue

In my response I have been somewhat selfish—taking note of how others take me and answering accordingly. I have used first person, which is part of my style, and given that this is a conversation, have more frequently than perhaps I should, used self-references. I do want to express my appreciation and even amazement at how carefully and deeply my readers have treated this project. I only wish I could have had the time and space to do an equally deep and particular response to the many points I have not covered.

Notes

1. Israel Finkelstein and Neil Asher Silberman, *The Bible Unearthed: Archeology's New Vision of Ancient Israel and the Origin of its Sacred Texts* (New York: The Free Press, 2001).

2. Bruno Latour and Peter Weibel, *Iconoclash:Beyond the Image Wars in Science, Religion and Art* (Cambridge: MIT Press, 2002).

3. Clara Pinto-Correia, *The Ovary of Eve: Egg and Sperm and Preformation* (Chicago: University of Chicago Press, 1997).

4. Donna J. Haraway *Modest_Witness@Second Millenium. FemaleMan_ meets_ Oncomouse* (New York: Routlege, 1997), p. 88.

5. Gerhard Dohrn-Van Rossum, *History of the Hour: Clocks and Modern Temporal Orders* (Chicago: University of Chicago Press, 1992).

6. Don Ihde, "Jazz Embodied: Instrumentation," in *Spontaneous Combustion*, ed. Steen Meier (Copenhagen: Copenhagen Jazz House, 2001), 41–45.

7. Kevles writes: "In the early 1890s sound seemed to be the door to a technology explosion. In medicine the stethoscope had become a staple in the physician's

black bag, and percussion of the chest had become a routine method of sounding out disease. The possibilities of recording sounds on a phonograph inspired other writers. . . ." Bettyann Holzmann Kevles, *Naked to the Bone: Medical Imaging in the Twentieth Century* (New Brunswick: Rutgers University Press, 1997), 13.

8. Andy Clark, *Natural Born Cyborgs: Minds, Technologies, and the Future of Human Intelligence* (Oxford: Oxford University Press, 2003). Also see my review in *Nature* 424, 7 (August 2003): 615.

Select Bibliography

Books

Hermeneutic Phenomenology: The Philosophy of Paul Ricoeur. Evanston: Northwestern University Press, 1971.

Sense and Significance. New York: Humanities Press, 1973.

Listening and Voice: A Phenomenology of Sound. Athens, OH: Ohio University Press, 1976.

Experimental Phenomenology. New York: G.P. Putnam's Sons, 1977; Albany: State University of New York Press, 1986.

Technics and Praxis: A Philosophy of Technology. Dordrecht: Reidel, 1979.

Existential Technics. Albany: State University of New York Press, 1983.

Consequence of Phenomenology. Albany: State University of New York Press, 1986.

Technology and the Lifeworld. Bloomington: Indiana University Press, 1990.

Instrumental Realism: The Interface between Philosophy of Technology and Philosophy of Science. Bloomington: Indiana University Press, 1990.

Philosophy of Technology: An Introduction. New York: Paragon House, 1993.

Postphenomenology: Essays in the Postmodern Context. Evanston: Northwestern University Press, 1993.

Expanding Hermeneutics: Visualism in Science. Evanston: Northwestern University Press, 1998.

Bodies in Technology. Electronic Mediations Series. Vol. V. Minneapolis: University of Minnesota Press, 2002.

This bibliography does not list abstracts, encyclopedia entries, book reviews, translations of books or articles, or reprinted entries in multiple sources.

Monograph

On Nonfoundational Phenomenology. Publikationer fran institutionen for pedegogik, Fenomenografiska notiser 3 (Goteborgs, 1986).

Books Edited

Coeditor, with Richard M. Zaner. *Phenomenology And Existentialism*. New York: Capricorn Books, 1973.

Editor, *Paul Ricoeur, The Conflict of Interpretations*. Evanston: Northwestern University Press, 1974.

Coeditor, with Richard M. Zaner. *Dialogues in Phenomenology*. Selected Studies in Phenomenology and Existential Philosophy. Vol. V. The Hague: Martinus Nijhoff, 1977.

Coeditor, with Richard M. Zaner. *Interdisciplinary Phenomenology*. Selected Studies in Phenomenology and Existential Philosophy. Vol. VI. The Hague: Martinus Nijhoff, 1977.

Coeditor, with Hugh J. Silverman. *Hermeneutics and Deconstruction*. Selected Studies in Phenomenology and Existential Philosophy. Vol. IX. Albany: State University of New York Press, 1985.

Coeditor, with Hugh J. Silverman. *Descriptions*. Selected Studies in Phenomenology and Existential Philosophy. Vol. X. Albany: State University of New York Press, 1985.

Coeditor, with Evan Selinger. *Chasing Technoscience: Matrix of Materiality*. Bloomington: Indiana University Press, 2003.

Contribution to Books

"Language and Experience." In *New Essays in Phenomenology: Studies in the Philosophy of Experience,* ed. James Edie. Chicago: Quadrangle Press, 1969, 50–57.

"Auditory Imagination." In *Phenomenology in Perspective*, ed. F. Joseph Smith. The Hague: Martinus Nijhoff. 1970, 202–215.

"Sound and Music." In *Aisthesis and Aesthetics*, ed. Erwin Strauss. and Richard Griffith. Pittsburgh: Duquesne University Press, 1970, 252–258.

"Sense and Sensuality." In *A Phenomenology of Eros*, ed. F. Joseph Smith. The Hague: Martinus Nijhoff, 1972, 61–73.

"Discussion of Aphasia." In *Language and Language Disturbances*, ed. by Erwin Strauss. Pittsburgh: Duquesne University Press, 1974, 137–142.

"A Phenomenology of Man-Machine Relations." In *Work, Technology and Education*, ed. Walter Feinberg and Henry Rosemont. Urbana: University of Illinois Press, 1975, 186–203.

"Wittgenstein's 'Phenomenological Reduction'." In *Phenomenological Perspectives*, ed. Phillip Bossert. The Hague: Martinus Nijhoff, 1975, 47–60.

"The Technological Embodiment of Media." In *Communication Philosophy and the Technological Age*, ed. Michael. Hyde. Tuscaloosa: University of Alabama Press, 1982, 54–72.

"The Experience of Media." In *Interpersonal Communications*, ed. Joseph Pilotta. Washington DC: University Press of America, 1982, 69–80.

"On Hearing Shapes, Surfaces and Interiors." In *Phenomenology: Dialogues and Bridges*, ed. Bruce Wilshire and Ronald Bruzina. Albany: State University of New York Press, 1982, 241–251.

"The Historical-Ontological Priority of Technology Over Science," In *Philosophy and Technology*, ed. Friedrich Rapp and Paul Durbin. Dordrecht: Reidel, 1983, 235–252.

Foreword to *The Impossible Coloring Book: Oscar Reutersvard's Drawings in Japanese Perspective* by Oscar Reutersvard. New York: Perigree Books, 1983, 3–6.

"Technology, Utopia and Dystopia." In *Research in Philosophy and Technology Vol. 6*, ed. Paul Durbin. Greenwich: JAI Press, 1983, 107–126.

"Phenomenology and the Phenomenon of Technology." In *Philosophy and Science in Phenomenological Perspective*, ed. Kho K. Cho. The Hague: Martinus Nijhoff, 1984, 111–122.

"Technology and Cultural Variations" In *Research in Philosophy and Technology Vol. 8*, ed. Paul Durbin. Greenwich: JAI Press, 1985, 17–33.

"Technologies as Others: Alterity Relations." In *Hermeneutic Phenomenology: Lectures and Essays*, ed. Joseph Kockelmans. Washington DC: University of America Press, 1988, 245–256.

"Self Presentation." In *Analecta Husserliana*, ed. Eugene Kaelin and Calvin Schrag. Dordrecht: Kluwer, 1989, 353–359.

"Technology in the Renassance." In *Interpreting the Italian Renaissance*, ed. Anthony Toscano. Stony Brook: Forum Italicum, 1991, 113–118.

"Text and the New Hermeneutics." In *On Paul Ricouer: Narrative and Interpretation*, ed. David Wood. London: Routledge, 1991, 124–139.

"New Technologies/Old Cultures." In *New Worlds, New Technologies New Issues*, ed. Stephen Cutcliffe, Stephen Goldman, Manuel Median, and Jose Sanmartin. Bethlehem: Lehigh University Press, 1992, 91.

"Technologies as Cultural Instruments." In *Phenomenology and Indian Philosophy*, ed. D.P. Chattodadhyaya, Lester Embree, and Jitendranath Mohanty. Albany: State University of New York Press, 1992, 207–215.

"Technology and Cross-Cultural Perception." In *Japanese and Western Phenomenology*, ed. Phillip Blosser. Dordrecht: Kluwer, 1992, 221–234.

"Response to Borgmann and Sanchez." In *Research in Philosophy and Technology*, *Vol. 13* ed. Frederick Ferre. Greenwhich: JAI Press, 1993, 350–253.

"Technology and Cultural Revenge," In *Phenomenology and the Cultural Disciplines*, ed. Martin Daniel and Lester Embree. Dordrecht: Kluwer, 1994, 251–264.

"In Praise of Sound." In *Landmark Essays: On Voice and Writing*, ed. Peter Elbow. Davis: Hermagoras Press, 1994, 165–174.

"Image Technologies and Traditional Cultures." In *Technology and the Politics of Knowledge*, ed. Andrew Feenberg and Alaistar Hannay. Bloomington and Indianapolis: Indiana University Press, 1995, 147–158.

"Paul Ricoeur's Place in the Hermeneutic Tradition." In *The Philosophy of Paul Ricoeur*, ed. Lewis Hahn. Chicago: Open Court Press, 1995, 59–70.

"Image Technologies and 'Pluriculture'." In *Cross-Cultural Conversation*, ed. Anita N. Balslev. Atlanta: Scholars Press, 1996, 101–118.

"The Tension between Technological and Social Development." In *Social Development: Between Intervention and Integration*, ed. Jacob Rendtorff, Adam Diderichsen and Peter Kemp. Copenhagen: Rhodos International Science and Art Publishers, 1997, 80–100.

"The Structure of Technology Knowledge," In *In Shaping Concepts of Technology*, eds. Mark deVries and Arley Tamir, Dordrecht: Kluwer, 1997, 7–79.

"Bodies, Virtual Bodies and Technology." In *Body and Flesh*, ed. Donn Welton. Oxford: Blackwell, 1998, 349–357.

"Phil-Tech meets Eco-Phil." In *Research in Philosophy and Technology Vol. 18*, ed. Carl Mitcham. Greenwich: JAI Press, 1999, 27–38.

"Expanding Hermeneutics." In *Hermeneutics and Science*, ed. Marta Feher and Olga Kiss. Dordrecht: Kluwer, 1999, 346–349.

"Perceptual Reasoning." In *Hermeneutics and Science*, ed. Marta Feher and Olga Kiss. Dordrecht: Kluwer, 1999, 13–24.

"Jazz Embodied: Instrumentation." In *Ojeblikkets Antaendelse [Spontaneous Combustion]*. Copenhagen: Copenhagen Jazz House, 2001, 41–44.

"Phenomenology and Technoscience," In *The Reach of Reflection: Issues for Phenomoneology's Second Century,* ed. Steve Crowell, Lester Embree, and Samuel Julian. Electron Press, 2001, 504–516.

"A Phenomenology of Technics." In *Philosophy Of Technology: The Technological Condition,* ed. Robert Scharff and Val Dusek. Malden: Blackwell, 2002, 507–529.

"Heidegger's Philosophy of Technology." In *Philosophy Of Technology: The Technological Condition,* ed. Robert Scharff and Val Dusek. Malden: Blackwell, 2002, 277–292.

"Literary and Science Fictions: Philosophers and Technomyths." In *Riceour as Another: The Ethics of Subjectivity,* ed. Richard Cohen and James Marsh. Albany: State University of New York Press, 2002, 93–105.

"The Tall and the Short of It: Male Sports Bodies." in *Revealing Male Bodies* ed. Nancy Tuana, William Cowling, Maurice Hammington, Greg Johnson, and Terrance MacMullan. Bloomington: Indiana University Press, 2002, 231–246.

"An Interview with Don Ihde." In *Chasing Technoscience: Matrix of Materiality,* ed. Don Ihde and Evan Selinger. Bloomington: Indiana University Press, 2003, 117–130.

"If Phenomenology is an Albatross is Postphenomenology Possible?" In *Chasing Technoscience: Matrix of Materiality,* ed. Don Ihde and Evan Selinger. Bloomington: Indiana University Press, 2003, 131–146.

Foreward to *Unforeseen History,* by Emmanuel Levinas. Bloomington: University of Illinois Press, 2003, vii–ix.

"Visualism in Science." In *Visual Information,* ed. Salvador Soraci and Kimiyo Murata-Soraci. Westport: Praeger, 2003, 249–260.

"Auditory Imagination," In *The Auditory Culture Reader,* eds. Michael Bull and Less Back. Oxford: Berg, 2003, 61–66.

"What Globalization do we want?" In *Globalization, Technology and Philosophy,* ed. David Tabachnick and Toivo Koivukosi. Albany: State University of New York Press, 2004, 75–92.

"Simulation and Embodiment." In *Yearbook of the Institute of Advanced Studies on Science, Technology and Society,* ed. Arno Bammé, Günter Getzinger, and Bernhard Wieser. Munich: Profil, 2004, 231–244.

"1000 Thousand Years of War: Interview with Manuel DeLanda." In *Life in the Wires: The Ctheory Reader,* ed. Arthur and Marilouise Kroker. Ctheory Books, 2004, 135–154.

"Philosophy and Technology," In *World and Worldhood,* ed. Peter Kemp, Dordrecht: Springer, 2004, 91–102.

Journal Articles

"Aristotle's Metaphysics: The Idea of God," *The Philosophical Forum* 19 (1961–2): 73–82.

"Parmenidean Puzzles," *The Southern Journal of Philosophy* 4, no. 2 (1966): 49–54.

"Commentary on Sound and Music," *The Psychiatric Spectator* 4, no. 6 (1967): 18–19.

"Rationality and Myth," *The Journal of Thought* 2, no. 1 (1967): 10–18.

"The Secular City and the Existentialists," *The Andover Newton Quarterly* 7, no. 4 (1967): 188–198.

"Some Auditory Phenomenon," *Philosophy Today* 17 (1973): 3–11.

"Some Parallels between Analysis and Phenomenology," *Philosophy and Phenomenological Research* 27, no. 4 (1967): 577–586.

"From Phenomenology to Hermeneutic," *The Journal of Existentialism* 8, no. 30 (1967–8): 111–132.

"Leisure in a Work Society," *Educational Theory* 19, no. 4 (1969): 424–430.

Coauthor, with T. Slaughter. "Listening." *International Philosophical Quarterly* 10, no. 2 (1970): 232–251.

"Language and Two Phenomenologies," *The Southern Journal of Philosophy* 8, no. 4 (1970): 399–408.

"On Perceiving Persons," *International Philosophical Quarterly* 10, no. 2 (1970): 232–251.

"God and Sound," *International Philosophical Quarterly* 10, no. 2 (1970): 232–251.

"Paris and Praxis," *Social Theory and Practice* 1, no. 1 (1970): 48–57.

"Parmenidean Meditations," *The Journal of the British Society for Phenomenology* 1, no. 3 (1970): 16–23.

"A Philosopher Listens," *The Journal of Aesthetic Education* 5, no. 3 (1971): 69–76.

"Youthcult and Youthmyth," *The Journal of Aesthetic Education* 6, no. 3 (1972): 193–210.

"Bach to Rock: A Musical Odyssey," *Music and Man* 1 (1973): 1–10.

"Vision and Objectification," *Philosophy Today* Spring (1973): 3–11.

"Phenomenology and the Later Heidegger," *Philosophy Today* Spring (1974): 267–279.

"The Experience of Technology," *Cultural Hermeneutics* 2 (1974): 267–279.

"Technology and Human Self-Conception," *The Southwestern Journal of Philosophy* 10, no. 1 (1979): 23–24.

"Technology and Humanism," *Cross Currents* 29, no. 2 (1979): 237–240.

"Interpreting Hermeneutics," *Man and World* 13, no. 3–4 (1980): 325–343.

"Phenomenology and Deconstructive Strategy," *Semiotica* 41 (1982): 5–24.

"Technology and Human Values: A Philosopher's Worries," *Weaver of Information and Perspectives on Technological Literacy* 5, no. 2 (1987): 2–4.

"Phenomenology and Architecture," *The Pratt Journal of Architecture* Spring (1988): 63–68.

"Deconstructing Visual Illusions," *Proceedings of the Russellean Society* 15 (1990): 59–72.

"Image Technologies and Traditional Culture," *Inquiry* 35, no. 3/4 (1992): 377–388.

"Recent Hermeneutics in Gadamer and Ricoeur," *Semiotica* 102 (1994): 157–162.

"Philosophy of Technology, 1975–1995," *Techne: Journal of the Society for Philosophy and Technology* 1, no. 1/2 (1995). [Electronic Journal]

"This is Not a Text, or, Do We Read Images?," *Philosophy Today* 40, No. 1/4 (1996): 125–131.

"The Structure of Technology Knowledge," *International Journal of Design Education* 7 (1997): 73–79.

"Thingly Hermeneutics: Technoconstructing," *Man and World* 30, no. 3 (1997): 369–381.

"Why Not Science Critics?," *International Studies in Philosophy* 29 (1997): 45–54.

"Whole Earth Measurements," *Philosophy Today* 41, no. 1 (1997): 128–134.

"Technology and Prognostic Predicaments." *AI and Society* 13 (1999): 44–51.

"Technoscience and the 'Other' Continental Philosophy," *Continental Philosophy Review* 33 (2000): 59–74.

"Timeline Travails," *Science* 287 (2000): 803.

"Millenial Essay. Putting Technology in its Place: Why don't Europeans

Carry Mayan Calendar Calculators in their Filofaxes?" *Nature* 404 (2000): 935–936

"Millenial Essay. Epistemology Engines: An Antique Optical Device Has Powered Several Centuries of Scientific Thought," *Nature* 406 (2000): 21.

"Multistability and Cyberspace," *Transforming Spaces: The Topological Turn* [Electronic Journal]. Darmstadt (2002). Accessed 11 October 2004. http://www.ifs.tu-darmstadt.de/radkoll/Publikationen/transformingspaces.html.

"Was Heidegger Prescient Concerning Technoscience?," *Existentia: An International Journal of Philosophy* 11 (2001): 373–386.

"Shapes, Surfaces and Interiors," *Soundscape* 2, no. 1 (2001): 16–17.

"How Could We Ever Believe Science Is Not Political?," *Technology and Society* 24, no. 1 (2002): 179–189.

"Beyond the Skin Bag," *Nature* 424, no. 6949 (2003): 615.

"Pragmatism, Phenomenology and Philosophy of Technology," *The Proceedings for the UTCP International Symposium on Pragmatism and the Philosophy of Technology in the 21st Century* 2 (2003): 50–59.

"Book Symposium: Bodies in Technology," Eduardo Mendieta, Evan Selinger, Don Ihde *Journal of Applied Philosophy*, 20, no. 1 (2003): 95–111.

"Interview with Don Ihde, May 9th, 2003," Anders Albrechtslund. [Electronic Publication] (2003). Accessed on 22 March 2005. http://www.filosofi.net.

"Has the Philosophy of Technology Arrived? A State-of-the-Art Review," *Philosophy of Science* 71, no.1 (2004): 117–131.

"The Ultimate Phenomenological Reduction," *Interfaces: Image Text Language* 1, no. 21/22 (2004): 59–68.

"Experimental Realism and Empirical Idealism in Informatics: A Virtual Interviewer of Don Ihde and West Churchman," Kristo Ivanov, Umea University Informatics [Electronic Journal] (2003). Accessed 11 October 2004. http://www.informatik.umu.se/~kivanov/IhdeChurchman.html.

Coauthor, with Evan Selinger. "Merleau-Ponty and Epistemology Engines," *Human Studies: A Journal for Philosophy and the Human Sciences* 27, no. 4 (2004): 361–376.

Contributors

Albert Borgmann is a professor in the department of philosophy at the University of Montana. Among his publications are *Technology and the Character of Contemporary Life, Crossing the Postmodern Divide, Holding On to Reality: The Nature of Information at the Turn of the Millennium,* and *Power Failure: Christianity in the Culture of Technology.*

Richard Cohen is the Isaac Swift Distinguished Professor of Judaic Studies and the coordinator of the Judaic Studies Program at the University of North Carolina. Among his publications are *Ethics, Exegesis and Philosophy: Interpretation after Levinas* and *Elevations: The Height of the Good in Rosenzweig and Levinas.*

Robert Crease is a professor in the Department of Philosophy at Stony Brook University and a historian at Brookhaven National Laboratory. Recent books include *The Prism and the Pendulum: The Ten Most Beautiful Experiments in Science, Making Physics: A Biography of Brookhaven National Laboratory,* and *The Play of Nature: Experimentation as Performance.*

Andrew Feenberg holds the Canadian Research Chair in Philosophy of Technology in the School of Communication of Simon Fraser University. He is the author of *Lukacs, Marx and the Sources of Critical Theory, Alternative Modernity, Questioning Technology, Transforming Technology,* and *Heidegger and Marcuse: The Catastrophe and Redemption of History.*

Peter Galison is the Mallinckrodt Professor of the History of Science and of Physics at Harvard University. His books include *How Experiments End, Image and Logic,* and *Einstein's Clocks, Poincare's Maps.* He coproduced a documentary film on the politics of science, *Ultimate Weapon: The H-bomb Dilemma* and is now working on a second, *Secrecy* about the architecture of the classification and secrecy establishment.

Donna J. Haraway is a professor in the Department of the History of Consciousness at the University of California, Santa Cruz. Some of her publications include Modest_Witness@Second_Millennium. *Femaleman©_Meets_Oncomouse: Feminism and Technoscience, The Companion Species Manifesto: Dogs, People, and Significant Otherness, Simians, Cyborgs, and Women: The Re-Invention of Nature, Primate Visions: Gender, Race, and Nature in the World of Modern Science,* and *Crystals Fabrics and Fields: Metaphors that Shape Embryos.*

Don Ihde is a Distinguished Professor in the Department of Philosophy at Stony Brook University. An acclaimed international speaker and scholar, he directs the Technoscience Research Group and is the author of thirteen books, including *Listening and Voice, Experimental Phenomenology, Technology and the Lifeworld, Instrumental Realism, Expanding Hermeneutics,* and *Bodies in Technology.*

Lenore Langsdorf is the William and Galia Minor Professor of the Philosophy of Communication in the department of speech communication at Southern Illinois University, Carbondale. She is the author of numerous articles and chapters in edited volumes, and is coeditor of and contributor to *Recovering Pragmatism's Voice: The Classical Tradition, Rorty, and the Philosophy of Communication* (with Andrew Smith) as well as *The Critical Turn: Rhetoric and Philosophy in Contemporary Discourse* (with Ian Angus).

Hans Lenk is a professor of philosophy at Karlsruhe University and honorary Dean of the European Faculty of Land Use and Development, Strasbourg. A former president of the German Philosophical Society, he is now Vice President of FISP and member of the Institute International de Philosophie. He is the author of 1,200 articles and more than 110 books, including most recently *Grasping Reality, Kleine Philosophie des Gehirns,* and *Denken und Handlungsbindung.*

Judy Lochhead is a professor and chair of the Department of Music at Stony Brook University. The focus of her teaching and research is recent music in the concert tradition. A forthcoming book, *Reconceiving Structure: Recent Music/Music Analysis,* will address the music of such composers as Anne LeBaron, Eleanor Hovda, Rachel McInturff, Laurie Anderson, and others.

Carl Mitcham is a professor of Liberal Arts and International Studies at Colorado School of Mines. One of the leading American philosophers of technology with emphasis on ethics, Mitcham is the author of *Techno-logical Reflection on Campus* and has also edited and coedited a number of volumes including *Visions of STS: Counterpoints in Science, Technology, and Society Studies, Philosophy and Technology: Readings in the Philosophical Problems of Technology*, and *Ethics and Technology.*

Finn Olesen is a professor of information studies at the University of Aarhus, Denmark. He has published numerous articles on actor network theory, technology, sociotechnical practices in health care, posthumanity, and metaphors in medical communication.

Andrew Pickering is a professor of sociology and a member of the Unit for Criticism and Interpretive Theory at the University of Illinois. His books include *Constructing Quarks: A Sociological History of Particle Physics, The Mangle of Practice: Time, Agency and Science*, and an edited collection, *Science as Practice and Culture*. He is currently working on a book on the history of cybernetics in Britain.

Trevor Pinch is a professor and chair of the Department of Science and Technology studies at Cornell University. His recent publications include *The Golem: What Everyone Should Know About Science* (with Harry Collins), *The Golem at Large: What You Should Know About Technology* (with Harry Collins), *Analog Days: The Invention and Impact of the Moog Synthesizer* (with Frank Trocco), and *How Users Matter: The Co-Construction of Users and Technology* (with Nelly Oudshoorn).

Evan Selinger is a professor in the Department of Philosophy at Rochester Institute of Technology. Recent publications include two coedited books, *Chasing Technoscience: Matrix for Materiality* and *The Philosophy of Expertise*, as well as articles in *Continental Philosophy Review, Critical Review, Philosophy Today, Journal of Practical Philosophy, Human Studies, Phenomenology and the Cognitive Sciences*, and *Public Affairs Quarterly*.

Robert C. Scharff is a professor and chair of the Philosophy Department at the University of New Hampshire. He has been editor of *Continental Philosophy Review* since 1995 and is the author of *Comte After Positivism* and coeditor, with Val Dusek, of *The Philosophy of Technology: The Technological Condition—An Anthology.*

Vivian Sobchack is associate dean and a professor of Film and Television Studies at the UCLA School of Theater, Film and Television. Her books include *Screening Space: The American Science Fiction Film, The Address of the Eye: A Phenomenology of Film Experience*, and *Carnal Thoughts: Bodies, Embodiment and Moving Image Culture.*

Paul B. Thompson holds the W.K. Kellogg Chair in Agricultural, Food and Community Ethics at Michigan State University. He is the author of *The Spirit of the Soil: Agriculture and Environmental Ethics, Food Biotechnology in Ethical Perspective*, and *The Ethics of Aid and Trade* and coeditor of *The Agrarian Roots of Pragmatism.*

Peter-Paul Verbeek is a lecturer in the Department of Philosophy at the University of Twente, Enschede, The Netherlands. He is the author of *What Things Do: Philosophical Reflections on Technology, Agency, and Design* and a number of articles on the philosophy and ethics of technology and industrial design.

Donn Welton is a professor in the Department of Philosophy at Stony Brook University. He has written *The Origins of Meaning* and *The Other Husserl*, and edited *The Essential Husserl* and *The New Husserl.*

Name Index